SOUTHERN LITERARY STUDIES

Fred Hobson, Editor

MAKING HISTORY

MAKING HISTORY

The Biographical Narratives of

Robert Penn Warren

JONATHAN S. CULLICK

Louisiana State University Press

Baton Rouge

MM

Designer: Melanie O'Quinn Samaha
Typeface: Sabon
Typesetter: Coghill Composition Co., Inc.
Printer and binder: Thomson-Shore, Inc.

Library of Congress Cataloging-in-Publication Data

Cullick, Jonathan S.
    Making history : the biographical narratives of Robert Penn Warren /
    Jonathan S. Cullick.
        p.   cm. — (Southern literary studies)
    Includes bibliographical references and index.
    ISBN 0-8071-2558-X (cloth : alk. paper) — ISBN 0-8071-2603-9 (paper :
    alk. paper)
    1. Warren, Robert Penn, 1905– —Knowledge—History. 2. Literature and
history—Southern States—History—20th century. 3. Biographical fiction,
American—History and criticism. 4. Historical fiction, American—History
and criticism. 5. Warren, Robert Penn, 1905– —Technique. 6. Southern
States—In literature,   7. Biography as a literary form. 8. Narration
(Rhetoric) 9. Autobiography. I. Title. II. Series.
PS3545.A748 Z662 2000
813′.52—dc21   99-057982

For Cheryl

Contents

Conclusion

Acknowledgments

I greatly appreciate the assistance of Steven Weisenburger. His thorough commentaries on my drafts, and his insights into narrative theory and other matters during our many friendly discussions, have proven to be invaluable. I am grateful to others who offered very helpful suggestions on various stages of the manuscript: Fred Hobson, William Bedford Clark, John Cawelti. Thanks also to William Freehling, Thomas Blues, and Jonathan Allison. Thanks to Wendy Jacobs for her careful copyediting of the manuscript. I would like to acknowledge John Easterly and Les Phillabaum at Louisiana State University Press, for their support of this project.

The Special Collections department of the University of Kentucky M. I. King Library deserves recognition. I thank the reference librarians for their friendly assistance in the archives, where I made much use of the Kentucky Collection and the Robert Penn Warren Collection.

The chapter on Warren's biography of John Brown was originally published in *Mississippi Quarterly* 51 (Winter 1997–98): 33–54, and is reprinted with permission. Parts of the chapter on *All the King's Men* have appeared previously in *Studies in American Fiction* 25 (1997): 197–210, and are reprinted with permission. Selections from "The World of Daniel Boone" (copyright © 1963 by Robert Penn Warren) are reprinted by permission of William Morris Agency, Inc., on behalf of the author. A small portion of the chapter on Daniel Boone was presented at the regional meeting of the Kentucky-Tennessee American

Studies Association and published in the 1996 edition of their journal, *Border States*.

Special thanks to my father, Mr. Isaac Cullick, for his encouragement. Finally, my greatest appreciation goes to my wife, Cheryl, for accompanying me in this journey.

Abbreviations

MAKING HISTORY

Introduction

Robert Penn Warren's first and final books were biographical narratives, a significant fact that previous scholarship has underestimated. Warren's first published book was a work of nonfiction, *John Brown: The Making of a Martyr* (1929), after which he put down biography to write fiction. He wrote biographical works in verse, for example, *Brother to Dragons* (1953), *Audubon: A Vision* (1969), and *Chief Joseph of the Nez Perce* (1982), but he did not return to prose biographical narratives until the final decade of his life and career, with the publication of *Jefferson Davis Gets His Citizenship Back* (1980) and *Portrait of a Father* (1988). There are occasional exceptions. Three critically neglected essays appeared in *Holiday* magazine: a couple of articles on the birth of Texas, which focused on personalities such as Sam Houston and Jim Bowie, appeared in 1958. More notably, "The World of Daniel Boone" appeared in 1963. The 1970s brought publication of biographical and critical assessments of literary figures: "Hawthorne Revisited: Some Remarks on Hell-Firedness," "John Greenleaf Whittier: Poetry as Experience" in *John Greenleaf Whittier's Poetry*, and *Homage to Theodore Dreiser*. However, a gap of fifty years rests between the biographical examinations of major historical figures—John Brown and Jefferson Davis.

These early and late narratives differ greatly from each other. The works on John Brown and Jefferson Davis (and Robert Franklin Warren, Robert Penn Warren's father) strike a reader with an obvious development in tone: the narratorial voice shifts from the sarcasm and cynicism of the *John Brown* narrator to the empathetic voice of the *Jefferson Davis* and *Portrait of a Father* narrators.

Though we might easily cite the artist's maturity to account for such differences, this answer is too facile, given Warren's penetrating investigations into the search for self-definition and the uses of the past. We must ask specifically *how* the artist grew. What specific narrative features did the novelist/historian discard or employ along the way? What does the difference between the early and late biographical narratives say about his philosophy of history? My investigation into these questions demonstrates that Warren's narrative technique reflects his philosophical position.

All the King's Men perhaps best articulates Warren's philosophy. Warren replaces the traditional "timeline" of history with a "matrix," as illustrated by Jack Burden's spiderweb analogy. This paradigm becomes a model for ethical action, a secularized version of the Christian doctrine of Original Sin (i.e., that mutual fallibility unites all individuals in what Cass Mastern would call "the common guilt of man" [*AKM* 187]). In Warren's model, because each individual affects every other, all individuals are in a communion with all others past, present, and future. Because all individuals are fallible, the sins of the precursors are the sins of posterity. In this paradigm, the past is an instrument of liberation rather than a burden because it affirms the common humanity of ancestors and inheritors. Jack Burden learns this lesson by the end of the novel as he and Anne Stanton make what Marshall Walker calls their "Miltonic departure from an Eden of false hopes,"[1] toward their postlapsarian entrance into "the awful responsibility of Time" (*AKM* 438). We may thus refer to Warren's paradigm of the past as his "concept of historical connection."

Critics have long observed this concept in Warren's works. L. Hugh Moore calls it the "theory of historical interrelated-

---

1. Marshall Walker, *Robert Penn Warren: A Vision Earned* (New York: Barnes and Noble, 1979), 106.

ness," and James Justus calls it the "Doctrine of Complicity."[2] I am arguing that the matrix paradigm is not just a philosophical or ethical position; it is also a textual position. Warren encodes the matrix paradigm into the level of the discourse as well as the story.

Warren's narrators and protagonists progress toward historical connection with three tropes: return, reconciliation, and redemption. The narrator returns to the historical scene, reconciles (that is, revises or reconstructs) conventional historical narratives, and thereby gains knowledge that redeems him from the burden of the past. Reconciliation is the most significant of these devices, because by critiquing previous historical constructions and self-reflexively creating new ones, the narrators articulate their views of the past and formulate their present identities. The sections of reconciliation show Warren attempting both to demythicize and show respect for historical figures. He interrogates previous historians' representations, replacing them with conventions of realism, yet without destroying the romantic or heroic implications that make cultural histories significant. As John Burt has noted, Warren is both drawn to and repelled by romanticism; for example, the struggles between and within the plots of *All the King's Men* are struggles between realism and idealism.

Return, reconciliation, and redemption serve as instruments for illustrating connection within the matrix of time. They personalize history. In every biographical narrative Warren argues that history must be experienced on a personal level for it to be meaningful. Thus, for example, historical figures must be humanized to become more accessible to moderns. In an interview with Frank Gado, Warren states, "Social tensions have a parallel in the personal world. The individual is an embodiment of external circumstances, so that a personal story is a social story."[3] In

2. L. Hugh Moore, *Robert Penn Warren and History: "The Big Myth We Live"* (Paris: Mouton, 1970), 65; James Justus, *The Achievement of Robert Penn Warren* (Baton Rouge: Louisiana State University Press, 1981), 41.

3. Robert Penn Warren, "A Conversation with Robert Penn Warren" (Interview with Frank Gado, 1966), in *Talking with Robert Penn Warren,* ed. Floyd

other words, history is constituted not just of social, technological, economic, and political components but of every individual who experiences and embodies those components. All elements in history converge on the personal level, and it is this personal convergence that gives history meaning.

Because understanding history requires connecting with the people who lived history, Warren wrote historical narratives in the biographical and autobiographical modes. Warren argues that we do not understand history by studying only politics and economics. We must get inside the minds of the people who lived the past, "for we are their children in the light of humanness / and under the shadow of God's closing hand."⁴ Warren states in an interview with Bill Moyers that the most significant problem facing individuals in an increasingly technological and bureaucratic age is loss of unique identity. Biography and autobiography personalize history. They restore identity.

At this point the modernist agenda of Warren's biographical narratives becomes clear. The historian, like the novelist, can reintegrate the fragments of modern humanity. Narration permits the historian and novelist to treat the individual as a complete entity rather than as a particle of some larger, deterministic structure. In his introduction to Warren's works in *The History of Southern Literature*, James Justus identifies Warren's intention: "to humanize the participants of history, to free them from the confining categories invariably designed for them, not merely by the needs of historians but by certain impulses in us all to reduce and compartmentalize in order to make sense of the complex affairs of complex men."⁵ The historian's and novelist's role is to reconstruct historical figures for the modern age, a kind of aesthetic completion of the South's political-economic reconstruction.

Watkins, John T. Hiers, and Mary Louise Weaks (Athens: University of Georgia Press, 1990), 70.

4. Robert Penn Warren, *Selected Poems, 1923–1975* (New York: Random House, 1976), 243.

5. James Justus, "Robert Penn Warren," in *The History of Southern Literature*, ed. Louis D. Rubin, Jr., et al. (Baton Rouge: Louisiana State University Press, 1985), 452.

Perhaps the most intriguing aesthetic aspect of Warren's historian-narrators is their discourse. As his narrators achieve an understanding of historical connection, they employ discourse that places less distance between themselves and the objects they study. This characteristic most accounts for the difference between Warren's early and late narrators. Warren loses trust in the idea of a neutral narrator. In *John Brown,* Warren implicitly claims objectivity for his narrative by exposing the biases of prior historians. However, with *Jefferson Davis* and *Portrait of a Father,* Warren gives up all claim to objectivity.

Seymour Chatman's terminology from narrative theory is helpful here. All of these narrators may be described as "overt" as opposed to "covert," because their explicit commentaries and tones make their voices highly "audible." Another useful distinction, to borrow Wayne Booth's terms, is that the early narrators attempt to be "narrator-observers" (detached from the stories they narrate) rather than "narrator-agents" (participants in the stories they narrate). The narrator of *John Brown* is overt but an observer. The narrators of *Jefferson Davis* and *Portrait of a Father* are overt agents. Between these biographical narratives, the narrators of novels such as *All the King's Men* and *World Enough and Time* develop from observers into agents.

The novels become laboratories in which Warren explores and ultimately dismisses the idea of narratorial objectivity. *All the King's Men* and *World Enough and Time* particularly demonstrate this development, since their narrators are "self-conscious." The "self-conscious" narrator, as the term is used by Seymour Chatman (and by Wayne Booth before him), examines and comments upon his own discourse.[6]

In a sense, it is as if the *John Brown* narrator begins to doubt his own neutrality after he finishes the biography. Before writing more conventional histories, he becomes self-conscious about his claim to objectivity and takes an exploratory detour into fiction for several decades. He becomes Jack Burden, then the metafic-

6. Seymour Chatman, *Story and Discourse* (Ithaca: Cornell University Press, 1978), 228.

tional *World Enough and Time* narrator. Like Burden, he emerges from his fictions "out of history into history" (*AKM* 438), writing narratives that are histories and not quite histories, no longer capable of wearing the mask of detachment and objectivity. The narratives of Jefferson Davis and Robert Franklin Warren become an impressionistic collage of genres: history, biography, meditation, portrait, speculation, and autobiography.

This last mode is the most significant. Autobiography represents the ultimate connection with the historical object of study. The early narrator of *John Brown* affects a detached stance, going to such lengths to assure the reader of his detachment that he makes his presence obvious. The mature narrator of *Jefferson Davis* and *Portrait of a Father* purposefully writes himself into his histories. Like Jack Burden, he cannot divorce himself from the past nor can he maintain the false pose of neutrality. Warren's matrix paradigm ultimately forces a shift in mode. The final biographical narratives are autobiographical because, given his call for historical connection, autobiography becomes the most appropriate mode.

This study will show that Warren's vision of history is not only worthy of the analysis it has received from philosophical, ethical, theological, political, and psychological perspectives. From a historiographical point of view, Warren's vision also calls for analysis on the textual level. True to his reputation as a New Critic, Warren's techniques reflect his historical explorations and themes. My approach examines what we might call the "narrative syntax" of Warren's historical vision.

One note about the order of the chapters. Chapter I presents an overview of Warren's uses of the past in his biographical narratives. All subsequent chapters are arranged by genre; texts are then addressed chronologically within this arrangement. Chapters II, III, and IV explore the nonfiction narratives, from the early works on John Brown and Daniel Boone to the late works on Jefferson Davis and Robert Franklin Warren. (Chapter II traces Warren's writing about race, from *John Brown* to *Segregation: The Inner Conflict in the South* and *Who Speaks for the Negro?*.) Chapters V and VI focus on the fictional biographical narratives, *All the King's Men* and *World Enough and Time*. Chapter VII examines biography in poetry, from "The Ballad of Billie Potts" to *Chief Joseph of the Nez Perce*. The conclusion considers Warren's biographical scholarship on literary figures: Hawthorne, Melville, Whittier, and Dreiser.

Two additional notes about terminology: First, occasionally I use the terms *story* and *discourse*. For convenience, I am using Seymour Chatman's distinction between "story" (*what* happens in a narrative, the *content*, the *showing*) and "discourse" (*how* things happen in a narrative, the *technique*, the *telling*). The difference is essential when discussing, for instance, the concept of historical connection that Jack Burden learns in the *story* of *All the King's Men* and the ways in which he reflects the concept in the *discourse* that he uses as he narrates.

Second, throughout this study, I use the term "biographical narrative" rather than "biography." The Warren texts discussed here invite explication particularly because of their complication of the boundary between fiction and nonfiction. For example, Warren's narrative of Jefferson Davis is both a portrait of Davis and meditation upon history, the Davis monument in Kentucky, and the author's own life. It is an impressionistic mixture of biography, philosophy, autobiography, and speculation. The text does not easily conform to the generic distinctions of fiction and nonfiction.

In all of his biographical studies, Warren's main concern is, to use Richard Gray's terms, "the notion of history rather than any series of historical events." Thus, it makes sense to refer to these works not as biographies per se but as narratives in which, while the central subject is the exploration of an individual's life, the author's objective extends to other concerns. In reference to Joseph Conrad, Warren coins the term "philosophical novelist" to mean the writer "for whom the documentation of the world is constantly striving to rise to the level of generalizations about values." This type of writer "is willing to go naked into the pit, again and again, to make the same old struggle for his truth."[7]

---

7. Richard Gray, *The Literature of Memory: Modern Writers of the Ameri-*

Along these lines, we might refer to Warren as a "philosophical biographer," and Warren's studies of historical figures might more appropriately be called "biographical narratives," a term that allows some extension of the conventions of traditional biography.

---

can South (Baltimore: Johns Hopkins University Press, 1977), 70; Robert Penn Warren, "The Great Mirage" (1951), in *New and Selected Essays* (New York: Random House, 1989), 160.

I

Return, Reconciliation, Redemption
Uses of the Past in Warren's Biographical Narratives

> Without a sense of time, there can be no sense of identity.
> —Robert Penn Warren, "The Use of the Past"

Warren's protagonists and narrators struggle between a desire to liberate themselves from the past and a need to shape their identities in the context of the past. In his biographical narratives, Warren redresses their separation by initiating a new paradigm of historical causality; according to this paradigm, the past is present, an *available* rather than a separable, distant experience. Warren employs three strategies to construct the new framework. He returns to the past in order to reconnect personally. He revises historiographical misconceptions so that the past will reconcile with the present. Finally, he demonstrates that knowledge gained through return and reconciliation redeems us from the concept of the past as a burden, permitting one to be connected to the past rather than haunted by it. Warren's paradigm ultimately constitutes a history that is more usable for the present.

In "The Use of the Past," Warren identifies the cause of Americans' ignorance of history as America's mission "to make all things new." While such a progressive vision contributes to America's success, America moves forward only by jettisoning the past and disconnecting itself from its history. America's providential view of history thus creates an illusion of cultural innocence and omnipotence, and perpetuates the illusion that perfection is possible: "The sense of being freed from the past, of being reborn, of being forever innocent, did give America an abounding energy, and undauntable self-reliance, and an unquenchable optimism. . . . But sometimes virtues have their defects. . . . [Americans] felt themselves to be a Chosen People, who . . . could never sin in God's sight. Furthermore, they came to feel that God's will and their own were miraculously identical." Warren expresses concern that Americans fail to recognize the ethical dimension of their own and their nation's actions, because they fail to acknowledge their connection to the forces of history. Thus Warren refers to Americans as "moral narcissists," warning that we must rescue ourselves from this mode of thinking, for "without a sense of time, there can be no sense of identity" to assist us in navigating toward the future.[1]

In order to go forward into the future, throughout his writings Warren attempts to bridge the separation by returning to and recovering the past. The recovered past must be a more accurate record in order to act as a corrective upon the present. Cleanth Brooks writes of his friend and colleague: "Warren was not content with abstractions. His truth must be concrete and have concrete applications. Thus Warren loved America, but he had to accept the dark chapters of American history."[2] Recovering (or disclosing) the "concrete" truth and "dark chapters" of history requires re-examining the accepted past. To re-examine, one must return. However, as is noted in "The Use of the Past," such backward movement and self-examination are at odds with America's forward-looking vision. The tropes of return, reconciliation, and redemption conceive a new framework for perceiving causality in history.

We may envision Warren's new paradigm for history as a "matrix." It contrasts with the traditional paradigm of time as a "vector," time as a line with each event having a clearly demar-

1. Robert Penn Warren, "The Use of the Past," in *New and Selected Essays* (New York: Random House, 1989), 32, 35, 50.

2. Cleanth Brooks, "Homage to R. P. Warren," in *"To Love So Well the World": A Festscrift in Honor of Robert Penn Warren*, ed. Dennis L. Weeks (New York: Peter Lang, 1992), 15.

cated point of origin and termination. When events are plotted onto a timeline, the points form vectors (line segments of finite length and specific direction). Because it thus breaks time down into a sequence of segmented, successive vectors, the timeline creates an illusion of historical closure by depicting past events as complete, separate, and distinct from the present. The vector paradigm may be visualized as a straight road, such as the highway in the opening of *All the King's Men*. As individuals proceed, they lose the ability to delineate the details of the receding horizon. Visibility becomes impressionistic, with the horizon discernible more by general appearance than specific details. Even at its best, this historical recession oversimplifies history. As Warren comments during an interview with Edwin Newman, "What we remember from history is human stances, the sense of human values, rather than issues. . . . All becomes legend."[3] At worst, the recession of the "landscape" results in historical fragmentation and compartmentalization.

Warren revises this view by conceiving a matrix as a new model for historical construction and ethical action. Jack Burden's "spiderweb" analogy in *All the King's Men* illustrates the ethical implications of the matrix paradigm. While researching Cass Mastern's journals, Burden discovers that Cass began to feel responsible for the unexpected consequences of his actions. Cass's affair with his best friend's wife resulted in suffering that extended within and beyond the triangle of betrayal, and Cass realized that "all had come from my single act of sin and perfidy, as the boughs from the bole and the leaves from the bough. . . . The vibration set up in the whole fabric of the world by my act had spread infinitely" (*AKM* 178). In one of the most significant passages of the novel, Burden develops his spiderweb metaphor for time:

> [Cass] learned that the world is all of one piece. He learned that the world is like an enormous spider web and if you touch it,

3. Robert Penn Warren, "Speaking Freely" (Interview with Edwin Newman, 1971), in *Talking with Robert Penn Warren*, ed. Watkins, Hiers, and Weaks, 197.

however lightly, at any point, the vibration ripples to the remotest perimeter and the drowsy spider feels the tingle and is drowsy no more but springs out to fling the gossamer coils about you who have touched the web and then inject the black, numbing poison under your hide. It does not matter whether or not you meant to brush the web of things. Your happy foot or your gay wing may have brushed it ever so lightly, but what happens always happens and there is the spider. (*AKM* 188–89)

In Burden's web conception, time is a matrix of actions with intended and unintended consequences. History is not movement forward in a linear sense but action within a network of causes and effects. Because the term "matrix" derives from the Latin words for "womb" and "mother," the matrix offers a vision of time as a climate within which people act. It represents time not as progression but as interconnection among multidirectional causes and effects. In the vector paradigm, time proceeds only in one direction. In the matrix paradigm, actions and consequences radiate outward and back inward again.

Because it is monodirectional, the vector paradigm focuses attention upon recency; there is a past or future that can be called "distant." Graphically, a timeline depicts space between events, creating the illusion that events are separated by the amount of time that passes between them. The matrix paradigm recognizes interconnectedness (i.e., repetition and return), thereby providing a means for recognizing personal responsibility for the consequences of actions. Unlike vectored history, matrixed history compels responsible action. Jack Burden, for example, commences his narrative on a highway. When he shifts his perception of history to the metaphor of the web, he enters "the awful responsibility of Time." The ethical growth of Warren's protagonists hinges on just this paradigmatic shift from the vector to the matrix.

L. Hugh Moore defines Warren's model as a "theory of historical interrelatedness" that challenges individuals to construct ethical actions out of the chaos of time: "Man is responsible morally if not physically for any consequences of his acts, thought, or mere existence, even though frequently he cannot know or guess these consequences. . . . [An individual] is free to choose even though he cannot know the outcome of his choice and even though his choice may make little or no difference in the physical world; indeed, the result may be exactly the opposite of what he intended." Moore clarifies this theory by cautioning that it "should not be interpreted as implying a moral plan to the universe, for there is nothing orderly, logical, planned, or predictable about the operation of the web of history." Similarly, James Justus refers to this ethical position as the "Doctrine of Complicity," which is "the central conviction that none is without guilt."[4] Because all human beings are fallible, the sin of one is the sin of all. Because the sins of the fathers are repeatable, they are also the sins of the sons.

This view secularizes the doctrine of Original Sin, uniting all people across time and within any particular time by referring to history rather than theology or metaphysics. Original Sin is well documented in Warren's work. William Bedford Clark confirms, "Virtually all readers of Warren's work have identified the pedal point of his characteristic music as a pervasive sense of Original Sin." Robert S. Koppelman refers to this secular ethical formulation as "a brand of spirituality [that] is always grounded in the reality of lived experience . . . [Warren's] modernist spirituality."[5] In *Wilderness*, Aaron tells Adam that history can take the place of God as the reason for all things. The matrix paradigm illustrates that all individuals affect all others, placing all people in communion with one another.

From a fundamentalist religious perspective, Ashby Wyndham (*At Heaven's Gate*) recalls a time when he did not realize the interrelatedness among human beings: "I taken no thought and it was my sin. . . . You throw a rock in a pond and it don't

4. L. Hugh Moore, *Robert Penn Warren and History*, 65, 16; Justus, *Achievement of Robert Penn Warren*, 41.

5. William Bedford Clark, *The American Vision of Robert Penn Warren* (Lexington: University Press of Kentucky, 1991), 62; Robert S. Koppelman, *Robert Penn Warren's Modernist Spirituality* (Columbia: University of Missouri Press, 1995), 4.

make but one splash but they is ripples runs out from it" (*AHG* 120). Ashby's "sin" is his ignorance of the effects of his actions; his redemption occurs when he acknowledges those effects in his statement of confession. Such interrelatedness reflects Faulkner's description of history in *Absalom, Absalom!* as "that pebble's watery echo." In an essay on Faulkner, Warren writes, "There is, then, a contamination implicit in the human condition—a kind of Original Sin, as it were. . . . But it is possible . . . to achieve some measure of redemption through love."[6] Warren agrees with Faulkner's connection of past and present but departs from Faulkner by conceiving of a connection that is not deterministic. For example, Percy Munn in *Night Rider* envisions himself and the other members of the protective association as bound by invisible threads. While realizing that the organization gives him an identity, Munn seeks to identify himself by acting separately and autonomously. Although one involuntarily inherits a history, one also inherits the free will to act upon time. One may also receive these inheritances within the vector model (i.e., inheritances are linear since they are transferred through lineage). But in the matrix model the inheritance is accompanied by responsibility. In the vector model, Jack Burden acts upon and is acted upon by time but without the sense of accountability that the matrix model affords.

The image of the web and the pebble in water appear throughout Warren's work (e.g., *Night Rider, At Heaven's Gate, All the King's Men, Band of Angels, Wilderness*). In *Wilderness,* connection and complicity lead to hope, for they confirm humanity's interdependence. Unlike many Faulkner characters (such as Ike McCaslin and Quentin Compson), many of Warren's narrators, protagonists, and minor characters discover and assert their authority to act within the matrix of history. They recognize and accept their complicity in history, their responsibility for others, and their humility before the awesome web of

6. William Faulkner, *Absalom, Absalom!* (New York: Vintage, 1987), 326; Robert Penn Warren, "William Faulkner" (1946), in *New and Selected Essays* (New York: Random House, 1989), 206.

time. They arrive at this knowledge by returning to and reconciling with their past, thereby acquiring the knowledge necessary to earn redemption for the future.

Redemption from the burden of the past is available only to those who concurrently recognize both their connection to the past and their ability to act upon the present and future. As Leonard Casper points out, in Warren's world, "Salvation can be earned by subscribing to responsibility. It must be earned in the world and in time." Thomas Connelly concurs, noting that in Warren's fiction salvation results "when one [comes] to terms with his own complicity in history."[7]

By combining to construct a new program for ethical action, these three tropes also form a new historical realism. Reconnecting with the past, and renegotiating the relationship between the myths of the past and the needs of the present, are tools with which Warren certifies his biographical narratives as authentic records. As with other historians, Warren's "realism" depends not just on the facts he produces but on certain conventions of realism. In "The Discourse of History," Roland Barthes describes the traditional convention of objectivity as "the deficiency of signs of the utterer. . . . The historian is claiming to allow the referent to speak all on its own." Barthes is referring to the suppression of the first-person pronoun in putatively "realist" narratives, in which the writer actually substitutes an "objective persona" for his/her "emotional persona." Thus "objectivity" becomes a convention that makes the text appear to be a transparent medium for its subject. However, as Barthes and other narrative theorists have noted, there is always "friction" between "the time of uttering" (discourse time) and "the time of the matter of the utterance" (story time).[8] Warren's three

---

7. Leonard Casper, *Robert Penn Warren: The Dark and Bloody Ground* (Seattle: University of Washington Press, 1960), 181; Thomas Connelly, "Robert Penn Warren as Historian," in *A Southern Renascence Man: Views of Robert Penn Warren,* ed. Walter B. Edgar (Baton Rouge: Louisiana State University Press, 1984), 15.

8. Roland Barthes, "The Discourse of History," trans. Stephen Bann, in *Comparative Criticism,* ed. E. S. Schaffer (Cambridge: Cambridge University Press, 1981), 9–11.

tropes—particularly the trope of reconciliation—call attention to this friction because their presence makes the narrative self-conscious about its articulation of the past. Warren does not attempt to achieve an objective voice, for he acknowledges the necessity of myth. Warren may not achieve truth but he does construct meaning with the particular tools that he employs. Warren's "truth" is found in the dynamics of interconnection, as depicted by the matrix.

The trope of return initiates the necessary bridge to the past in Warren's narratives, and it calls attention to the narratives' realist agenda. In the novels, Percy Munn (*Night Rider*) returns by night to the scene of his crime; Jerry Calhoun (*At Heaven's Gate*) unconsciously struggles against the artificial world of his surrogate father, Bogan Murdock, by returning to his grandfather's and father's home; Jack Burden's story (*All the King's Men*) is precipitated by traveling home by car to both Willie's boyhood home and Burden's Landing in the opening of the novel; Brad Tolliver (*Flood: A Romance of Our Time*) and Jed Tewksbury (*A Place to Come To*) are intellectuals who leave their homes in the South but, because of a deracinated existence, must return and renegotiate their relation to home. Even in the interpolated narratives within the novels, characters such as Willie Proudfit, Ashby Wyndham, and Munn Short explain how, like the Prodigal Son, they strayed and returned home. Or, in Warren's poetry, R.P.W. (*Brother to Dragons*) returns to Kentucky with his father to see Smithland, revealing the importance of the region he knows as home:

> Perhaps never to come back, for I did not know
> What here remained, at least for me;
> And to this day have not gone back, but hold,
> In my heart, that landscape. (*BD* 131–32)

In much of the nonfiction (*Segregation, Jefferson Davis, Portrait of a Father*), Warren travels home in planes, in automobiles, and in his memory. Particularly in these three narratives and *Brother to Dragons,* the narrator uses the return journey as an invitation for the reader to participate in the backward motion with the autobiographical narrator, even to focalize through the narrator.[9] The act of cycling back, physically or in memory, is essential for reconnecting with the past. By having the protagonist start from the present and move anachronously, Warren also emphasizes that time is a matrix, for the backward motion of return violates the unidirectional, forward motion of the vector. The narrative structure—the return—reflects the new conception of the structure of time.

The purpose of making the return trip is to reconcile with the past. Because it involves examining constructions of history, reconciliation is the most significant and pervasive trope in the Warren canon. Through reconciliation, Warren constructs a "vision of the self reconciled and spiritually reunited with the larger forces of Place, Nature, and Time." Neil Nakadate also identifies the importance of reconciliation in Warren's work: reconciliation between pragmatism and idealism, between the generations, between the races, between the past and present, and between individual and community.[10] In the context of my study, reconciliation means revision for the purpose of constructing a more realistic text. There are different perceptions of history that must be revised so that they can reconcile with one another. To reconcile the ledgers of the past and present, Warren's revisionary history strips away myths setting the past on a stage of heroism. The accounts of the past and present must be settled, or reconciled, because the past might not be reconstructed into history accurately by scholars or by the popular imagination. Tropes of reconciliation also validate the narrative as "true." Warren revises by critically examining and "correcting" the narratives of previous historians, a strategy that proposes to certify his text's documentary status.

9. "Focalization" is Gerard Genette's term to describe the perceiving character's point of view. See *Narrative Discourse,* trans. Jane E. Lewin (Ithaca: Cornell University Press, 1980).
10. Koppelman, *Warren's Modernist Spirituality,* 14; Neil Nakadate, "The Narrative Stances of Robert Penn Warren" (Ph.D. diss., Indiana University, 1972), 177–78.

That there are distinct conceptions of history open to reconciliation indicates a difference between what we call "the past" and what is called "history." The "past" includes all prior occurrences; as such, it is an ideal, inaccessible in the practical world. "History," however, is the selection and deflection of certain past events according to an established notion of historicity, involving inclusions and exclusions of events culled from the larger "past." In contrast to the "past," "history" creates the illusion that events are complete and understandable. A culture subsumes an individual event into the structure of its agreed-upon history, thereby maintaining the coherence of its past. "History" thus becomes the set of stories a culture tells about itself, the accepted version of its own past. The motive for wanting events to cohere culturally and politically illustrates what Warren and Brooks called the "human craving to have things put in order."[11] Though they were speaking of fiction, the same principle applies to history.

The process of selecting events from the past in order to construct history results from what Hayden White calls a "need or impulse to rank events with respect to their significance for their culture." Genres provide the conventions needed to produce such a ranking. Just as fictional episodes are plotted to conform to the structure of a particular genre, moments from the past are validated as distinct episodes worthy of being considered historical when they are reconstructed according to a genre. As Hayden White argues, a plot is an entity that exists prior to events, and an event is validated as historical in direct proportion to the extent to which it contributes to the development of the plot. Sequences of real-life events do not intrinsically cohere to genres of tragedy or comedy, but once they are plotted according to a genre, and once a reader recognizes the genre, the event is understandable. Therefore, a genre performs a social function, for it permits a culture to agree upon the significance of a historical event. A narrative genre enables a community to create its own

11. Cleanth Brooks and Robert Penn Warren, *Understanding Fiction*, 2nd ed. (New York: Appleton-Century-Croft, 1959), 274.

history and identity by creating its own epics, tragedies, heroes, and villains. The problem with such stories is that they create what White calls an "illusory coherence."[12] Reconciliation, through revision, corrects the illusion but, ironically, only by substituting other illusions in its place. The act of revising or "correcting" endows the new story with the status of truth.

In order to revise commonly held perceptions of the past, Warren divides an event itself from all of its traditional constructions by exposing the story-telling process by which it is represented as history. This exposure of the past calls into doubt the accuracy of commonly accepted historical plots and implicitly attempts to legitimate the accuracy of the facts in Warren's narrative. Warren has commented, "[Facts] are deadly things. Facts may kill. For one thing, they can kill myths."[13] However, by killing myths, Warren does not destroy history. As a historian, Warren is similar to the artist-naturalist in *Audubon: A Vision;* just as Audubon kills birds for the purpose of making them come alive in art, Warren demythicizes history so as to make it live. The killing of myths permits the survival of history, a more "usable past" (to take Van Wyck Brooks's term). Warren demythicizes historical figures in order to revive them for the present. Thus, in each biographical narrative, Warren revisits a significant historical character and peels away the layers of myth that have concealed the real individual behind a screen of heroic representations.

Warren states that modern Americans see in historical events "only a kind of gross symbol, not a human experience of infinite complication."[14] Canonizing historical figures as heroes or as villains renders them irrelevant by oversimplifying their lives. By

---

12. Hayden White, *The Content of the Form: Narrative Discourse and Historical Representation* (Baltimore: Johns Hopkins University Press, 1987), 14, 43–44, 51, ix.

13. Robert Penn Warren, "The Uses of History in Fiction" (Panel discussion with Ralph Ellison, William Styron, and C. Vann Woodward, 1968), in *Talking with Robert Penn Warren,* ed. Watkins, Hiers, and Weaks, 109.

14. Warren, "Speaking Freely" (Interview with Newman, 1971), 196.

refusing to clothe historical figures in glories or evils they never wore, Warren refuses to hold past individuals to standards they could not possibly have reached. Warren seeks to honor historical figures by acknowledging their fallibility as well as their greatness.

Warren wrote about America's creation of heroes in "A Dearth of Heroes," an *American Heritage* essay written as an introduction to Dixon Wecter's 1941 study, *The Hero in America: A Chronicle of Hero-Worship.* The essay argues for the importance of studying heroes: "If the hero is the embodiment of our ideals . . . then to analyze him is likely to mean an analysis of ourselves. By a man's hero ye shall know him. . . . To create a hero is, indeed, to create a self."[15] Summarizing Wecter, the article specifies aspects of the American self that are ensconced in America's heroes. America was founded upon abstractions, the ideas articulated in the Declaration of Independence, which have fed the nation's persistent preoccupation with its own future and expansion. With its attention drawn toward spatial and temporal distance, the American vision is ambivalent about attachment to a particular place and a shared past. Americans possess a peculiar sense of mobility: rather than situate themselves into history, they consider themselves immune to the forces of history. Lacking connection, America looks elsewhere for an identity, specifically to collective symbols such as heroes (the American flag being another example of such a symbol).

The process of demythicizing makes legendary figures more real, in turn enabling the present culture to identify with them. In "The Use of the Past," Warren addresses the importance of this task: "There is no absolute positive past available to us, no matter how rigorously we strive to determine it—as strive we must. Inevitably, the past, so far as we know it, is an inference, a creation, and this, without being paradoxical, can be said to be its chief value for us. In creating the image of the past, we create ourselves." Reconciling past with present requires attend-

---

15. Robert Penn Warren, "A Dearth of Heroes," *American Heritage,* October 1972, 4.

ing to how history is constructed. But myths are nonetheless necessary. Summarizing Warren's revision of myths, L. Hugh Moore notes: "Because history is full of danger for man, he needs a myth. Since much of history has no meaning inherent in it, man must make sense of it."[16] The empiricism and pragmatism of modernity challenge the construction of new myths because they have destroyed old beliefs. Therefore, Warren sets out not to obliterate myths but to revise them so that they will be more applicable to a modern age. He accomplishes this by creating his secular version of Original Sin, the "Doctrine of Complicity" (cf. Justus, *Achievement*), a matrixed ethic much needed in a modern age of historical separation.

It must be noted that the "Doctrine of Complicity" is still a myth. After interrogating myths and dismissing idealized views of the past, the idea that all are guilty of original sin becomes the most important myth Warren finds worth salvaging. Robert White observes: "In the end, Warren insists that we must return to a by now largely abandoned view of human nature . . . the view that man is brother to dragons, that he is guilty of 'original sin.' "[17] Thus, Warren's historical realism substitutes previously idealized (or romantic) myths with myths he deems more usable for the modern world.

Although this study concerns Warren's prose narratives, we may find one of his most succinct instances of the reconciliation process in a poem from *Promises*, "Founding Fathers, Nineteenth-Century Style, Southeast U.S.A." The speaker regards daguerreotypes of ancestors, but in looking into the camera to have their portraits taken, the men stare from the pictures toward the present with "severe reprehension" and "eyes that now remark our own time's sad declension." The subjects of the portraits judge the present just as viewers in the present judge the past. The speaker describes how they lived, married, raised children, worked, "longed for an epic to do their own deeds right honor,"

16. Warren, "The Use of the Past," 51; Moore, *Robert Penn Warren and History*, 20.

17. Robert White, "Robert Penn Warren and the Myth of the Garden," *Faulkner Studies* 3 (1954): 66.

and died. The speaker also observes "those, the nameless, of whom no portraits remain." Acknowledging all of the forebears, famous and common, the speaker exhorts the reader, noting that "now their voices / come thin . . . But beg us only one word to justify their own old life-cost":

> So let us bend ear to them in this hour of lateness,
> And what they are trying to say, try to understand,
> And try to forgive them their defects, even their greatness,
> For we are their children in the light of humanness,
> and under the shadow of God's closing hand.[18]

The poem implies that the fathers are no different from the sons; all are capable of moments of greatness and all are susceptible to moments of failure. By suggesting that the progeny learn to forgive them, the poet removes the forebears from the proscenium that makes them appear legends and heroes. The poet places the ancestors into a realistic construction to supersede the romantic narratives that have characterized them. By interrogating the myth, the poet unites the progenitors and the progeny within the same matrix, making history more alive, accessible, and relevant.

William Bedford Clark comments that in Warren's thought, "History, read honestly, offers us no model for a Golden Age. . . . To seek to renew in some pristine sense the flawed covenant of the Founders is an exercise in useless sentimentality. But neither would it be wise, Warren insists, to renounce their dream out of hand."[19] Glorifying the past, according to Warren, is just as destructive as repudiating it altogether. Both courses, the former by reverence and the latter by ignorance, result in the uncritical repetition of past actions. The proper approach toward the past thus becomes respect rather than reverence. Regarding the ancestors as heroes removes them from common experience, robbing them of their weaknesses and humanity. Self-righteous criticism of ancestors assumes that one is disconnected from the

---

18. Warren, *Selected Poems, 1923–1975*, 241–43.
19. Clark, *American Vision of Robert Penn Warren*, 100.

past. Because the effects of human actions are ultimately unpredictable and unknowable, an individual's best approach to history is humility in communion with the forebear. According to Warren, because all acts have consequences that may or may not be intended or predicted, the "proper attitude" for all humanity to take toward history is "humility."[20] Warren's "proper attitude" means that history should be neither a burden nor hero-worship. So that the present may more readily identify with the past, history should be transmitted in a realistic mode, which is more accessible to the modern reader than a romantic narrative.

By the end of "Founding Fathers," the fathers appear more real, more human, and their children have greater access to their glories and failures. This poem thus argues for connection. It calls upon the children to show empathy—to hear, understand, and forgive the fathers—because both the children and the fathers have directed their lives within the same "light of humanness" and have surrendered to their limitations "under the shadow of God's closing hand." They are all in the matrix. Whether Warren's narrators and protagonists experience salvation depends upon whether they acknowledge their place as members of the matrix. Such acknowledgement depends upon recognizing the fallibility of their ancestors.

The speaker of the poem teaches the same lesson that Jack Burden learns: history is not a burden but an instrument of liberation, because it affirms the humanity both of those who lived in the past and those who inherit the past. This redeeming knowledge can be learned only through historical reconciliation, a process that dominates the Warren canon of biographical narratives from *John Brown: The Making of a Martyr* to *Jefferson Davis Gets His Citizenship Back* and *Portrait of a Father*. Throughout these works Warren audits the ledgers of the past, critiquing and revising the historical record as necessary.

Return and reconciliation ultimately result in the kind of knowledge that redeems one from the burden of the past, meaning not that one is completely liberated from the past but that

---

20. Moore, *Robert Penn Warren and History*, 89.

one has accepted it rather than being defeated by it. Barnett Guttenberg notes, "The burden of responsibility is liberating. . . . Responsibility for one's being means that one is the creator of his being, and that he is therefore free to choose what his world will be."[21] In the conclusion of *All the King's Men*, Jack Burden is freed from the burden of the past by acknowledging the importance of history and his own responsibility in time. The past is still present to him, but unlike Faulkner's Quentin Compson, for him it is now a "usable history" that will aid him in navigating his way into the future. Redemption is often apparent in the act of confession, as in the interpolated narratives of the novels. Ashby Wyndham's story is his confession to the police. Willie Proudfit and Munn Short tell their stories respectively to Percy Munn and Jeremiah Beaumont, to share the self-knowledge that they have gained through their sins and redemptions. Articulating this knowledge is a public act of self-definition requiring the teller to externalize his identity.

In an essay widely regarded as one of his major epistemological statements, Warren argues that "only by knowledge does man achieve his identity . . . because [knowledge] gives him the image of himself." Through knowledge one achieves self-definition, a state of separation. However, knowledge also makes one realize that one's own experience is universal, that one is in a state of "osmosis of being" with the rest of the world. Warren illustrates the redeeming quality of knowledge with the following metaphor: "Man eats of the fruit of the Tree of Knowledge, and falls. But if he takes another bite, he may get at least a sort of redemption."[22] In *Brother to Dragons*, Thomas Jefferson communicates the importance of using historical knowledge for redemption, by admitting that even though he told Adams "That the dream of the future is better than / The dream of the past," the truth is "That without the fact of the past, no matter / How terrible, we cannot dream the future" (BD 118). Jefferson's kins-

21. Barnett Guttenberg, *Web of Being: The Novels of Robert Penn Warren* (Nashville: Vanderbilt University Press, 1975), 55.

22. Robert Penn Warren, "Knowledge and the Image of Man," *Sewanee Review* 63 (1955): 186–87.

man, Meriwether Lewis, pursues this thought: "For nothing we had, / Nothing we were, / Is lost. All is redeemed, / In knowledge" (*BD* 120).

An example of redemption through knowledge and confession is "Blackberry Winter," a Prodigal Son story in which the narrator at age forty-four, revisits one day of his childhood to acknowledge his complicity in time. Seth observes that in childhood, time is not a pattern of separate moments but an atmosphere within which events emerge: "When you are nine years old, what you remember seems forever; for you remember everything and everything is important and stands big and full and fills up Time and is so solid that you can walk around and around it like a tree and look at it" (BW 64). The story is an initiation narrative; the storm that floods the landscape and the stranger who confronts Seth's father both intrude upon the garden of Seth's youth. Seth narrates the story as a man in his forties recalling how time appeared during his prelapsarian existence, before events seemed to become fragmented from each other. The young Seth's perception of time eschews both vector and matrix paradigms, for events have no clear points of origin or termination. In fact, time never moves:

> You are aware that time passes, that there is a movement in time, but that is not what Time is. Time is not a movement, a flowing, a wind then, but is, rather, a kind of climate in which things are, and when a thing happens it begins to live and keeps on living and stands solid in time like the tree that you can walk around. And if there is a movement, the movement is not Time itself, any more than a breeze is climate, and all the breeze does is to shake a little the leaves on the tree which is alive and solid. (BW 64)

By recalling when time was a "climate in which things are," the older Seth prefigures the narrator of *Jefferson Davis Gets His Citizenship Back*, who recalls having learned about the Civil War not necessarily from home or school, "but from the very air around him" (*JD* 9). In *Jefferson Davis Gets His Citizenship Back* Warren recalls a "sense of changelessness" (*JD* 3) that he

experienced in his boyhood. Because the effects of the Civil War
are still being felt, the past is a strong presence; thus, "time
seemed frozen, because nothing seemed to be happening there
on that remote farm except the same things again and again"
(*JD* 8).

There are parallels between Seth's story and Jack Burden's
ethical discovery of historical interconnectedness. Like Burden,
the older Seth recounts his own story, though the spatial limitations of the short story offer Seth the opportunity to narrate not
a thread of successive events but a description of one day in his
life. The older Seth, then, does more than recall his initiation
into the world of experience. He depicts a conflict between two
notions of time: climate and movement. Linear movement is
depicted by the stranger walking with deliberation through the
woods at the beginning of the story, and by the changes that
the boy observes throughout the story (such as the dead poults,
the garbage washed out from under Dellie's cabin, and Dellie's
change of life). The boy himself matures by taking part in the
movement, moving away from his mother's rule by violating her
order not to walk barefoot, and ultimately moving away from
his father's rule by following the stranger "all the years."

However, Seth returns. "Blackberry Winter" is a Prodigal Son
story, similar to the confessions made by the narrators of the
interpolated narratives within the novels: Willie Proudfit, Ashby
Wyndham, Cass Mastern, Munn Short, and Hamish Bond.
(James Justus, in the first chapter of *The Achievement of Robert
Penn Warren*, entitled "Fathers and Sons," gives the most thorough discussion of this theme of the son who leaves and returns
to the father.) Seth's narrative is in the confessional mode, culmi-
nating in the admission of his sin: "But I did follow him, all the
years" (BW 87). The act of narration, then, is an act of return.
He recounts his memories of his mother and father, and Dellie
and Old Jebb, with a sensitivity that suggests nostalgia—a romantic desire to reconnect with the past and with the sense of
connection that he experienced in his youth: "When you are a
boy and stand in the stillness of woods . . . you feel your very
feet sinking into and clutching the earth like roots" (BW 64).

Equally significant is the interplay between past and present in this story. The older Seth comes to the same realization as Warren's narrator in *Jefferson Davis Gets His Citizenship Back*: "There are two kinds of memory. One is narrative, the unspooling in the head of what has happened, like a movie film with no voices. The other is symbolic—the image, say, of a dead friend of long ago" (*JD* 1). Memory can be chronological or symbolic, the latter of which is the more enduring. In his narration, Seth chooses to present his memory not as an unwinding spool of thread but as an image, as if it were something solid, something that "begins to live and keeps on living and stands solid in Time." The adult Seth recalls events from one day in his life. The concluding sentence of the story indicates that Seth has been physically—but, more important, also spiritually or emotionally—led astray. His "following" the stranger ever since that one day implies that he has had many experiences, after that day, that repudiate home and parents. Yet Seth chooses not to narrate events of the years between the story time (when he was nine years old) and the time of his discourse (when he is forty-four years old). Thus that one significant day has existed in his memory like an image, a symbol, a "tree that you can walk around" or "a kind of climate in which things are." By revisiting it through narration, Seth recognizes his complicity within the matrix of time, and his narration becomes an act of redemption.

II

The Making of a Historian
The Biography of John Brown

And still they come, these young iconoclasts, aflame with
crusading zeal and bent on telling the oldsters where they
get off with their historical hero-worshipping.
—Avery Craven, Review of *John Brown*, 1930

To topple an idol from its pedestal was not enough; the idol
must be hacked in pieces and the pieces trampled in the
mud of innuendo and scorn.
—William MacDonald, Review of *John Brown*, 1930

In later texts Warren demythicizes historical figures
for the purpose of making them more accessible
to a modern audience. His objective is to enable
readers to connect with the subject. *John Brown: The Making of
a Martyr* fails because Warren destabilizes myths as an exercise
for its own sake, with no attempt at connection or redemption.
Reconciliation becomes mere revision. As we will see, in later
works such as "The World of Daniel Boone," Warren struggles
against the influences of romantic historians yet concedes his
debt to them. He realizes that he cannot achieve absolute realism, and the result is a dialogue with the past. In contrast, in
John Brown Warren dismisses his precursors. Asserting his own
realist voice above theirs, he enters into a monologue that ne-

glects to recognize that, like them, he proceeds from a "narratorial" agenda. Although many critics have identified Warren's youthful sarcastic tone as the weakness of the Brown biography, the actual flaw is that Warren does not interrogate his own agenda as forcefully as he examines those of prior biographers. Instead, he assumes that his voice is the only objective one in the debate over Brown. His ability to question his own authority as forcefully as he could question other historians would require decades of maturity.

Robert Penn Warren was years away from writing his most mature and reflective statements on history when he researched and wrote *John Brown*. Nevertheless, in that biography, we can see the earliest step toward history taken by a man of letters who would spend a lifetime struggling with the past. As many have noted, the biography anticipates the major themes of later works: the conflict between individual idealism and social complexities, the problem of identity and self-knowledge, the seductions of power.[1] Similarly, many critics have identified John Brown as the "prototype," "progenitor," and "ancestor" of Warren's later fictional protagonists.[2] Though these appraisals are essential to an understanding of Warren's historical fictions, a full appreciation of the work after *John Brown* requires attention not only to Warren's development of the protagonists and their related themes but also to Warren's development as histo-

1. For example, see Louis D. Rubin, Jr., *The Wary Fugitives: Four Poets and the South* (Baton Rouge: Louisiana State University Press, 1978), 337; Walker, *A Vision Earned*, 87; Justus, *Achievement of Robert Penn Warren*, 1; Hugh Ruppersburg, *Robert Penn Warren and the American Imagination* (Athens: University of Georgia Press, 1990), 24–25. My argument, however, takes its origin from L. Hugh Moore's *Robert Penn Warren and History*, which proposes that history is the central subject in Warren's work.

2. See Casper, *The Dark and Bloody Ground*, 92; Charles H. Bohner, *Robert Penn Warren* (New York: Twayne, 1964), 31; John L. Stewart, *The Burden of Time* (Princeton: Princeton University Press, 1965), 447–48; Justus, *Achievement of Robert Penn Warren*, 210; Connelly, "Robert Penn Warren as Historian," 15; Ruppersburg, *Robert Penn Warren and the American Imagination*, 25; C. Vann Woodward, Introduction to *John Brown: The Making of a Martyr*, by Robert Penn Warren, Southern Classics Series (Nashville: J. S. Sanders, 1993), xvi.

rian. In his introduction to the 1993 reprint of *John Brown*, C. Vann Woodward observes that "the biography reveals much about the biographer as well as about his subject."[3] The historian-narrator of *John Brown* is also a prototype for the narrator of the later histories. This early experiment in biography was not only about "the making of a martyr." It was also about the making of a historian.

In *John Brown*, as in all of Warren's work, the most significant protagonist is the historian-narrator, and the most essential theme—upon which all the other themes are based and to which they all return—is how the historian-narrator constructs the historical figure. Critics of *John Brown* have focused on Warren's biases and his political and moral themes, yet the essential issue in *John Brown* is that Brown existed for Warren as an embedded myth whose layers had to be peeled back. Brown was a text Warren had to demythicize in order to reconcile heroic versions of the past with the needs of a cynical modern age.

Warren began the biography with the intention of researching Brown, but instead he discovered the ontological and epistemological problem of constructing the biography. He discovered that he had to audit the records of John Brown's biographers to create a version of Brown that would be more accessible to modern readers. The result was a biography that Warren proposed as authentic and definitive, one that replaced the heroic conventions of previous biographies with its own conventions of verisimilitude.

To understand Warren's objectives and his failures in *John Brown*, some background is necessary. In 1929 Warren was a twenty-four-year-old graduate student whose association with Allen Tate at Vanderbilt University earned him an introduction to literary agent Mavis McIntosh; she obtained for him a commission from publisher Payson & Clarke to write a biography of Brown. Intent on historical accuracy, Warren thoroughly familiarized himself with all of the definitive biographies of his subject, even taking a trip to Harper's Ferry, where he inter-

---

3. Woodward, Introduction to *John Brown*, xvii.

viewed the last surviving witness of the infamous raid.[4] While a Rhodes Scholar at Oxford he completed the biography in his spare time, and though it was probably "the most readable account and the most penetrating appraisal of the gaunt fanatic yet to appear,"[5] the book sold poorly due to the effects of the Great Depression on the publishing industry. Adding to the dismal sales were the negative reviews directed against what one reviewer labeled Warren's "de-heroizing process" and what another reviewer called "an indictment, not an unbiased biography."[6] The book was not received well. The epigraphs to this chapter typify the severity of reviewers exasperated by Warren's adolescent attempt at the fashionable, ironic, witty Strachean style. Reviews that did praise the book noted its thorough research and penetrating analysis but nevertheless charged it with failing to appreciate the complexity of its subject.[7]

Even sympathetic Warren scholars have cited the "young writer's recklessness," an intention "to burn John Brown in effigy,"[8] and a failure "to present the past in all its complexity

4. Bohner, *Robert Penn Warren*, 29.

5. Stewart, *The Burden of Time*, 141.

6. From reviews of *John Brown* by, respectively, Florence Finch Kelly, "John Brown Sits for a Critical Portrait," *New York Times Book Review*, 12 January 1930, 7, and Avery Craven's review in *New York Herald Tribune Book Review*, 12 January 1930, 17. For more positive reviews, see Allan Nevins's review ("Martyr and Fanatic," *New Republic*, 19 March 1930, 134–35), which praises Warren's accuracy and insight, and the anonymous review in *Historical Outlook*, a journal for history teachers, which notes that Warren "has judiciously re-evaluated the facts and events of Brown's life" (*Historical Outlook* 21 [1930]: 186).

7. For example: "There is in it a certain quality of keen analysis and ability for pointed statement, but the temptation to clever manipulation and overstatement is too great" (Craven's review, 17); "John Brown is dramatized, made vital, and to a certain extent he grips the reader's imagination. But he is not made understandable. . . . [One familiar with the history] cannot feel that such an estimate tells the whole story" (Kelly's review, 7); "Warren's book, for all its interest and value, does not get at the heart of that figure" (F. L. Robbins's review, *Outlook*, 13 November 1929, 153). See also mixed reviews by Dexter Perkins, "Figures in Perspective," *Virginia Quarterly Review* 6 (1930): 614–20; and R. H. Gabriel, "Seven American Leaders," *Yale Review* 19 (1930): 590–96. Gabriel states that the work, though unscholarly, identifies biographical problems and thus should stimulate further enquiry.

8. Casper, *The Dark and Bloody Ground*, 91.

and ambiguity."[9] Such assessments are generally accurate and deserved; yet, with the advantage of historical hindsight, these same critics have noted the book's flaws with much more patience than its earliest reviewers. Recognizing the superior work that followed *John Brown,* Warren scholars have appropriately treated the book as apprentice work. Beyond the cynicism and inexperience of a novice historian, critics see *John Brown* as important despite its flaws because it laid a foundation for Warren's career. Marshall Walker notes that with the publication of this biography, the young writer "demonstrated the readiness to 'enter history, not to flinch from history' that has typified his career."[10]

If Warren's first historical work is a failure, it is therefore a fortunate one. What William Havard says of Warren's fiction can be applied to the nonfiction as well: "The striking feature of Warren's effort is the tremendous scope of his quest"; thus, if he occasionally fails, "it is a noble failure." Similarly, from William Bedford Clark, this "very failure was an eloquent witness to the ambitious nature of his vision and offered an undeniable promise of greater things to come."[11] The book is a significant gateway into Warren's later work. In *Who Speaks for the Negro,* Warren himself comments on *John Brown* with the hindsight of thirty-five years: "That book was shot through with Southern defensiveness, and in my ignorance the psychological picture of the hero was presented too schematically. But even so, the work on the book was my real introduction into some awareness of the dark and tangled problem of motives and values" (*WSN* 320). Warren said in an interview with Richard Sale: "*Brown,* I guess, was an approach to fiction because it presented a psychological problem to deal with and the question of narrative."[12]

9. L. Hugh Moore, *Robert Penn Warren and History,* 27.
10. Walker, *A Vision Earned,* 237.
11. William C. Havard, "The Burden of the Literary Mind: Some Meditations on Robert Penn Warren as Historian," in *Robert Penn Warren: A Collection of Critical Essays,* edited by Lewis Longley (New York: New York University Press, 1965), 182; Clark, *American Vision of Robert Penn Warren,* 36.
12. Robert Penn Warren, "An Interview in New Haven with Robert Penn Warren" (Interview with Richard Sale, 1969), in *Talking with Robert Penn Warren,* ed. Watkins, Hiers, and Weaks, 137.

John Brown establishes the intention that characterizes Warren's entire career: to reconcile the past with the present—to reconstruct events from the conventional historical record by
exposing the plots by which those events have been historicized,
so as to create (to borrow Van Wyck Brooks's term) a more "usable past." Warren managed to "discover the real Brown amidst
all the legends and folksay, and the distortions or calculated
omissions of earlier partisan biographies."[13] The cynical misrep-
resentation of Brown was ironically the consequence of a sometimes too ambitious attempt to expose what the writer saw as
previous misrepresentations.

To inaugurate his own text as the authoritative version, Warren employs paratextual markers that he never again uses in his
biographical narratives, specifically, the map of Harper's Ferry
on the flyleaf, the photograph of John Brown, the illustrations
of various historical scenes, the bibliography, the index, and even
the author's personal footnotes that unintentionally appeared in
the first edition.[14] Without these paratextual elements, this book
could easily be classified as a less successful meditation on biography rather than an attempt to write a conventional nonfiction
biography. The book's status as "nonfiction biography" is therefore unstable.

The most significant paratextual element is the subtitle, "The
Making of a Martyr," an indication that Warren's objective is to
record not only the history of how Brown lived but also the history of how Brown has been represented by biographers. This
text is not simply *about* John Brown. It is concerned with how
Brown has been constructed—how he has been "made"—as a
historical figure. From the beginning Warren set out to write history about the "making" of history. While Warren's book has
been criticized for its unreliability, throughout *John Brown* Warren addresses the problem of creating an accurate biography of

---

13. John L. Stewart, "Robert Penn Warren and the Knot of History," *English Literary History* 26 (1959): 103.
14. Gerard Genette has noted that certain paratextual elements distinguish
history from fiction. See "Fictional Narrative, Factual Narrative," *Poetics Today*
11 (1990): 772.

a mythologized figure. The result is a biographical narrative that says as much about the problems of the biographer as about his subject.

Warren focuses on two subjects: Brown as individual and Brown as historical creation. The first Brown was (to borrow Warren's words from *Audubon: A Vision*) "only himself," but the second "Brown" was the hero of American myth. Brown died in 1859, but "Brown" has lived on because he was plotted into history. Warren examines the two ways that this heroic "Brown" was "made." First, Warren examines the biographies that have recreated John Brown. Second and more significant, Warren examines how Brown manipulated the historical record so as to create himself. Warren explicitly interrogates these previous texts of Brown's life and discovers their unreliability for his own research. Throughout the biography, Warren recognizes the difficulty of writing an accurate life—a text upon layers of untrustworthy texts. Because he cannot access his subject directly, Warren calls attention to the texts—those created by biographers and those created by Brown himself—that stand not as windows to the past but as screens that obstruct the past.

Warren audits previous biographies of Brown to locate biases and inaccuracies within constructions of Brown's life. His bibliography exposes the unreliability of these other accounts. The essay section, "Bibliographical Note: A Matter of Opinions," critiques the unreliability of—and the presence of personal agendas within—previous accounts. In the essay Warren notes that James Redpath, the writer of the 1860 biography, was an abolitionist who omitted Brown's complicity in the Pottawatomie Massacre so as to ensure Brown's status as a martyr to promote the Union cause. Warren particularly critiques the definitive biography, written in 1910 by Oswald Garrison Villard, for relying upon Brown's family as an authoritative source, dismissing Brown's minor crimes as errors, and ignoring the more serious crimes altogether (see *John Brown* 442–43).

By censuring Hill Peebles Wilson and Villard for neglecting Brown's "elaborate psychological mechanism for justification" (*JB* 446), Warren justifies his own authorial intrusions into

Brown's mind. Censuring those biographers for lack of accuracy seems to authorize his own narrative and justify his cynical tone. The treatment of Brown's biographers in the "Bibliographical Note" may in part account for the sarcastic tone for which Warren has been criticized. Some, for example, note that the tone is the result of this book being an "Agrarian's attempt to demythologize a Northern martyr." (In an interview with Marshall Walker, Warren agreed with this assertion but added that this was not a "conscious motive," since his work on the biography began before "the Agrarian conversations.")[15] Throughout the biography Warren's intrusive voice reacts against the historical constructions of Brown. As Ruppersburg notes, Warren "rarely stands in awe of [historical figures]," because to Warren the "Great Men of History" are really "spokesmen, commentators, symbols, even, like Brown, exploitive opportunists, relatively isolated from the elements of which history is made."[16] The "Bibliographical Note" demonstrates that Warren also does not stand in awe of the biographers of historical figures. His voice in the biography reflects his skeptical stance toward John Brown and the processes by which he has been "made." Moreover, through his tone and critiques of other biographers, he seeks to legitimate his own narrative. Paradoxically, though, in exposing the biases of other biographers, he neglects to acknowledge his own agenda—to bring John Brown down from the pedestal.

Warren demythicizes not only by examining how biographers have constructed Brown but also by investigating how Brown constructed himself. The biography proceeds chronologically, according to convention, though as noted, with emphasis upon the construction of events and not just events themselves. Warren begins with Brown's genealogy and formative years, focusing on Brown's later reconstructions of these events. The narrative

15. Walker, *A Vision Earned*, 86; Robert Penn Warren, "Robert Penn Warren: An Interview" (Interview with Marshall Walker, 1969), in *Talking with Robert Penn Warren*, ed. Watkins, Hiers, and Weaks, 150; see also Justus, *Achievement of Robert Penn Warren*, 209; Stewart, *The Burden of Time*, 447; Walker, *A Vision Earned*, 86.

16. Ruppersburg, *Robert Penn Warren and the American Imagination*, 26.

considers his earliest abolitionist readings and writings, coupled with his religious fervor, ambition, and restlessness. Warren concentrates on the decade leading up to the Harper's Ferry raid, tracing Brown's legal and illegal political activities during the conflicts over "Bleeding Kansas," with particular emphasis on the Pottawatomie Massacre, a violent raid on his political opposition. Warren investigates Brown's charisma, his creation of a band of supporters, his fundraising efforts, his formation of a sort of paramilitary school, his plans for a provisional government, and his use of the news media. The biography culminates in the Harper's Ferry raid, assessing reasons for its failure. The book closes with the aftermath of the raid—Brown's trial and execution.

The narrator persistently reminds us that Brown was always conscious of his place in national and cosmic events, and for this reason he was meticulous about textualizing himself for political purposes. A major theme of the biography is how Brown imposed himself upon history through letters, speeches, and a sophisticated style of public relations and media manipulation. As Warren presents him, Brown was trying to write a narrative of his political and spiritual success. With such self-textualizations, Brown was his own first biographer, a kind of American "self-made" man.

The first self-textualization Warren investigates is Brown's name. The first chapter, "But Not in a Rented House," recounts an episode from Foxe's *Acts and Monuments,* the execution of a heretic named "John Brown" who was martyred in the early sixteenth century. Warren speculates that if John Brown ever read this account, "he may have wondered if that fellow who bore his name had any connection with himself" (*JB* 11). The speculation continues: when the nineteenth-century John Brown was executed, "some of his friends half-mystically reflected on the similarity of name and fate" (*JB* 11). Warren emphasizes that these two Browns had no actual family connection, nor was there any connection with the Peter Brown who sailed on the *Mayflower,* though "John Brown firmly believed this man to be the father of his line" (*JB* 11). This opening revises not only

traditional conceptions of who Brown might have been; it also
revises the very conventions of biography. Usually, a biography
begins with some tracing of the subject's genealogy so as to define the subject, but Warren challenges Brown's misconceptions
about his genealogy. Warren does this in one other text, *Audubon: A Vision*, which begins with a preface that corrects the "official version" of Audubon's identity as the Lost Dauphin and
cites other "embellishments" and "legends." The first section of
the poem is entitled "Was Not the Lost Dauphin." Similarly,
Warren defines Brown only in terms of who he was *not*. The
identity of Warren's "Brown" is more a product of self-composi-
tion than genealogy.

The chapter also investigates Brown's childhood, which was
spent reading history books, and Warren concludes that "from
them it seems he took the habit of dramatizing himself a little;
he learned the meaning of ambition" (*JB* 20). As a boy of twelve,
he had his first glimpses of slavery, which "led him 'to declare or
swear eternal war with slavery'" (*JB* 19). With undercutting
irony, Warren comments and questions: "In any case these are
the details that John Brown related after he had become the relentless Kansas Captain John Brown. . . . Had he come across
the story of Hannibal's infant oath on the altar of Baal? Or in the
book he knew best the story of the voice calling at night to the
child Samuel?" (*JB* 19). From examining the name and earliest
formative experiences, Warren explicitly seeks not just the foundation of Brown's later views but the origin of Brown's own
script for his life.

Warren recounts how young Brown decided to enter the min-
istry (an ambition cut short due to ill health) and later hid a
runaway slave. After a search party left the cabin, Brown went
out to locate the slave, who had run outside to hide. Brown
found him and later recalled, " 'I heard his heart thumping before I reached him' " (*JB* 21). Warren sardonically marvels at
the amazing acoustics of the region and quips, "Incidentally, he
seized on the opportunity to again swear eternal emnity against
slavery" (*JB* 21). Warren narrates these incidents ironically to
emphasize that such legendary moments in Brown's life have

been constructed by Brown himself. Brown told of such events years later, plotting them in such a way as to fit into the plot of his public life. A moment from his childhood becomes an epiphany: hearing the heartbeat of one slave prefigures Brown's later ability to recognize the suffering of all slaves. Warren has commented that Brown "lives in terms of grand gestures and heroic stances. . . . Brown lives in the dramatic stance of his life . . . he lives in noble stances and noble utterances."[17] To Warren, such events were created in hindsight, and they have been created or revised to agree with the heroic plot into which they are placed.

Warren's assessment of previous biographies in the "Bibliographical Note," and his examination of Brown's genealogy and childhood in the first chapter, interrogate the subsequent legend of Brown's life. By exposing the truth of Brown's genealogy and by encouraging a skeptical view of early events that Brown plotted as epiphanies in his life script, Warren questions the historical authenticity of Brown's legend.

Brown structured his life according to two plots; we might call them the savior plot and the martyr plot. The notion of creating himself as a martyr would not occur to him until years later, at his trial. In Warren's narrative, the principal role that Brown constructed for himself was that of savior: Brown would be a kind of Moses or Christ, freeing slaves from their physical bondage and the American South from its spiritual bondage. In the chapter entitled "The Birth of a Nation," Warren describes speeches Brown made to those who joined his band: "John Brown told them that God had created him to be the deliverer of the slaves, just as Moses was of the children of Israel" (*JB* 261). In the second chapter, "The Merchant Prince," Warren writes: "He had faith in the will of God, and that faith was so great, perhaps, that he began to know what thing God willed. And to foreknow was to will also; at last his own will and the divine will were one" (*JB* 63). As I have shown in Chapter I, Warren would label such thinking "moral narcissism," the illu-

17. Warren, "Robert Penn Warren: An Interview" (Interview with Walker, 1969), 155.

sion that one's intentions are commensurate with and sanctioned by God's will.[18] Warren distrusts this providential view of history because nations and individuals can use it to justify any policy or action. As Ruppersburg notes, "Warren apparently suspects that Brown consciously exploited High Law absolutism to justify his actions."[19] Though Warren would not write "The Use of the Past" until almost fifty years after *John Brown*, the ideas are already apparent as he calls into question Brown's method of plotting his life according to biblical typology.

Facing trial, Brown shifted roles from savior to martyr. He could take advantage of his new position by transforming himself into a passive leader, a martyr. To Warren, this transformation began even as the Harper's Ferry raid concluded. Awaiting the inevitable attack by the Marines, Brown began to justify himself to both his followers and his captives inside the armory. In this passage, worth quoting at length, Warren's narrator exceeds his authority as an objective historian and performs the fictional act of becoming omniscient so as to enter Brown's consciousness:

> He cast back for something more personal, more intimate, more powerfully his own to justify him in the extremity. "Gentlemen," he said to the prisoners, "if you knew my past history, you would not blame me for being here." . . . His words were almost like the reveries of age—the reveries in which old men try vaguely to piece out some chain of cause and effect, of reason and deed, to account for themselves and their place. . . . It was as if, for the first time, John Brown was thinking of himself as a mere victim, and not as an active agent who willed the deed. (*JB* 376)

The passage continues with Brown thinking that perhaps the project failed due to a defect in his own faith, that perhaps if his will had been stronger he would have succeeded. Thus, the rationalization that Brown offered to his band, his captives, and to himself is one that never questioned whether the moral righ-

---

18. Warren, "The Use of the Past," 32–33.
19. Ruppersburg, *Robert Penn Warren and the American Imagination*, 25.

teousness of his mission really justified his means. Brown main-
tained faith in the righteousness of violence in the cause of an
absolute moral position and thereby cast himself as a martyr
rather than a criminal. He refused to consider a plea of insanity,
for "it would have meant a repudiation of himself. . . . It would
have meant that he himself was nothing" (*JB* 401). Brown realized that an insane man would not make a satisfactory martyr.

Warren reminds the reader of what he states back in the first
chapter, that in his youth Brown "had learned to dramatize himself" (*JB* 428). Warren charges Brown with dramatizing himself
as a martyr by lying in court (*JB* 412) and by selectively reading
and quoting from the Bible in his cell to find justification: "He
found his vindication there as he had always found vindication,
and again it clearly pointed out his way to him. 'I am just as
content to die for God's eternal truth and for suffering humanity
on the scaffold as in any other way,' he wrote to his younger
children" (*JB* 429). The section on Brown's efforts at martyr-
dom concludes as it begins: with Brown being controlled by
events beyond his power. After his execution, the Civil War begins; according to Warren, the war and the Emancipation Proclamation "defined John Brown," for "John Brown was a cipher, a
symbol, in this argument, which had so little concern one way
or the other with what sort of a fellow he really was" (*JB* 432).
Just as later Warren characters like Willie Stark find themselves
defined by historical accidents (e.g., the notoriety Willie receives
after the fire-escape accident at the school), John Brown's transformation into a myth is validated by chance as well as by de-
sign.

In the first chapter, I argued that Warren challenges myths by
exposing the processes by which they were created. Throughout
the Brown biography, Warren also challenges myths by interrogating the individual events of which they are composed. Warren
reveals that as Brown resorted to more dubious methods, such
as theft and murder, he also employed more sophisticated methods of media control. As William Bedford Clark notes, Brown's
manipulation of media helped to create Brown's "most enduring

and enigmatic text—his self-created Self."[20] The sixth chapter, "A Little Company By Ourselves," presents the central controversial event in Brown's life—the Pottawatomie Massacre, in which Brown and his band killed opponents and stole their horses, guns, and other items so as to supply themselves and their cause with provisions. This event was and still is a major event in Brown's life because it provided Brown with the fame he needed to gain support for the Harper's Ferry raid. This event is also controversial because for Brown to remain a heroic figure it had to be revised or completely erased from the historical record by both Brown and his sympathetic biographers. Warren resurrects the events of the massacre to question the heroic savior-martyr plot of Brown's life. In other words, as a future New Critic, Warren locates an event that has been excluded from the plot and inserts it so as to call the unity of the entire plot into question.

After the massacre, the men traded the horses they had stolen to get rid of the most obvious evidence of the crime and also obtain faster horses. However, "the terms of [this] transaction will never be known," because, as Warren writes: "The sons who survived John Brown even denied for years his presence on the Pottawatomie on the night of May 25. When the truth was out at last and the world had prepared a motive—a motive which would fit the martyr—there were confessions from the sons. The world had justified the murderer; the Browns knew that it is a little more difficult to justify a horse thief" (*JB* 166). The "truth" of this event depends upon the motives of the storytellers. Because the severity of the crime paradoxically implies the sincerity of convictions, Brown's execution of his opponents fits into the martyr plot. However, petty thievery does not flatter a martyr.

Knowing the damage that such information could inflict upon the story he was constructing for himself, Brown hired a press agent so that he could "become to some people who could forget or excuse Pottawatomie, or deny his share in it, a sort of hero

---

20. Clark, *American Vision of Robert Penn Warren*, 39.

and defender" (*JB* 176). Warren treats the press agent with
irony. Abolitionist reporter James Redpath "knew that what the
Free State cause needed to consolidate . . . was a hero," and
whereas previous men were "not good copy," "Old John Brown
would do admirably" (*JB* 183). Similarly, Brown's letter to his
wife following the crime is in reality, according to Warren, "his
official announcement" denying any involvement in the crime.
Warren comments: "That was all he had to say about Pottawatomie. It was the story he wanted the world to accept" (*JB* 176–
77). Years later, while drawing up a constitution for the
provisional government that he was preparing to establish if necessary, Brown wrote a preamble stating his absolute belief that
slavery was a declaration of war, justifying any act, however dis-
honest or violent: "And so, a little tardily, the events of Pottawatomie received their definition" (*JB* 281). The Pottawatomie
crimes had certainly received their definition within Brown's
own consciousness, but this document, Warren argues, is a public statement giving the crimes a context. By investigating the
process of defining prior events, Warren exposes Brown's apparatus for imposing versions of himself onto popular audiences.

In the seventh and eighth chapters, "Letters of Marque from
God" and "Passing the Hat," Warren makes his most extensive
summation of Brown's rhetorical ability to manipulate audiences
whenever he was speaking and writing on behalf of his cause.
Warren comments that Brown "always managed delicately to
adjust the extent of his connection with Pottawatomie to the
stomach of his audience" (*JB* 203). He notes that "with his more
ambitious scale of action he gave a new dignity to the business
by drawing up a Covenant" (*JB* 207), implying that Brown realized the rhetorical function of official documents. In these chapters Warren wryly cites Brown's "genius for saying the
impressive thing, at the impressive moment" (*JB* 210). Warren
exposes Brown's strategies for marketing himself, "to create for
the world at large" a "picture of the hero": "Brown knew well
enough that the pen was mightier than the sword, but he saw no
reason why one should not use both; and the battle he lost by
the sword was converted magically into a victory won by the

pen" (*JB* 216). In other words, Brown would falsify numbers, maximizing the casualties of the enemies and minimizing his own. At one point Warren calls Brown's pen and even Brown's name his "weapon" for responding to criticism (*JB* 302, 306). In his hands the pen and oratory were weapons eventually meant to conquer his enemies by first conquering his supporters. One particular example is most illustrative for its colorful narration and humorous tone. Brown asked Mrs. Stearns, the wife of a well-known philanthropist, to give her opinion on a speech that he was writing. A sort of farewell address to be delivered to a congregation, the speech explained that dwindling financial resources would force him and his followers to disband and terminate their abolitionist efforts. While delivering the speech to her, "John Brown lifted his eyes now and then to watch the effect on Mrs. Stearns" (*JB* 240). Warren comments: "In all probability Mrs. Stearns was the entire audience for which John Brown intended his farewell. That audience was completely converted and completely ashamed. . . . Mrs. Stearns was in the mood for selling all her goods and giving the money to the poor Captain John Brown" (*JB* 241). Mrs. Stearns prodded her husband, who gave Brown a check for $7,000. Warren's terse commentary: "The two paragraphs of 'Old Brown's Farewell' are one of the highest paid literary productions on record" (*JB* 241). The purpose of describing this scene at length is that it illustrates Warren's point that to Brown, "Vocabulary was simply a very valuable instrument" (*JB* 246). Warren portrays Brown using discourse pragmatically to shape and impose images of himself.

Warren even accounts for disparate versions of the events at Harper's Ferry by concluding that Brown must have continued his efforts to revise events by giving false statements to the authorities. Given Warren's sardonic comments throughout the biography, some of the statements in this section seem dissembling or contradictory in their deferential tone: "It is unpleasant to recall John Brown's words, for they rob the scene of something of the worth which his courage had earned and the dignity which was its due" (*JB* 389). According to Marshall Walker, in Warren's construction of Brown, ulterior motives follow Brown all the way to the execution, for Brown "realized that death on the scaffold would provide him with the inestimable advantage of becoming a myth."[21] To the end, Brown tries to enforce the myth that he had become.

What makes all of these observations, investigations, and disclosures about Brown's life useful to Warren is that they demythicize the hero. In Warren's text, "The idea of the martyr is fairly melted back into the impure elements of history."[22] Brown and his supporters envisioned Brown to be a man driven by absolute principles. However, his willingness to shape the message according to the particular situation reveals Brown as a pragmatic man as well, negotiating his absolutes as a method of upholding those very same absolutes. In this regard, critics are correct in noting that Brown is the forerunner of protagonists like Willie Stark and Jeremiah Beaumont, who discover that reaching the goal of an ideal paradoxically requires employing means that violate that ideal. Instituting an ideal requires using the very political and financial machinery that may be antithetical to the ideal. Warren presents Brown as a shrewd politician who accepted that setting his sights on more daring political acts would require shaping his discourse into marketable versions of his message.

While Brown is certainly a prototype of Warren's later protagonists, he is so for reasons in addition to those that critics have conventionally identified. Other Warren scholars have noted that Brown prefigures Warren's later conflicts between idealism and political reality, and between individual identity and public persona. But Brown prefigures more. His discourse sets the standard for Warren's later protagonists.

Because Warren exposes and criticizes this discourse, the narrator is also a prototype. William Bedford Clark has suggested that Warren's examination of John Brown's writings resembles Burden's use of Mastern's journal and the narrator of *World Enough and Time* examining Jeremiah Beaumont's journal.[23]

21. Walker, *A Vision Earned,* 87.
22. Ibid., 86.
23. Clark, *American Vision of Robert Penn Warren,* 38.

For example, the historian-narrator of *World Enough and Time* comments on Jeremiah Beaumont, "It was a drama he had prepared, an ambiguous drama which seemed both to affirm and to deny life, to affirm and to deny humanity. . . . It may be that a man cannot live unless he prepares a drama" (*WEAT* 5). In writing his journals, Jeremiah purposefully leaves behind a "lifescript" for the historian to work from. Like Brown, he is a "selfmade" man in the sense that he considers how his decisions will construct his private and public identities. After Beaumont kills Fort, he takes pleasure in condemning the act, as though cleansing himself of the corruption and returning to the society of others; this is just one of his many intentional efforts to reconstruct himself publicly. Such ironies are not lost on the narrator. When Jeremiah and Rachel attempt suicide, the narrator recognizes their noble effort to escape the dishonor of execution in Roman fashion. But they fail, and in wry tones reminiscent of the Brown narrator, the narrator comments, "So after the fine speeches and the tragic stance, the grand exit was muffed. The actors trip on their ceremonial robes" (*WEAT* 401). As in *John Brown,* the narrator exposes the historical truth, thereby demythicizing the players. As the historian of *John Brown* exposes the layers of historical revision in his "Bibliographical Note," so the historian of *World Enough and Time* often "protests" (to use Woodward's term) the incompleteness of the historical record. The narrator surveys the scraps of letters and newspaper clippings that remain, and he finally comments, "We have what is left, the lies and half-lies and the truths and half-truths" (*WEAT* 3). These protests make the reader "skeptical" of the "narrator's pretensions," "and that . . . is the author's intention. Otherwise, why does the narrator protest so much?"[24] The biographer of *John Brown* exposes the historicity of his subject by disclosing to the reader the fallibility of the historical record as it has been created and distorted by historians and by the historical personage himself. Thus the *John Brown* biographer prefigures Warren's later narrators.

24. C. Vann Woodward, *The Future of the Past* (New York: Oxford University Press, 1989), 230.

We see another example in *All the King's Men*. Like John Brown, Willie Stark is an idealist who compromises his ideals. Burden demythicizes Willie by exposing the apparatus with which he constructs public images of himself. Willie is a "self-made" man who composes plots and images of himself as methods for establishing his power. Among these images are the large photographs of him in drugstores and pool halls, his casting himself into an American success story, the photo session when an image of him as a family man is staged, his apprenticeship in speechwriting and oratory, his son's success on the gridiron, and his hospital. Stark's political rise is not only the result of his learning how to put aside ideals and employ compromise, corruption, and intimidation in political games. His political success was very much the result of his learning to revise and publicize representations of himself. Warren's relation to John Brown in 1929 prefigures Jack Burden's relation to Willie Stark. In 1946 Warren's ironic tone resurfaces in Burden's wry and sardonic comments; more important, his interrogation of the historical record also reappears, as protagonists and narrators are shown manipulating the historical record. The difference is that Brown and Stark impose themselves into history; Warren and Burden take these figures "out of history into history" by exposing their historiographical impositions.

The discourse of Brown and Stark is linear—monological. They dominate an audience through manipulation and deception, and as Warren suggests, they compromise values in that process. For example, though Brown would invoke history when he needed a precedent, he would also revise history as necessary to his purposes: "John Brown never looked back; his past and history were simply an instrument for framing astounding future" (*JB* 310, *sic*). Similarly, theology was also a political instrument: "When [an issue] was transposed into terms of theology there was no hope of settlement" (*JB* 314). And American values like freedom could also be useful; in Brown's paramilitary "school" his student-disciples "learned, above all, what virtue can lie in a word; the word 'Freedom' obscured every selfish motive, and transformed, in the public mind if not in the recesses of their own more realistic minds, every act of criminality or violence into something worthy and excellent" (*JB* 264). These three examples—history, theology, and freedom—demonstrate how concepts conventionally considered enlightening became tools of concealment in Brown's agenda. Though these are traditionally considered cohesive elements for a community, Warren's Brown employs them against communities. According to Warren, Brown uses dialectic rhetorical situations to serve his linear purposes.

Because Warren discloses the methods with which the public version of John Brown has been constructed, this biography anticipates Warren's continued investigations into the rift between private self and public persona. For example, *John Brown* introduces one type of scene that reappears throughout Warren's historical fictions. As Brown and his band travel to Harper's Ferry at night, the narrator notes that none could have answered the question of why they were there except for Brown, who "might have found a readier answer, but it, like the other answers, would not have told the whole story. . . . He marched down the road to Harper's Ferry because he could not do otherwise" (*JB* 348–49). This moment anticipates characters like Percy Munn in *Night Rider* and Jeremiah Beaumont in *World Enough and Time*, questioning their motives as they ride at night to commit their crimes. Their public selves have driven their private decisions, but with the darkness concealing their public identities, their private identities emerge, leading them to ask themselves why they are there. Public and private selves exist in dialogue or, sometimes, in debate.

In *John Brown* Warren's omniscient narrator enters Brown's private self behind the public image and reveals the discursive means by which that public image has been created. He emphasizes "the importance of the individual's private self over whatever public persona he might assume."[25] The biography demonstrates that the private John Brown (like the private Jeremiah Beaumont and Willie Stark) is a reality, but the public ver-

25. Ruppersburg, *Robert Penn Warren and the American Imagination*, 27.

sion is a fiction. And with all of these protagonists, the fictional public version eventually encroaches upon the private self. Individuals come to believe their fictions to the point that the validity of the private self comes under question. Identity in Warren's novels, then, is a product of historical representation. History and identity are in dialogue, constructing each other, but sometimes they are in conflict.

Warren's biography proposes itself as a corrective because he enters the discord between history and identity by examining how the hero is a person "made" by himself and by others. Such a self-conscious narrative connects past to present. By demythicizing—by removing the public construction and leaving only the private self—Warren forces the hero to become human. Thus, the "hero" becomes accessible and connected to the present. This approach to historiography permits a more authentic response to history than hero-worship permits. Burden learns how to act responsibly when he discovers that history is a matrix rather than a timeline—that all events and actions are connected like the points of a spiderweb. Warren removes historical figures from the abstractions that separate them from the world and places them within this matrix of time. When Warren "calls upon the testimony of the past to counter, rather than foster, a myth,"[26] he does not destroy history. He revives historical figures by acknowledging that they are individuals "with virtues and weaknesses, products of their era and environment" who "become great because their society comes to see them as such, or because they come to view themselves as such, not because of innate ability or vision."[27] Because destabilizing the images of heroes makes historical figures more human than heroic, it makes history more accessible.

However, Warren makes John Brown inaccessible, and this is where the biography fails. The major problem with *John Brown* is that Warren performs the demythicizing process for its own sake. In *John Brown* Warren does not return to his home soil or

26. Clark, *American Vision of Robert Penn Warren*, 35.
27. Ruppersburg, *Robert Penn Warren and the American Imagination*, 27.

seek redeeming knowledge; he approaches the trope of reconciliation in a vacuum. Whereas historical revision becomes a vehicle for significance in his more mature works, in *John Brown* revisionism is an aesthetic beyond which the young biographer does not reach. One reviewer (William MacDonald, in the epigraph at the head of this chapter) was not entirely far from the truth by accusing Warren of not only toppling the idol from his pedestal but hacking the idol into pieces.

In later works Warren strips away heroic textualizations to create a sense of connection with the historical figure. The narrator and reader join the historical subject in what L. Hugh Moore defines as "historical interrelatedness," and the knowledge that all are joined within the same matrix of time redeems them from the burden of history.[28] In *John Brown* Warren makes no such attempt at connection or redemption. His approach to reconciling the ledgers of past and present is less forgiving. He is concerned only with revising the past rather than reconciling with the past. Warren critiques and dismisses all prior representations of Brown without offering any redeeming representations. He tears away the idealistic portrayals from history, but he does not stop to tend the wounds.

As in "The World of Daniel Boone," Warren uses a dialogical approach in *John Brown*. The "Bibliographical Note" and bibliography bring other texts and voices into the debate. However, like Jack Burden narrating the Cass Mastern story, Warren asserts his narratorial voice over all of the others. In this regard, L. Hugh Moore delivers the sharpest and most precise criticism: "In *John Brown*, then, Warren is guilty of the very things he has warned against, a one-sided attack, ignoring the tremendous complexities which he believes inhere in any historical event or any human motivation."[29] Warren begins by calling for dialogue, but he develops into a monological narrator.

The monological voice proposes to "correct" the previous biographers, but he does not interrogate his own agenda with the

28. L. Hugh Moore, *Robert Penn Warren and History*, 65.
29. Ibid., 28.

same diligence. Warren criticizes Villard, Wilson, and Redpath for creating their own versions of Brown, but he does not recognize that he, too, is creating a version of Brown, a "realistic" version. Instead, he substitutes previous biographers' conventions of idealized history with his own conventions of realism. The main convention Warren employs is the examination of how Brown and others after him have textualized him. The other convention is the cynical tone with which Warren, like Jack Burden, persistently attempts to legitimate the narrative as authentic. The narratorial voice is so concerned not to take on characteristics of hero worship that it swings too far in the opposite direction by taking on an exaggerated, affected, academic detachment. What makes *John Brown* an immature text is not simply the presence of these conventions; it is the author's unexamined assumption that such conventions are synonymous with objectivity. As a young biographer Warren was astute in questioning the authority of prior biographers, but he also failed to question his assumption that he was writing the definitive text.

As a narrator, the young Warren resembles the young Jack Burden, presuming the inviolability of his own neutrality and distancing himself from the historical object with his condescending rhetoric. His overt tone expresses disapprobation to create the detachment of a superior observer, but this pose of objectivity actually calls attention to his lack of objectivity. His affected neutrality undercuts itself.

In later biographical works, Warren disabuses himself of these false assumptions. The works become more reflective and more patient with their objects as the author, like the maturing Jack Burden, acknowledges complicity with the past. For example, in *The Legacy of the Civil War* (1961) Warren comes to realize that there are "the heroic, charged images that our hearts and imaginations strenuously demand . . . the image of John Brown, abstracted from his life and from history, standing on the scaffold and drawing a pin from the lapel of his coat and offering it to the executioner to use in adjusting the hood. Such images survive everything—logic, criticism, even fact if fact stands in the way. They generate their own values. For men need symbols for their aspirations" (*LCW* 32–33). In later historiographical projects, Warren's style of demythicizing changes. Woodward states that the Brown project "was the first but not the last venture into history that Warren made, though the later ones were more in the nature of reflections on history."[30] In later biographical narratives, the fallibility of the historical figure affirms the humanity of those who lived in the past and those who inherit it. The acknowledged fallibility of the narrator also serves an affirmative function in the later narratives. In addition to *John Brown*, Warren's other early writings on race show ambivalence. "The Briar Patch," his contribution to the 1930 Agrarian manifesto *I'll Take My Stand*, maintains academic distance from the topic. The later narratives, *Segregation: The Inner Conflict in the South* and *Who Speaks for the Negro?* show an author who has become discontent with the voice of a detached narrator. Although they are not biographical narratives, they are personal narratives, grounded in interviews and shaped by the autobiographical impulses of the narrator. They are narratives of connection.

Segregation opens with the narrator's return home, described as an inevitable act within the matrix of time: "But I went back, for going back this time, like all the other times, was a necessary part of my life. I was going back to look at the landscapes and streets I had known—Kentucky, Tennessee, Arkansas, Mississippi, Louisiana—to look at the faces, to hear the voices, to hear, in fact, the voices in my own blood" (*Seg.* 229). He travels along the road that becomes archetypal in Warren—first a runway that he sees "drop away, like a dream" (*Seg.* 229), and then Highway 61. As he drives along the highway, he sees in the headlamps of the automobile an image that stands in counterpoint to the voices within him: "a glimpse of the black faces and the staring eyes. Or the figure, sudden in our headlight, would rise from the roadside, dark and shapeless against the soaked blackness of the cotton land" (*Seg.* 230). Like Seth, the narrator is a fugitive from home, with the voices and images of his native region haunting him until he must return to confront or reunite with them.

30. Woodward, Introduction to *John Brown: The Making of a Martyr*, xv.

Whether to confront or reunite is precisely the struggle that characterizes the narrator's reconciliation process. The voices that remain with him are those of the people with whom he identifies, the white people he will interview. But the black images that he sees (or imagines he sees) cast shadows upon the interviews. They are also the voices he will hear again nine years later when he interviews leaders of African-American civil rights organizations and writes *Who Speaks for the Negro?*. For the present book, he interviews white leaders of segregationist organizations. He is in an ambivalent relationship with the past and his home region; they are his burden and his hope.

Both books are part of the same process, of which *Segregation* is the beginning. *Segregation* presents neither a complete return nor reconciliation. Warren always remains somewhat outside his own process. He notices that even the whites, his own people, are suspicious of him. Visiting a fort, he sees a boy who turns from him, and "occasionally there would be a stiffening, a flicker of suspicion, an evasion or momentary refusal of the subject" (*Seg.* 235). Checking into a motel, Warren observes the desk clerk glancing at the license plate on his car: "My Tennessee license, and Tennessee accent, hadn't been good enough credentials in Clarksville, Mississippi" (*Seg.* 236). Warren attributes these encounters to "suspicion of the outlander, or of the corrupted native" (*Seg.* 237). However, if others are unwilling to interact with him, he demonstrates similar detachment. He attends one interview of a black activist, but with the detachment of Jack Burden he states, "I've just come along to watch, I'm not involved" (*Seg.* 250). His departure leaves little room for redemption: "I know what the Southerner feels going out of the South, the relief, the expanding vistas. . . . I feel the surge of relief. But I know what the relief really is. It is the relief from responsibility. . . . It is the flight from the reality you were born to" (*Seg.* 260–61). These statements are echoes of Jack Burden's flight to the American West, in direct contrast to Barnett Guttenberg's claim of self-liberation through responsibility.

Nonetheless, *Segregation: The Inner Conflict in the South* succeeds because it concludes with a serious examination of racial issues and hopeful articulation of solutions that the future might bring. Warren's tentative departure from the South echoes R.P.W.'s exit from Smithland at the conclusion of *Brother to Dragons:* "But now I passed the gate into a world / Sweeter than hope in that confirmation of late light" (*BD* 132). *Segregation* concludes with the realization that the South has a moral problem; however, the redemptive process of creating a solution will make the South a moral leader for the nation.

Warren reflects upon the most significant problem facing the South, "self-division" (*Seg.* 261), noted in the subtitle of the book, *The Inner Conflict in the South.* The reconciliation process begins in earnest as he points out that "division between man and man" is a symptom of "division within the individual man" (*Seg.* 262). He catalogs the polarities that create internal divisions within each southerner. Each white citizen is torn "between his own social idealism and his anger at Yankee Phariseeism . . . between his social views and his fear of the power state . . . between his social views and his clan sense . . . between his Christianity and his social prejudice . . . between his sense of democracy and his ingrained attitudes toward the Negro," and so forth (*Seg.* 262). Warren does not attempt to negotiate the conflict presented in each of these dichotomies, but he takes the initial step toward resolution by identifying them and arguing, "I don't think the problem is to learn to live with the Negro. . . . It is to learn to live with ourselves. . . . I don't think you can live with yourself when you are humiliating the man next to you" (*Seg.* 268).

A more complete step toward resolution appears with the publication of *Who Speaks for the Negro?,* which makes a much more realized attempt at return, reconciliation, and redemption. The book begins with the voice of a narrator who seems discontent with his decision to leave the South in hopes of finding "relief from responsibility." Showing a clear development from detachment to connection, the narrator's foreword, written in the first person (as is the entire work), states his objectives in personal terms: "I have written this book because I wanted to find out something. . . . This book is not a history, a sociological analysis, an anthropological study, or a *Who's Who* of the Negro Revolution. It is a record of my attempt to find out what I could find out" (*WSN* n.p.).

In the first chapter Warren revisits his segregationist essay, "The Briar Patch," from *I'll Take My Stand*. He states that he "never read that essay after it was published," and "in fact, while writing it, I had experienced some vague discomfort" (*WSN* 10–11). He acknowledges that his attempt to define and defend a humane conception of segregation was not only misguided, it was also a tacit admission of flaws in the South: "[my] self-consciousness indicated an awareness that in the real world I was trying to write about, there existed a segregation that was not humane" (*WSN* 11). He concludes, "I could never again write the essay" (*WSN* 12). This prefatory critique of "The Briar Patch" was necessary before Warren could proceed with a serious study of race relations. *Who Speaks for the Negro?* presents another return to the region of his origin. By opening the book with a retraction of his previous essay, Warren also returns to himself. As he acknowledges responsibility for writing a text that demands correction, he performs an act of reconciliation with himself, which prepares him to reconcile with others and with the past. Warren exposes the faults of his earlier work as an act of connection.

In a similar passage, Warren re-examines his behavior during one night in 1939. While waiting for someone in a car on a street adjacent to the Louisiana State University campus in Baton Rouge, Warren saw a white man beating a black boy. He comments: "I had felt some surge of anger, I had put my hand on the latch of the door, and then had, in that very motion, stopped," because he had been overcome with "that paralyzing sense of being totally outside my own community" (*WSN* 13). Fortunately, someone else intervened; Warren admits, "I had been saved. I had not had to get 'involved' " (*WSN* 13). Warren recounts this autobiographical scene in the confessional mode. Like Seth returning to a day of his youth in "Blackberry Winter," Warren recognizes and uses narrative to represent his complicity.

The acts of narrating and interviewing manifest a shift from detachment to connection. The interviews demonstrate Warren's development from a detached observer to an audible and participatory narrator. In *The Achievement of Robert Penn Warren*, James Justus thoroughly analyzes the narrator of *Who Speaks for the Negro?*: "This book is very much Warren's. While he generally allows his spokesmen their own formulations, he does not hesitate to editorialize or even moralize."[31]

Warren's re-examination of his own attitudes in "The Briar Patch" during the episode near the LSU campus, and his involvement with the interviews, reactivate a process that began only at the end of *Segregation*. The earlier text concluded with a self-interview that has the appearance of rigorous self-reflection. But this self-interview is still symptomatic of division, because it suggests two selves, like Jack Burden's speaking of himself in the third person. Warren's examination of "The Briar Patch" in *Who Speaks for the Negro?* also suggests division, but of an entirely different kind. While the *Segregation* self-interview implies a division of two contemporaneous selves, the self-analysis of *Who Speaks for the Negro?* implies a difference between past and present selves, an indicator of intellectual maturity.

Who Speaks for the Negro? concludes with a substantial section of commentary. As in the conclusion of *Segregation*, the text weighs the balance of historical debts, and it expresses hope for a repair of self-division. In an attempt to reconcile conflicting accounts of the past, Warren considers and criticizes the notion that white Americans must make reparations to black Americans in the form of monetary compensation. He employs rhetorical questions in the service of his argument: are debts owed to "Caucasions who have been penalized by history"; how can such a debt be calculated; would taxes for reparations be expected from those whose ancestors came to America after the Civil War; would African nations who sold their ancestors into slavery also be expected to pay? (*WSN* 434–35). The list of questions implies that some debts cannot be paid, only forgiven. In a movement toward redemption, Warren concludes by admitting that with its

31. Justus, *Achievement of Robert Penn Warren*, 147.

treatment of slaves and their descendants, Western civilization is condemned by its own standards of liberty, justice, and Christian charity (*WSN* 441). Whites must realize that solving the race problem is important to their self-preservation, for full integration, legal and social, will help to make all people contributing members of society. As in *Segregation,* he concludes with a call for integration, an end to both social segregation and self-division: "In the diminishment of others there is a deep diminishment of the self" (*WSN* 443–44).

Segregation and *Who Speaks for the Negro?* are best considered process pieces rather than finished productions. They are records not of the author's conclusions and prescriptions but of his struggles with the issues. These books do not give all the answers, and some of the answers they do give are no doubt debatable, but they do raise significant questions, and they show the mind of a white southerner seriously attempting to determine how to make the necessary and inevitable transition in his thoughts about race relations. National history and current social issues are ultimately personal matters. The presentation of this knowledge to white readers of the 1950s and 1960s is the real achievement of these books.

Thirty years earlier, in *John Brown,* we can see a movement toward the personal engagement and philosophical histories that Warren would produce later in his career with *Segregation* and *Who Speaks for the Negro?,* and also with "The World of Daniel Boone," *The Legacy of the Civil War: Meditations on the Centennial, Jefferson Davis Gets His Citizenship Back,* and *Portrait of a Father.* As words like "portrait" and "meditations" in these titles indicate, Warren's conception of history was that it could unite traits of "fact" and "truth" by uniting both an archivist's concern for accuracy and a philosopher's concern for significance. For all of its immaturity, *John Brown* tends toward these more reflective histories in its substitution of conventions of realism for conventions of romanticism in the construction of historical narratives. It is an important text in the Warren canon. *John Brown* has been called "an essay in philosophical biography";[32]

32. Walker, *A Vision Earned,* 87.

the book shows, in Justus's terms, "a poet's sensitivity to the interstices of the record."[33] Warren himself agreed with this assessment. During a panel discussion at Vanderbilt in 1956, Warren called the book "a step toward fiction."[34] It was a step toward philosophical history as well.

We may admit that the genre of conventional nonfiction biography may not have been the best vehicle for Warren. As Louis D. Rubin, Jr., suggests, "The factual requirements of straight biography [were] too restrictive to permit Warren to let his imagination go fully to work."[35] Nevertheless, in *John Brown* we see the author attempting to go "beyond *what* happened to include the *how* and the *why*."[36] *John Brown* is "the first full-blown evidence of Warren's philosophy of history which he would employ in later prose and poetry."[37] By the time he writes *A Place to Come To,* Warren's first-person narrator Jed Tewksbury can comment on his own "angry, hard, bantering tone" as he writes his autobiography. In a passage that echoes how the young Warren may have approached his biography of Brown, Jed reflects, "That tone represents, I suppose, an unconscious will to detach myself from the scene that is my subject," but Jed also questions that if he remains detached, "what can I now be writing about? For what else can I be and where else can I belong?" (*PTCT* 15).

Like Jed, Warren's metahistorical approach becomes more reflective on the nature of time, more empathetic to the historical figures, and in the novels and later nonfiction histories, more willing to acknowledge the presence of individuals who do not compromise principles or discourse. In his discussion of *John*

33. James Justus, "Warren and the Narrator as Historical Self," in *Time's Glory: Original Essays on Robert Penn Warren,* ed. James A. Grimshaw (Arkansas: University of Central Arkansas Press, 1986), 110.

34. Robert Penn Warren, "Fugitives' Reunion: Conversations at Vanderbilt" (Panel Discussion, 1956), in *Talking with Robert Penn Warren,* ed. Watkins, Hiers, and Weaks, 20.

35. Rubin, *The Wary Fugitives,* 337.

36. Woodward, Introduction to *John Brown,* xiv.

37. Thomas Connelly, "Robert Penn Warren as Historian," in *A Southern Renascence Man: Views of Robert Penn Warren,* ed. Walter B. Edgar (Baton Rouge: Louisiana State University Press, 1984), 15.

Brown in *Who Speaks for the Negro?*, Warren comments: "It is far from the book I would write now" (*WSN* 320). As all writers do with their apprentice work, Warren would step away from the biography of Brown. But this biography will always be Warren's essential entrance into "the awful responsibility of Time."

III

Returning to the Dark and Bloody Ground
"The World of Daniel Boone"

> We can look back on this moment . . .
> —"The World of Daniel Boone"

As we have seen thus far, "Founding Fathers," "Blackberry Winter," *Segregation*, and *Who Speaks for the Negro?* demonstrate the dominant tropes of Warren's historical narratives. The use of these tropes is particularly instructive in Warren's later biographical narratives. His historical explorations in nonfiction, poetry, and fiction, including the interpolated autobiographical narratives within the novels, focus not on the events but on the characters of history. In particular, these works reconcile past and present by examining the processes with which historical figures have been plotted into narratives by themselves and their biographers. To illustrate how Warren's uses of history coalesce in biographical narratives, one short work provides an instructive example.

From 1958 to 1963 Warren wrote three essays for *Holiday* magazine. The first two were historical narratives, "Remember the Alamo!" and "How Texas Won Her Freedom." Warren wrote the third essay, "The World of Daniel Boone," as a travel story and biographical narrative. Though virtually ignored by Warren scholarship, this article offers a small-scale study of Warren's uses of the past in biographical narrative.

As travel literature, the article describes the region ("the world") where Boone explored and settled, providing road directions for readers to follow. The article supplements the readers' travel through the Boonesborough area with background information about Boone's life. As the title indicates, Warren paints a portrait of the region that Boone settled, the "world" that he "created."

However, Warren extends the term "world" to suggest the world that created Boone. What is most significant for critical study is that the article explores how historians, writers of fiction, and poets have constructed Boone, transforming the man into a character in a narrative.

Thirty years earlier, Warren subtitled his biography of John Brown *The Making of a Martyr,* indicating that his interest was not just in the historical figure but in the process of "making" him a legend. Similarly, the "world" in the title of the Boone article indicates the author's concern with the narratives that represented Boone during and subsequent to his life. Like the John Brown biography, the Boone narrative proposes itself as a corrective to previous historical accounts.

Because realistic narration depends not just upon the accuracy of the data but also upon the use of certain literary conventions, Warren employs the tropes of return and reconciliation to legitimate his narrative. Both tropes are evident in the opening sequence of the article, worth quoting at length:

> On U.S. 60, east out of Lexington, that is probably the way you will go—out past the great horse farms of Kentucky, the hunt club and the swelling pastures and white paddocks and stone walls and noble groves. It is beautiful country, even now. It was once thought to be Eden.
>
> At Winchester you turn south on U.S. 227. The country is more rugged now, the limestone breaking through but the bottoms rich. Eastward is the wall of the mountains. You find the river, the Kentucky, and the high modern bridge spanning it. There, by the highway, in a posture of eternal and unconvincing alertness, is the statue: *Daniel Boone.*
>
> To the right of the bridge opens a romantic gorge, to the left

lie the flats. There on the low ground is where Boonesborough was. It is not there now. But on hot Sunday afternoons people still come here to a modest little resort, to cool off in the river, to strew their sandwich papers and idly read the names growing dim on an unpretentious stone—the names of the men who, on this spot, opened Eden.

You can read the names and go—back to Winchester, perhaps, and take the Stanton road, State 15, and find the side road off to Pilot Knob. If you climb it, you will be standing where Daniel Boone stood when he first saw this country. (WDB 162)[1]

By addressing the reader with the second-person pronoun and by employing the narrative-present tense ("you find the river") and present-temporal adverbs ("it is not there *now*," "people *still* come here"), Warren establishes a contemporary stance to close the disconnection between past and present. The narrative invites the reader to stand where Boone stood and see what he saw, either literally by travel or imaginatively by means of Warren's prose. (This kind of "invitation" also appears at the end of *Chief Joseph of the Nez Perce*, as Warren asks the reader to empathize with Chief Joseph's perspective.) Consequently, the opening statements invoke the presence of the past, eliminating any distance between Warren, the reader, and the subject of the narrative. The author and the reader join the historical subject in the matrix of time.

This joining appears in another travel narrative Warren wrote for *Holiday*, "Remember the Alamo!," which begins with road directions: "Go to the Military Plaza. . . . Keep on, over the river, till you hit Alamo Street. Turn left; you are almost there" (52). After taking the reader to the Alamo, the narrator expands his description of the region into a consideration of the Alamo's mythic implications: "Here is where they died. There were the great ones, who were to die in their greatness" (52). This article and its sequel, "How Texas Won Her Freedom," are worth read-

---

1. Quotations from "The World of Daniel Boone," copyright © 1963 by Robert Penn Warren are reprinted by permission of William Morris Agency, Inc., on behalf of the author.

ing for their similarities to the Daniel Boone article, though they are more laden with the factual recounting of the history of Texas and less concerned with explorations of historical construction.

As with the many Warren works (such as *Night Rider, All the King's Men,* "Circus in the Attic," *Segregation,* and *Flood*) that begin with travel sequences, the opening of the Boone narrative signals a return both to region and history. Charles Bohner has observed that like many other American novelists, Warren frequently uses the travel motif as an effective convention for opening a narrative.[2] More specifically, Marshall Walker suggests that the highway in Warren's work is "a symbol of modern man's confident and careless superficiality, his substitution of motion for meaning."[3] Yet for Warren, the highway also represents motion *toward* meaning. For example, "Circus in the Attic" begins with the narrator guiding the reader (addressed with the second-person pronoun) along the highway into Bardsville and up to the town's monument. Jack Burden commences his narrative by recalling his return home in a car along a highway that, because it is new, signals his separation from his place of origin: "To get there you follow Highway 58, going northeast out of the city, and it is a good highway and new. . . . You'll go whipping toward it, but it will always be ahead of you, that bright, flooded place, like a mirage" (*AKM* 1). In the opening of *Segregation,* describing his return to the South in the late 1950s, Warren focuses first upon the runway, then upon his continuing drive along Highway 61, "straight as a knife edge" (*Seg.* 230). Yet the straightness of the edge is not a line or vector, which would propel him into the future. Rather, Warren figures it as a link within the web of time, taking him back. Warren returns south in order to understand racial conflict in the South, a motion toward meaning. Thus, the return home is Warren's "backward glance"; it is a return to that point where the vibrations on the web and the ripples on the pond originated.[4]

2. Bohner, *Robert Penn Warren,* 61–62, 88.
3. Walker, *A Vision Earned,* 73.
4. In "The New Provincialism," Allen Tate states: "With the war of 1914–1918, the South reentered the world—but gave a backward glance as it stepped

The return to the past precipitates a reconciliation with the past. Reconciliation begins when the narrator observes a distinction between the romanticized conception of history and the modern tourists who ignore history. Just as Jack Burden views the landscape as a "mirage," the Boone narrator points out not that the land was Eden but that it was "once thought to be Eden." In an examination of Warren's use of the pastoral myth (as articulated by Henry Nash Smith), Robert White observes, "Warren has examined the myth of the garden of America, the myth of the primitive innocence of America—and found the myths not only inadequate, but essentially false."[5]

Indeed, his emphasis upon the passing of the idealized perception is a "correction" of the Eden myth. Warren criticizes the romanticized notion of Kentucky by citing historian Arthur K. Moore, who examined the eighteenth-century myth of Kentucky as America's paradise or promised land. Moore noted that "rumor transformed Kentucky into something rich and strange a century before the first settlements."[6] Warren quotes from Moore to describe what Boone saw while standing on Pilot Knob: "When he stood here and stared westward, he was looking not only at a forest stretching unbroken . . . but also, as historian Arthur K. Moore has said, at 'a fabled garden interpenetrated with myth' " (WDB 162). This passage romanticizes Boone while simultaneously emphasizing the mythical nature of the story. This establishes a tension between romanticism and realism that permeates the entire article.

Warren criticizes romantic constructions of the Boone story. However, there is a contradiction. He also refers to "the men who, on this spot, opened Eden," and throughout the article he relies upon references to Eden and the Promised Land. Warren seems ambivalent, simultaneously disbelieving yet being drawn to those "rumors" that "transformed" the frontier into a "fabled

---

over the border: that backward glance gave us the Southern renascence, a literature conscious of the past in the present" ("The New Provincialism," in *Essays of Four Decades* [Chicago: Swallow Press, 1968], 546).

5. White, "Robert Penn Warren and the Myth of the Garden," 66.

6. Arthur K. Moore, *The Frontier Mind: A Cultural Analysis of the Kentucky Frontiersman* (Lexington: University of Kentucky Press, 1957), 3.

garden." On the one hand, Warren interrogates the myth; on the other, he expresses nostalgia for it. Juxtaposing what he sees as a malaise of modernity against the mythical past, Warren sets out to "correct" the myths while implying that some myths do constitute a "usable past."

Warren acts as a tour guide not only through a region but also through the process of historical reconstruction. He emphasizes the passing of the romantic Edenic conception of the landscape; he contrasts the ambivalence of modern tourists (who "strew their sandwich papers and idly read the names") with the earnestness of those who "opened Eden"; and he notes "the names growing dim" on the modest monument. With these statements, Warren acknowledges the present disconnection from the past.

Were Warren to visit Boonesborough today, he would likely notice much more disconnection between past and present. The "romantic gorge" is now industrialized, the home of a quarry, with bulldozers digging the limestone out of the ground. The "names growing dim" on the "unpretentious stone" have been eroded away even more by the wind and rain, and have been replaced by the names and initials of vandals who have scratched their own identities into the monument. The present has overtaken the past. Boonesborough now exists only in a reconstructed version located away from the original site and within the minds of visitors who take the walking tour, at each marker looking upon meadows or picnic areas or parking lots, and reading a pamphlet that assures them, "Fort Boonesborough stood in the area in front of you." These ironies would not be lost on Warren.

Such ironies anticipate Warren's return to the Jefferson Davis Memorial in Fairview, Kentucky, in his 1980 portrait of Davis. The monument to Jefferson Davis is visited by people who barely know who Davis was; Warren questions whether the concrete monument is what history has come to in the modern world, and he wonders whether Davis looks at the scene disdainfully from another world. The opening passages from the Boone article do not explore the nature of the monument; such observations come later, in the Jefferson Davis portrait. However, "The World of Daniel Boone" observes that between past and present there is incongruence that must be reconciled. Whereas previous audiences have necessitated figuring Boone within a romantic narrative, a modern audience, which is apathetic at worst and skeptical at best, necessitates a new kind of narrative. As Warren (and Wecter) would argue, the hero reflects the culture that creates him.

Warren tries to provide such a narrative by "correcting" past historical accounts through a modern lens. As though taking a cue from Arthur K. Moore, who asserted that Boone was not the first white man to go into Kentucky, "though that honor has been bestowed upon Boone by legend,"[7] Warren peels away the layers of myths into which Boone has been embedded. To reconcile the ledgers of the past and present, Warren recovers texts by Boone himself and interrogates the texts of his biographers.

Warren sets out to "correct" prior representations of Boone by attempting to replace the first definitive narrative construction of Boone, John Filson's text, with a Boone who fits into a realistic narrative. Warren's method substitutes conventions of realism for conventions of romanticism. One such convention is Warren's almost dismissive references to Filson in the Boone story. Rather than citing Filson as Kentucky's first well-known historian, who conceived the popularly romantic image of Boone, Warren introduces Filson as follows: "Years later, in 1783, when Boone was the most famous man west of the mountains, a Pennsylvania schoolmaster named John Filson, then adventuring into Kentucky, set down a narrative that he got directly from Boone" (WDB 166). Warren's appositive phrases that define Filson use indefinite articles ("a Pennsylvania schoolmaster," "a narrative"), which imply that we have never heard of Filson before. Perhaps Warren anticipates that his audience, readers of a popular magazine, would not be familiar with Filson, as opposed to more well-known popular writers such as James Fenimore Cooper and Lord Byron, whom Warren later

7. Ibid., 48.

mentions without introduction. Yet the article's investigation into historical construction suggests that Warren was writing not just a travel story but a review of historical narratives, as he did in the "Bibliographical Note" that concludes his biography of John Brown. Thus, his introduction of Filson as an unknown puts Filson "in his place." As though to legitimate the verisimilitude of his own biographical narrative, Warren nudges the definitive biographer out of his canonical position.

Warren also counters Filson's statements with quotations from Boone that he selects to present Boone's simplicity and directness. Whereas Filson has Boone declaring that "peace crowns the sylvan shade,"[8] Warren quotes from less formal sources, such as the well-known inscription that Boone carved into a tree.

As a young man, Boone killed a bear and left an inscription on the bark of a tree, "the first of his several wilderness inscriptions: D. BOON KILLED A BAR ON TREE IN THE YEAR 1760" (WDB 164). Warren comments upon this early autobiographical text: "To make such inscriptions was, in the wilderness, a common habit. An inscription might have value as a record of exploration or ownership. But beyond such practical considerations, the act of marking down the name and date was an assertion of identity in the engulfing green blankness of the land" (WDB 164). With the public inscription, Boone fits into the same pattern as many Warren protagonists, from John Brown to Willie Stark, who assert themselves into history by creating public representations of themselves. Unlike Brown's and Stark's political agendas, Boone's self-representation seems a direct and honest statement of identity rather than a shrewdly constructed public persona. In language that echoes the simplicity and honesty of Ashby Wyndham (*At Heaven's Gate*), Warren quotes one of Boone's final letters: "for my part I am as ignerant as a Child all the Relegan I have to Love and feer god beleve in Jeses Christ Don all the

8. John Filson, *The Adventures of Colonel Daniel Boon, Formerly a Hunter: Containing a Narrative of the Wars of Kentucky* (London: John Stockdale, 1793), 22.

good to my Nighbour and my self that I Can and Do as Little harm as I Can help and trust on gods marcy for the Rest and I Beleve god never made a man of my prinspels to be Lost" (WDB 176). Warren presents such quotations from actual documents not only to provide historical accuracy; with their variant syntax and spellings, they suggest that the reader is hearing the "real" voice of the man rather than some constructed voice of myth.

Warren comments that "all his life he [Boone] was to wander through the mysteries of orthography with as gay an abandon as he ever roamed the greenwood" (WDB 162). Indeed, Boone's spelling was variant even by eighteenth-century standards. By comparing Boone's creative spellings to his wilderness wanderings, Warren attributes his orthography to the pioneer ethos, a kind of freedom from the correctness of civilization.

Warren presents Boone's writing as assertions of Boone's identity. He contrasts Boone's versions of himself with John Filson's version of Boone in a biography ostensibly dictated to Filson by Boone. Warren criticizes this narrative for its inaccuracy, which he attributes more to Filson, the man who knew how to read and write, rather than to Boone, the man who told the story: "Filson's account has come in for criticism, and certainly there was one great horse apple of a lie in it—the very language which Filson foisted on his hero . . . fancy, schoolbook language" (WDB 166). With this statement, Warren is referring to Filson's highly stylized language, which seems unlikely to have been spoken by the uneducated Boone, in sentences such as the following from the opening of Filson's *The Adventures of Colonel Daniel Boon* (1793): "Thus we behold Kentucky, lately an howling wilderness, the habitation of savages and wild beasts, become a fruitful field; this region, so favourably distinguished by nature, now become the habitation of civilization, at a period unparalleled in history."[9] Warren criticizes, even ridicules, such a romantic representation.

The problem with Warren's critique is that Filson's language was not as inappropriate for historical representation as Warren

9. Ibid., 1.

suggests. Filson's language was a narrative convention of the century in which he wrote; it was appropriate for its time. John Walton, Filson's biographer, observes, "That these were Boone's own words few believed; but that they expressed his philosophy was assumed by the readers who elected Boone the popular hero of the Romantic Revolution. . . . Filson was surely writing with an eye on the romantic mood of his readers."[10] In fact, Walton argues that "to him [Filson] must be given the credit for realizing the literary possibilities in the story of Boone's adventures."[11] J. Winston Coleman, whose histories include a biography of Filson, concurs, noting that Filson "wrote it [the Boone biography] up according to the contemporary literary taste."[12] It is that romantic literary taste that Warren writes against.

The most significant example of this tension is a passage in which Warren blatantly substitutes conventions of realism for romantic conventions. Warren recounts the death of Boone's son, James, in a frantic battle against a Native American tribe. While the raid is in progress there is no time to mourn when James is killed. Boone's party quickly buries the young man, and months later Boone makes a "solitary pilgrimage" to the grave:

> We can look back on this moment of lonely mourning in Powell's Valley—the most melancholy moment of Boone's life, by his own account—and see it as a moment that gives inwardness and humanity to an age. Beyond the cliches of romance of the frontier, beyond the epic record of endurance and the manipulations of land speculators and politicians, beyond the learned discussion of historical forces, there is the image of a father staring down at the patch of earth. . . . It is like that moment in the midst of the heroic hurly-burly of the *Iliad* when Hector . . . takes his son in his arms. (WDB 169)

This passage makes several significant points. As a romantic hero Boone stands upon a pedestal, distanced from the world below;

10. John Walton, *John Filson of Kentucke* (Lexington: University of Kentucky Press, 1956), 54–55.
11. Ibid., 50.
12. J. Winston Coleman, *John Filson, Esq.: Kentucky's First Historian and Cartographer* (Lexington, Ky.: Winburn, 1954), 8.

but as a typical father mourning his son he becomes real for the reader, an image upon which the experience and empathy of all parents may converge. Warren penetrates popular and scholarly constructions of history to arrive at the archetypal image of a mourning father. He reconstructs Boone into a more realistic image with which all readers may identify. Like the frontiersman slashing a path through the forest, Warren cuts through the "cliches of romance," the notions of epic, the "manipulations" of the modern commercial world, and the conventional historical scholarship, all of which, according to Warren, obscure realistic observation of a historical moment. (Such commercial "manipulations" may include popular media images of Boone created in the 1950s. Two examples are the NBC television series produced by Twentieth-Century Fox, and the 1956 Republic Pictures movie *Daniel Boone, Trailblazer,* produced by Albert C. Gannaway, which featured Bruce Bennett playing a Boone who fought brutal natives and greedy speculators with good humor and heroic references to his own destiny.) This passage removes Boone from romantic texts and refigures him as a character within a realistic text. By destabilizing the hero, Warren makes the hero appear real, thus relevant and accessible to an ambivalent or cynical modern age.

The process of revision demythicizes the hero, uncovering the individual who has been concealed behind a screen upon which heroic representations have been projected. Warren refuses to render Boone irrelevant by oversimplifying his life into a type of historical construction that Warren once derided as "a kind of gross symbol, not a human experience of infinite complication."[13] By viewing Boone without an interposing screen, the reader finds Boone more accessible. For example, in describing Boone's genealogy and childhood, Warren notes that "it would be another seventeen or eighteen years before he was ready to step forth into history" (WDB 164). Thus, the narrative reminds the reader that Boone was a human being before he was a legend.

Toward the conclusion of the Boone article, in a section

13. Warren, "Speaking Freely" (Interview with Newman, 1971), 196.

whose sardonic tone echoes Warren's criticisms of John Brown's biographers, Warren criticizes how historians and writers of fiction have characterized Boone within popular romantic narratives. In addition to the criticism of Filson, Warren cites Byron; Cooper, who "had merely changed Boone to Leatherstocking"; and a minor poet named Daniel Bryan, who published an epic of Boone's life in 1812. Warren approaches these romantic narratives from the perspective of a modern realist, noting that Bryan has the angels meeting over the Allegheny Mountains to decide who should civilize the West and electing Boone, who, according to Warren, was "conveniently waiting on a mountaintop . . . for the revelation of his destiny" (WDB 177). With his irreverent tone, Warren ridicules Bryan's Miltonic approach in passages such as the following from Bryan's *The Mountain Muse*:

> Inspire, immortal Spirits of the West! . . .
> With daring sweep arouse, till lofty song
> The bold sublimity of the new world
> Harmoniously proclaim; and loud resound
> The bloody brunts of the first Western Wars,
> And brave intrepid Boone's adventurous deeds.[14]

Warren criticizes this kind of historical construction, commenting that "the subject of the poem, Boone himself, did not like the work. Perhaps the gap was too great between the inflated verses . . . and his recollection of that May morning [when he went to his son's grave]" (WDB 177). In Bryan's rendition of the death of Boone's son, young James Boone is so virtuous that he soars above the world, but his Icarian flight comes to an untimely end when an Indian's arrow shoots him down.[15] It is, no doubt, such a narrative that Warren refers to when he places Boone at the grave of his son and comments, "We can look back on this moment . . . beyond the epic record of endurance."

14. Daniel Bryan, *The Mountain Muse: Comprising the Adventures of Daniel Boone; and the Power of Virtuous and Refined Beauty* (Harrisonburg, Ky.: Davidson and Bourne, 1813), bk. 5, lines 1, 16–20.

15. See ibid., lines 196–234.

Arthur K. Moore's influence upon Warren is apparent in this critical-bibliographical section of the article. Moore was particularly critical of Bryan for transforming Boone "into a preposterous Miltonic hero" and creating an "incredible portrait" that "revolted the real Boone."[16] Moore's most significant influence upon Warren, however, is not in any one statement about Boone but in the entire historiographical approach. Moore set out to correct what he saw as the inaccuracy of Frederick Jackson Turner's thesis of the American frontier. Similarly, Warren attempts to become a corrective voice in the biography of Boone. Like Moore, Warren struggles against precursors. Moore dismissed both Filson and Bryan, arguing that "no American writer of the nineteenth century had the gifts necessary to translate the frontier type to a large national context."[17] Warren also argues that no writer "got Boone down on paper" (WDB 177).

Yet this statement might seem to assume that Warren himself does "get Boone down on paper" with no interposing agenda. The passage of Boone mourning his son shows this assumption to be false, for Warren's consciousness does color the graveside scene with a romanticism of its own. However, Warren is not unaware of his own shift from covert narrator to overt narrator. With his direct addresses to the reader and the consuetudinary pronoun ("we can look back on this moment"), Warren erases the distance between himself and the historical object.

Unlike the *John Brown* narrator, the "Daniel Boone" narrator does not fail to acknowledge his lack of neutrality. Just as he paradoxically embraces the very Eden myth that he dismisses, Warren acknowledges his own complicity with other historians in trying to write a usable past. Warren admits, "We can only guess what the real Boone was, but the myth of Boone, the image of a certain human possibility, feeds something in the heart" (WDB 177). In the final paragraph of the article Warren recounts the very image that "feeds something in the heart," a description of Daniel Boone "alone in the wilderness, singing to the sunset

16. Arthur K. Moore, *The Frontier Mind*, 105, 146.
17. Ibid., 105.

out of his joyous heart" (WDB 177). This is a moment that appears in John Walton's biography of Filson. According to Walton, in 1770 a party of hunters who thought they were encamped in an isolated area of Kentucky, "were startled by the sound of a human voice raised in song not far from their camp. Approaching cautiously in the direction of the sound they soon saw a white man stretched full length on the ground, singing as loudly as he could. It was Daniel Boone." Walton refers to this incident as one of the "contemporary accounts [in which] Boone lived up to the romantic ideal."[18] Warren takes advantage of this scene, since it blends realism with romanticism. Warren places this romantic scene within a frame of realism: he documents the geography (the Green River area), the dates (1769–70), and the name of the scout (Casper Mansker) who discovered Boone singing. Documentation is, of course, a convention of historical verisimilitude, yet within that convention, Warren presents a romantic episode.

The depiction of this final moment indicates that Warren recognizes the necessity for some of the story's romanticism. Warren implies that myth is humanity's way to make sense out of what Jack Burden would call "the convulsion of the world" (*AKM* 438). During a discussion of Sam Houston in his interview with Bill Moyers, Warren discusses how the story's romantic or Homeric qualities make Houston significant to American history. This comment demonstrates that Warren is not opposed to myth or romance; in fact, he acknowledges their necessity and usefulness. What he does object to is the oversimplification of history. Again commenting on Sam Houston, Warren states, "It's the complexity that is engaging."[19] Warren objects not to myth, but to how myths can be abused when they obscure rather than illuminate the facts of history.

However much Warren criticizes the making of heroes and legends, when he instructs his readers to notice the "romantic

18. Walton, *John Filson of Kentucke*, 55.
19. Robert Penn Warren, "A Conversation with Robert Penn Warren" (Interview with Bill Moyers, 1976), in *Talking with Robert Penn Warren*, ed. Watkins, Hiers, and Weaks, 217–18.

gorge" as they cross the bridge to Boonesborough, he implicitly acknowledges that to be meaningful, history must go beyond its primary responsibility to document facts; it must "feed something in the heart." Warren demonstrates that he recognizes the need for legends and heroes when, even after criticizing Filson's portrayal of Boone's wandering through the wilderness, he comments, "It was a heroic wandering" (WDB 166), and when he writes: "So Daniel was alone, free to scout 'Kentucke' and taste the 'sylvan pleasures' of what he, in Filson's language, regarded as a 'second paradise.' He wandered at will, exalted in spirit" (WDB 167). Even in the passage that cuts through the "cliches of romance" as Boone visits James's grave, Warren concludes by comparing Boone to the epic character Hector. Warren's account admits a version of Boone as "a child of the forest. . . . His attitude toward life was touched with the mystic ambivalence of the true hunter" (WDB 172). At one point, Warren actually expresses regret for the loss of the romantic vision: "In the heart of Eden the palisades were rotting down. Soon Boonesborough itself . . . was to disappear without leaving a trace. . . . The classic figure of the Kentuckian—half beast and half hero, the artist of stomp-and-gouge and the child of nature ready to melt mystically into the curtain of green . . . that lank form in buckskin shirt, breechclout and leggings was about to retire into our romantic dreams and the pages of fiction" (WDB 174).[20] He complains that Boone country is now "an Eden, more in rhetoric than in fact," because lawyers and real estate speculators have replaced the heroes of the frontier and "the legal brief had replaced the long rifle as the weapon for taking Kentucky" (WDB 174). It has been observed that Warren has exhibited some nostalgia for the loss of the Kentucky of his youth: "In [Warren's]

20. This image of Boone echoes Jack Burden's conversation with Anne Stanton in *All the King's Men*, in which he describes Adam Stanton as an idealist: " 'He has lived all his life in the idea that there was a time a long long time back when everything was run by high-minded, handsome men wearing knee breeches and silver buckles or Continental blue or frock coats, or even buckskin and coonskin caps . . . who sat around a table and candidly debated the good of the public thing. It is because he is a romantic . . .' " (*AKM* 247).

youth, Kentucky was for him world enough, as it remains in memories and dreams, an Eden to which he occasionally returns, only to be saddened by its decline."[21] In his portrait of Boone, Warren is an ambivalent realist, trying to renegotiate romanticized notions of the past while expressing nostalgia for those very notions.

For all of his revision of romantic narratives, Warren constructs a romanticism of his own. The Boone narrative demonstrates the necessary coexistence of what Warren identifies as the historian's concern with actuality and the fiction writer's concern with imagination.[22] Even the cynical Jack Burden realized that "while the truth can set one free, it can also kill, and one should, therefore, be true to human values even if this sometimes necessitates being false to the facts of history."[23] Consequently, a realistic narrative is not merely one that is true to facts. Warren has commented to Bill Moyers, "I like these romantic stories of America. . . . I know we've had heroic ages, that it's Homeric."[24] Warren realizes that legends and heroes are still needed to make history meaningful, a particularly difficult endeavor in a modern world that destroys the sources of myth as it exploits nature and disregards humanity.

The Moyers interview is possibly Warren's most succinct and thorough articulation of the problems of modernization. In it Warren warns of what he sees as the possible consequences of the modern age—"the death of history." He argues that "only history keeps alive the human sense. . . . It's man's long effort to be human."[25] The need for history to appeal to "the human sense" indicates that Warren's historical realism is governed by narrative convention as much as by the romantic narratives.

Moreover, Warren's notion of "the human sense" indicates

21. Sister M. Bernetta Quinn, O.S.F., "Robert Penn Warren's Promised Land," *Southern Review* 8 (1972): 330–31.

22. Warren, "The Uses of History in Fiction" (Panel discussion with Ellison, Styron, and Woodward, 1968), 101.

23. L. Hugh Moore, *Robert Penn Warren and History*, 137.

24. Warren, "A Conversation" (Interview with Moyers, 1976), 218.

25. Ibid., 207–8.

that historiography need not consider realism and romanticism as mutually exclusive. Warren reaches for an informed but moving history, a kind of romantic realism of which the graveside episode is an example. The "realistic" text is the one that can be true to facts while evoking the stories that fulfill the need for "heroic stances." For example, Warren quotes from two of the pioneers' diaries, one that calls Kentucky "the garden where there was no forbidden fruit" and the other, described by Warren as "less literary and more realistic," which describes the ruggedness of the landscape (WDB 169). Then, in the next paragraph, Warren comments, "They were moving into the Promised Land" (WDB 169). Yet, again in the next paragraph, Warren writes: "The dream of the garden where there was no forbidden fruit did not last out the journey" (WDB 170). Warren is graphic in describing the hardships, particularly the violence, that ensued. When recounting the capture and deliverance of Boone's daughters, he comments, "This story had a happy ending," although he continues: "But in the murderous time now being ushered in, too many stories did not have happy endings" (WDB 171). The narrator vacillates between the romantic and the realistic. Warren constructs Boone according to the same dichotomy by which Henry Nash Smith defines the frontier hero: he is both a primitive and a builder of empires, asserting independence from the strictures of civilization while also making the virgin land safe for the settlement of civilization. The narrator straddles two narrative conventions.

Warren straddles a third convention as well: self-consciousness. Unlike his precursors, Warren's narrative is openly conscious of its opposition to prior narratives. His narrative dismisses previous romantic biographical accounts while simultaneously recognizing its debt to them. Because he persistently writes in relation to past biographers, Warren is continually in a dialogue with his own scholarly precursors. As Dominick LaCapra has observed, "Historiography is dialogical in that, through it, the historian enters into a 'conversational' exchange with the past and with other inquirers seeking an understanding of it."[26] Warren's return to the past, then, is a return to the scholars who preceded him, and his process of reconciliation is a struggle against their influence. As in the John Brown biography, Warren's approach is dialogical; he demythicizes by putting the range of voices and texts into a dialogue with or against each other. But then the overt voice of Warren's omniscient narrator takes over. In the earlier biography, which Warren wrote at the age of twenty-four, this dominant narratorial voice dismissed its precursors, but in the later work on Daniel Boone, the more mature narratorial voice speaks with the same idealism that it rebels against. As the conclusion of the Boone portrait shows, there is a desire to acknowledge or at least distill something of use from their influence, an attempt at redemption. For all of his criticism and sardonic tone, Warren does not completely dismiss prior biographers; they are his fathers, against whom he rebels and to whom he returns, the prodigal son.

Yet Warren does not terminate the journey exactly where he began. By maintaining a dialogue with his forebears—a dialogue that Warren established in *John Brown: The Making of a Martyr* and continued to the end of his career in *Portrait of a Father* —Warren reminds readers of the distinction between story and discourse, between the past as memory and history as the reconstructed past. It is the knowledge of this distinction that reminds the reader that every individual is complicit in the creation of history. Warren's contribution to historiography is not the replacement of a romanticized past but a conception of the past in which legends, heroes, and ideals are tempered through a filter of realism, the product being a more usable past for a modern age.

26. Dominick LaCapra, *History and Criticism* (Ithaca: Cornell University Press, 1985), 36.

IV

The Silent Monument and the Monumental Silence
Jefferson Davis and Robert Franklin Warren

> And now, all in my own countree,
> I stood on the firm land!
> > —Coleridge, *Rime of the Ancient Mariner*

> I will arise and go to my father.
> > —Luke 15:18, Parable of the Prodigal Son

In the time that elapses between the John Brown biography and the two later biographical narratives, Warren matures as a historian. Warren's final major works, the biographical narratives *Jefferson Davis Gets His Citizenship Back* and *Portrait of a Father*, demonstrate a substantial shift in his historical vision and historiographical technique. These texts are autobiographical. Wayne Booth's terminology is useful here. Warren clearly shifts from "narrator-observer" (detached from the story he narrates, as in *John Brown*) to "narrator-agent" (a participant in the story he narrates). Like Jack Burden, Warren clearly progresses from detachment in *John Brown* to connection in *Jefferson Davis Gets His Citizenship Back* and *Portrait of a Father*. Like the Mariner or the Prodigal Son, he returns and reconciles with the past, and tells his own story.

Warren becomes one of his own precursors, his later narratorial approach acting as a corrective to that of the apprentice-narrator of *John Brown*. The historian of *John Brown* displaced the voices of his elders, but the mature historian of *Jefferson Davis* and *Portrait of a Father* joins the displaced. His earlier voice, which spoke with certainty and affected neutrality, becomes one of the prior voices confronting him. As opposed to *John Brown*, in *Jefferson Davis* and *Portrait of a Father* Warren questions the validity of his endeavor to construct history. Like the Brown and Boone narratives, *Jefferson Davis* peels away historical constructions, but the book also confronts the stony silence of the historical object, an issue that dominates *Portrait of a Father* to an almost obsessive degree. In his early career Warren critically examined what previous histories said. In the two later projects, however, he struggles with what they have not said. He confronts the silent monument of Jefferson Davis, the president of the Confederacy, and the monumental silence of Robert Franklin Warren, his own father.

In these mature productions, Warren explores the nature of historical utterances. He finds that the object in the historian's study is silent, existing in memory rather than in actuality. Indeed, he finds the object silenced by the very voices that textualize it, for the process of narration imposes interpretations that the object is powerless to refute. Jack Burden discovers that "history is blind but man is not" (*AKM* 436). Past events intrinsically offer no meaning to the present; it is the narrating voice that provides meaning by constructing the event as narrative. Because "in creating the image of the past we create ourselves," narrators cannot help but impose their own identities and agenda.[1] Questions consequently arise: Whose voice qualifies to impose itself upon history? What credentials qualify one to speak for the silent objects of history? Who is adequate to the task of filling in the blanks and silences of history?[2]

1. Warren, "The Use of the Past," 51.
2. In this context I am interpreting "blind" to have its customary meaning of "neutral" as opposed to "disinterested." "Neutral" is also James Justus's interpretation ("Warren and the Narrator as Historical Self," 200).

Warren's final narratives seek to answer these questions. In *Jefferson Davis* Warren questions whether the monument is capable of speaking for Davis. In *Portrait of a Father* Warren questions whether the son, the father's living monument, can speak for the father. In both cases, the narrative itself acts as Warren's means to fill the silence.

The monument is the central image in *Jefferson Davis*. The setting is the entire monument site, including the surrounding grounds, the visiting tourists, the community, and the history of the monument's construction. In Davis's birthplace of Fairview, Kentucky, erection of the 351-foot obelisk commenced in 1917 and concluded in 1924, construction having been halted briefly owing to the rationing of materials during World War I. Since its completion, a Jefferson Davis birthday celebration has been held at the site every June, featuring "the Miss Confederacy Pageant, living history camps, artillery and infantry demonstrations, arts and crafts booths and music." There are picnic shelters, playgrounds, and a gift shop where visitors may purchase books about Davis and replicas of Civil War memorabilia. Marking the entrance to the monument site, a plaque quotes from Davis's address during his final visit to the birthplace in 1886: "Kentucky, my own, my native land . . . God grant that your sons and daughters may ever rise to illustrate the fame of their dead fathers."[3] As a son of Kentucky, Warren responds to this filial exhortation with his portrait of Jefferson Davis.

Warren compresses several time periods into the moment of narration. He constructs the narrative impressionistically rather than chronologically, his experiences and memories forming a matrix. He recalls boyhood visits to his maternal grandfather, teenage drives past the monument during its phases of construction, and his adult return to the 1979 annual celebration. The narrative looks back to Davis's virtues and failures in the Civil War and forward to Congress's restoration of his citizenship in 1978. Warren uses all of these occasions to explore the nature of

3. See Kentucky, Department of Parks, *Jefferson Davis Monument State Historic Site*, 1994.

memory, the function of history, the identity of the modern South, and the contrast between contemporary America and the heroic age that Davis represents. Critics have described the book variously as a "meditation," a "semi-fictional narrative based on fact," and an "impressionistic outline of Davis's tragic career."[4] Not a linear narrative, the book is a collage of moments, images, and themes drawn in by the vacuum of the monument's blankness.

The title of the Davis portrait signifies the importance of the historiographical process. *Jefferson Davis Gets His Citizenship Back* focuses not on the individual's life and historical significance but upon the ways in which the community constructs Davis as it constructs his monument. Warren's book is about "how the world has misunderstood [Davis] and attempted to make up for it by erecting monuments in his honor and more recently restoring the citizenship which was revoked."[5] Warren's title calls attention to the moment when modern Americans reconstructed Davis's identity by restoring the citizenship stripped from him in the aftermath of the Civil War. By successfully petitioning Congress (and southern-born president Jimmy Carter) to restore Davis's citizenship, loyal southerners used the political process to legislate Davis's transformation.

Warren directs the reader's attention not just to the historical figure's life but particularly to the monument, the celebrations, and the return of citizenship, recasting him from villain to misguided-but-well-intentioned patriot. Southern consciousness transforms Davis into a sentimental symbol, like the Confederate soldiers whose graves are still decorated in annual commemorations. Southerners loyal to the myth of the Lost Cause often create their symbols by acknowledging that the secessionists' ideology was wrong, while arguing that the Confederates' pride, honor, and commitment to that ideology deserve respect. For

---

4. Reviews of *Jefferson Davis Gets His Citizenship Back:* see respectively, J. W. Cooke, *Modern Age* 25 (1981): 310; M. Thomas Inge, *South Atlantic Review* 47, no. 3 (1982): 74; and Norman D. Brown, *Southwestern Historical Quarterly* 85 (1981): 93.

5. Inge, review of *Jefferson Davis,* 75.

example, the *Souvenir of Fairview, Kentucky,* a pamphlet distributed on the monument's dedication day, defends Davis: "His frankness and his sincerity during the violent debates in Congress were never questioned—even by his enemies."[6] In his portrait of Davis, Warren straddles a similar line. As in the previous biographical narratives, he criticizes romantic historical narratives even as he waxes nostalgic for them.

In "The Gamecock," his 1931 review of two Davis biographies, Warren's straddling between realism and romanticism is already apparent. He suggests that the first writer (Robert W. Winston) was biased against Davis, and he takes the second writer (Elisabeth Cutting) to task for her "sentimental symbolism" of Davis. Warren criticizes both biographers for the same fault: oversimplification of Davis, whether from a realistic or a romantic point of view.[7]

Lewis P. Simpson calls the Davis portrait Warren's "most sentimental essay on the South."[8] As a southern romantic, Warren returns to the South to celebrate Davis, but as a realist, he tries to reconcile the ways in which modern southerners have created the historical "Davis." *Jefferson Davis Gets His Citizenship Back* contains three main sections of return and reconciliation. In the first part of the narrative, Warren returns to his youth when he was introduced to Jefferson Davis and the monument. The second and longest major section recounts Davis's biography and critically analyzes his role in the South's Civil War defeat. In the third section, Warren returns to Todd County for the 1979 celebration, commenting upon this event and the restoration of Davis's citizenship.

As in many Warren texts, the trope of return initiates the narrative. The narrator in *Jefferson Davis Gets His Citizenship Back*

6. *Souvenir of Fairview, Kentucky. Dedication Day, June 7th, 1924* (Sturgis, Ky.: Ezell Publishing, 1924), 12.

7. See "The Gamecock," review of *High Stakes and Hair Trigger: The Life of Jefferson Davis* by Robert W. Winston, and *Jefferson Davis: Political Soldier* by Elisabeth Cutting, *New Republic,* 25 (March 1931): 158–59.

8. Lewis P. Simpson, *The Fable of the Southern Writer* (Baton Rouge: Louisiana State University Press, 1994), 149.

does not return by automobile, train, or airliner; instead, like Seth in "Blackberry Winter," the adult narrator returns home by means of memory: "There are two kinds of memory. One is narrative, the unspooling in the head of what has happened, like a movie film with no voices. The other is symbolic" (*JD* 1). As we have seen, Warren perceives time not in linear terms but as a matrix in which individual events have no clear points of origin and termination. The past is always present: for Seth, time is "a kind of climate in which things are" (BW 64). Similarly, for the young Warren, history is in the very air he breathes: "Time seemed frozen, because nothing seemed to be happening there on that remote farm except the same things again and again. . . . In the ever-present history there was, however, a kind of puzzlement. . . . I didn't get my impression of the Civil War from home. I got it from the air around me" (*JD* 8–9).

Like "Blackberry Winter," *Jefferson Davis* stresses the narrator's maturity. Seth recalls sighting the tramp from the window of his parents' home and imagining the man's journey through the woods and swamp beyond. Likewise, Warren recalls noticing the scenery that lay beyond his grandfather's home: "I am a small boy sitting tailor-fashion on the unkempt lawn, looking up at the old man, and then, beyond him, at the whitewashed board fence, and then at the woods coming down almost to the fence" (*JD* 1). His grandfather's farm is a very significant autobiographical image. In his 1953 "Self-Interview," Warren writes that his grandfather's farm is "among my most vivid recollections. . . . He [grandfather] was, I suppose, 'visionary' to me, too, looming much larger than life, the living symbol of the wild action and romance of the past. He was, whatever his own small part in great events may have been, 'history.' "[9] Both boys, Seth and Warren, literally and imaginatively regard scenery that transgresses the boundaries of home. Both ultimately leave the security of home by following their goals or desires "all the years" (BW 87). And both return as adults, by means of narra-

---

9. Robert Penn Warren, "A Self-Interview," in *Talking with Robert Penn Warren*, ed. Watkins, Hiers, and Weaks, 1–2.

tive, to achieve redeeming knowledge. These are Prodigal Son narratives.

The personal return to Todd County, like the return in the opening of *Segregation,* functions as a convention of historical realism. The use of personal recollections "establishes the author's credentials," because it suggests verisimilitude. James Justus notes that Warren uses personal experiences and memory to "ratify" his interpretations of history, employing "autobiography as a confirming seal." This is, therefore, a very different historian from the *John Brown* and "World of Daniel Boone" narrators. William Bedford Clark observes: "A historical awareness, a conviction that we may see ourselves in the past, becomes a persistent assumption in Warren's writings."[10] In *Jefferson Davis,* Warren makes no claim to objectivity. In fact, personal engagement becomes a structuring device. The pattern of the narrative conforms to the pattern of the mind, not chronological (linear) but as a collage of recollections and impressions (matrix).

For example, during the return to his childhood, Warren recalls his first sight of the monument, and he attempts to reconcile himself with this modern, concrete construction of Davis's identity. Initially, the monument has no meaning and then only superficial meaning for the boy. He hears the news that "not many miles off, in the settlement of Fairview, a big monument was going to be erected to Jefferson Davis, whoever the hell he was—a monument taller, maybe, than the Washington Monument. A monument meant jobs" (*JD* 20). As construction proceeds, the monument accrues new meanings for the young Warren. As narrator, he speculates that when he started driving past the rising monument in his teens, he must have been "unsure . . . I suppose, about the mystery of the pain, vision, valor, human weakness, and error of the past being somehow transformed into, glorified into, the immobile thrust of concrete (not

10. Cameron Freedman Napier, review of *Jefferson Davis Gets His Citizenship Back,* by Robert Penn Warren, *Alabama Historical Quarterly* 43 (1981): 154; Justus, "Warren and the Narrator as Historical Self," 111–12; Clark, *American Vision of Robert Penn Warren,* 27.

even the dignity of stone)" (*JD* 23). The monument is supposed to speak for Davis, but Warren questions what, if anything, it is capable of saying, and this analysis of the monument reveals an agenda. In recalling what went through his young mind, the older narrator records *current* impressions of his *earlier* impressions. In his boyhood he did not write about the monument's effects on him, nor does he specify what the monument means to him at the time of writing the narrative. Rather, he writes as an adult who recalls thoughts that went through his mind when he was a teenager.

We may call these recollections into question. Perhaps Warren actually did notice as a boy that "time seemed frozen," and perhaps the teenage Warren actually did pause before the monument to marvel at history being "transformed . . . into the immobile thrust of concrete." However, these sentiments sound more mature than the student-historian of *John Brown*. In other words, these meditations upon history sound too mature to have been the boy's thoughts.

Seymour Chatman's distinction between "perceptual" point of view (a character's actual, sensory experience) and "conceptual" point of view (a character's subjective impression) is illustrative. Chatman notes that while a narrator may "[look] back at his own earlier perception-as-a-character . . . that looking back is a conception, no longer a perception." When Warren-narrator (writing in 1980) "recalls" the thoughts of Warren-youth (looking at the monument in 1917 at the age of twelve), he reconstructs the youthful perception into an elderly man's conception. Gerard Genette points out that "the narrative of events . . . is a transcription of the (supposed) nonverbal into the verbal."[11] Warren puts into words what may have been, at most, a childhood impression of awe.

Similarly, in *Who Speaks for the Negro?*, Warren "recalls" a lynching that he never actually witnessed. He recalls seeing an oak tree in front of the jail, a sight from his childhood: "The

11. Chatman, *Story and Discourse*, 151–52, 155; Genette, *Narrative Discourse*, 165.

image of that tree which I still carry in my head has a rotten and raveled length of rope hanging from a bare bough, bare because the image in my head is always of a tree set in a winter scene. In actuality it is most improbable that I ever saw a length of rope hanging from that tree, for the lynching had taken place long before my birth. It may not even have been that tree" (*WSN* 11). He cannot look back on the moment without revising it by placing it into a winter setting and by inserting the rope suspended from a branch. His knowledge about the racist and violent context of the region creates an association with lynching when he sees a tree. His earlier perceptions are altered according to his current attitudes about the South.

Just as the monument revises the history of Davis, Warren revises those moments when he first gazed upon the monument. His ruminations upon the monument are those of an older man placing his mature ideas into the mind of the youth he once was. Warren's language itself acknowledges this possibility: "In any case, as I fumble at recollection and try to immerse myself in the dark flow of that moment, it seems that in facing the blank-topped monument I was trying to focus some meaning, however hard to define, on the relation of past and present, old pain and glory and new pain and glory" (*JD* 25). Warren "fumble[s] at recollection" and states that "it seems" he was working toward some meaning. He encloses his recollection of the moment within terms of uncertainty.

One significant passage, worth quoting at length, combines all of these themes—the impressions of childhood, the revision of the moment, the meaning of the monument, and the nature of time:

> Was the blank shaft that was rising there trying to say something . . . ? Was the tall shaft, now stubbed at the top, what history was? Certainly these words did not come into my fuddled head. Childhood and adolescence do not live much by words, by abstractions, for words freeze meaning in its living surge. . . . And, looking back years later, we know how hard it is to sink ourselves again into the old dark wordless flow. We have more

and more words now, and being truly adult is largely the effort
to make the lying words stand for the old living truth. (*JD* 24)

Warren questions whether the monument, a silent object, conveys any meaning. Can the monument speak for the historical
figure who can no longer speak for himself? This question applies to all historical constructions. The very presence of narratives and monuments signifies the pastness of the historical
events that they are created to preserve. Within the context of
this historiographical paradox, Warren acknowledges that he revises the moment from his youth by admitting, "These words
did not come into my fuddled head." However, he accounts for
his creative recollections by noting that in childhood there is a
"living truth" that adulthood is distanced from. Warren situates
the monument within an idealized context, a transcendent truth
that language obscures rather than discloses. As a realist analyz-
ing a monument, he questions how the community preserves stories of its own heroes, yet his recollections are those of a
romantic. Warren demythicizes the historical figure while he also
expresses the need for something in history that appeals to the
human need for meaning. Recall that in an interview with Edwin
Newman, Warren states: "What we remember from history is
human stances, the sense of human values, rather than issues."[12]
Warren strips away the "issues" of adulthood and realism in
order to uncover the "values" of idealism and childhood.

Warren evaluates Davis's life and Confederate presidency
from the perspective of a modern realist while maintaining Davis's status as the hero of a romantic narrative. We learn about
Davis's classical education and admission to West Point; that he
was an exceptionally kind slave master, a distinguished member
of the U.S. Congress, and also an idealist. Warren, knowing the
epic implications, then identifies Davis's idealism as his tragic
flaw: "The game of politics he had not learned (and never did
learn). . . . His weapon was forged of his learning, his devotion
to principle, his frigid dignity, his reputation for heroism and

12. Warren, "Speaking Freely" (Interview with Newman, 1971), 197.

honor, and, most of all, his logic" (*JD* 47). Davis did not realize that experience is more important than logic and principle, "and the incapacity of grasping such an idea was the tragic flaw in the midst of the hero's multifarious endowments" (*JD* 47). In this regard Davis differs from other Warren protagonists. He was an idealist, like John Brown, Jeremiah Beaumont, and Willie Stark, but unlike those characters he did not use the ends to justify the means. A typical Warren protagonist's downfall results from the employment of unethical actions in the pursuit of an ideal. Jefferson Davis's downfall resulted from ideals preventing the employment of any actions whatsoever.

Throughout these passages Warren refers ironically to Davis's secessionist insistence on states' rights, a principle that confounded his presidency by impeding wartime cooperation among the Confederate states and preventing him from making the decisions necessary to win the war. As Warren points out in *Jefferson Davis* and in *The Legacy of the Civil War,* southern states withheld equipment and troops from the war effort. The emphasis on states' and individuals' rights made the southerner "a first-class fighting man but a very poor soldier. . . . Disloyalty, sedition, profiteering and exploitation could all take refuge behind the barricade of civil rights" (*LCW* 36). In contrast, Warren points out that Lincoln suspended rights or seized Treasury funds, "implying that in violating [the Constitution] he was saving it" (*JD* 63). Sherman and Grant exemplify Davis's missing pragmatism. Sherman's concept of total war employed terror against civilians as a weapon; Grant's fully staffed army gave him the benefit of refusing prisoner exchanges, leaving his own soldiers to languish in southern prison camps (*JD* 66–67). Warren attributes the South's defeat to Davis's inability to be as pragmatic as his northern counterparts.

Hugh Ruppersburg argues that within these contrasts, "Warren gives his clearest definition of the Great Man": "the proof of greatness is the ability to meet the needs of the moment, to compromise personal principle if necessary to serve a higher principle or greater cause. The Great Man has mastered the art of pragmatism." Warren does repudiate both absolute idealism

(Davis) and absolute pragmatism (Sherman and Grant), favoring an appropriate balance between the two (Lincoln). Thus, Ruppersburg is correct: Warren is aware that Lincoln's "vision and pragmatism saved the American union."[13] Yet Warren's rhetoric undermines such straightforward explanations. He criticizes Davis, but as much as Warren holds Davis to realistic standards, he applauds the idealist's inability to conform to the fallen world around him. For example, in a statement that shifts accountability from the idealistic Davis and onto the pragmatic society, Warren comments, "Davis was what he was, and he was caught in the complications of the world he lived in—a world in which virtues could sometimes turn into liabilities" (*JD* 61). While criticizing Davis's failures, Warren credits him with the finest personal characteristics: "Honor, perhaps, more than victory, was, in the midst of ill fortune, ineptitudes, and even stupidities, his guiding star" (*JD* 68). Warren explains that Davis resisted the insult of shackles, refused to request a pardon, and "evidently preferred death to dishonor" (*JD* 75). Warren also offers a catalogue of wrongs committed against Davis. Many of his civil rights were violated: federal authorities denied him conferences with counsel, seized private correspondence with his lawyer, and arrested his wife only to harass him.

Throughout, Warren evaluates Davis's presidency and downfall using the rhetoric of an apologist rather than a critic. He charges that Davis's failure was his adherence to ideals that others failed to understand. Thus, Warren's narrative implies that while the South was destined to lose the war, it lost for the right reasons.

The analysis of Davis's presidency shifts abruptly into the present. In the third section of the book, Warren is seventy-four years old, returning to his hometown of Guthrie, Kentucky, and attending the celebration of Davis's restored citizenship at the monument. As in *John Brown* and "The World of Daniel Boone," in this section Warren most forcefully criticizes how modern southerners create their heroes. Warren mentions two

13. Ruppersburg, *Robert Penn Warren and the American Imagination*, 11, 13.

Davis biographers, John Craven and James Redpath, only to cite them for evidence rather than assess them negatively. Warren demonstrates patience toward his precursors. In a narrative that relies much upon his own subjectivity, he does not dismiss his precursors for their biases. Consequently, Warren turns his critical eye from scholarly histories to the modern South's popular constructions and consumptions of history. "Poised as he is on the boundary between two worlds—the world of his childhood reaching vicariously back to the War for Southern Independence and the world of 1981 lurching toward God knows what, Warren's pain and wonder are our own."[14] During the festivities, Warren observes the wide chasm between Davis's world of 1860 and the modern world that re-creates him.

Warren describes a play representing important events in Davis's life, which was performed on a stage set up in the parking lot behind the monument. Warren's account reads like a litany of the modern world's failures to represent history. Rain mars the rehearsals. Costumes are historically inaccurate. Lighting and sound equipment are poor. Throughout the performance, scenes of historical significance are disrupted by the persistent noises of the popcorn machine in the concession area, conversation among audience members, and "the usual quota of young children crunching bags of potato chips, giggling, punching each other, dragging chairs about and otherwise delighting their parents" (*JD* 97).

This is a parody of modern Americans' superficial use of history as a product to consume rather than a heritage to live by. "The World of Daniel Boone" sardonically observes a similar distinction between those who settled Boonesborough and modern tourists who merely visit. In "Remember the Alamo!" Warren writes that "the tourists began to come [to the Alamo] with jokes, giggles, respectful boredom or reverential whispers."[15] Similarly, on the second night of the Davis celebration, Warren watches slovenly dressed teenagers square-dancing in the park-

14. Cooke, review of *Jefferson Davis*, 312.
15. Warren, "Remember the Alamo!," *Holiday*, February 1958, 54.

ing area adjacent to the monument. In a section that echoes his own prior youthful inability to appreciate the monument, he notes their absence from the more serious celebrations, and wonders, "Had Jefferson Davis earlier been more than a name to most of them—if that?" (*JD* 101). Inclement weather makes the third night of festivities a "disaster." Most visitors retreat once the rain starts, but among those who stay for the performance is an elderly couple with a poodle that "paid close attention." Warren leaves for a more solemn personal ceremony in Guthrie: to visit the graves of his family and a poor white man named "Old Jeff." "Old Jeff" might appear to be a name Warren made up to create an antitype to Jefferson Davis in the narrative; however, this is not the case. Jeff Davis, nicknamed "Old Jeff" by the community in his old age, actually was a poor man who lived in Warren's hometown, and he is buried in the same cemetery as Warren's parents. Old Jeff's simple grave, reflective of his humble life, stands in ironic contrast to the famous man who shared his name. Consequently, the Jefferson Davis monument, for Warren, "stood there blank . . . and somehow, suddenly meaningless" (*JD* 110).

But Warren will not permit the monument to stand devoid of significance. Because it is silent, he speaks for it, imposing his own voice onto the blankness. The monument and the man it represents stand as a reminder—or a warning—to a modern age losing the values of Davis's time. Warren speculates, "More wryly, perhaps, [Davis] looks down on the well-meant and ignorant charade honoring his sufferings and triumphs" (*JD* 112), and he supposes that Davis "would no doubt reject the citizenship we so charitably thrust upon him" (*JD* 112), as Lincoln and Grant would reject "a nation that sometimes seems technologically and philosophically devoted to the depersonalization of men" (*JD* 113). Warren credits Davis (along with Lincoln and Grant) with being a heroic figure far removed from the world that modern Americans have created. But as a realist, Warren criticizes those who would idealize Davis by building a monument to him: the heroic Davis would reject any such popular revision or mythification of his identity.

Justus states that "the primary creation in this account is neither of the two Davises [Jefferson and "Old Jeff"] but rather a moral persona who in his drive to extract meaning from event is heavily committed to the affirmation of the merely human."[16] Warren's return and reconciliation in *Jefferson Davis* result in two kinds of redeeming knowledge. The first affirms that Davis was human and heroic, a flawed idealist deserving a monument, but not the one prepared for him by a society that has not learned both to embrace and critically assess history. The second affirms that subjectivity is both unavoidable and necessary in constructing history, demonstrating that autobiographical engagement makes history meaningful. These two visions in *Jefferson Davis* give the reader a model for responding to history. Like the narrator, any individual must make history meaningful by engaging in a personal dialogue with the silent monuments of the past.

In *Portrait of a Father* Warren attempts to initiate such a dialogue with the most significant monument of his own past, his father, but he faces the same problem as he encountered with the Jefferson Davis monument: the father is silent. This narrative, Warren's final historical excursion (he died two years after its original publication), represents the failure, or the surrender, of any attempt to achieve objectivity. *Portrait of a Father* is not so much about Robert Franklin Warren's life as Robert Penn Warren's struggle to write the history of that life. The portrait describes the blanks—the monumental silences—in the father's identity. The son struggles against his own inability to fill in those blanks. We saw that in his first biographical narrative, *John Brown,* Warren asserts his own voice over those of his precursors. In his last, *Portrait of a Father,* the progenitor nearly silences his son's voice.

Thus, the text's structure is confused. A *Mississippi Quarterly* review describes the book as "a little rambling at times and seemingly in need of occasional editing."[17] Even more than *Jef-*

---

16. Justus, "Warren and the Narrator as Historical Self," 115.

17. Kieran Quinlan, review of *Portrait of a Father,* by Robert Penn Warren, *Mississippi Quarterly* 42 (1989): 197.

ferson Davis, Portrait of a Father compresses time. The narrator always speaks from an explicit present frame, while his memory freely associates through the decades. Because the narrative is not divisible into clear sections, even the most general outline is impossible to discern. The following description of the first ten pages illustrates this point.

Whereas the opening of a conventional biography provides background on the subject's genealogy and life, in the initial paragraphs of *Portrait of a Father* the narrator explains that he possesses scant information about his father's personal and family history. His mother told him very little, though he does recall seeing some dates in a family Bible and he does have some vague information about his paternal grandparents, his grandfather having been a Confederate veteran who fought at Shiloh. From a brief digression into the Civil War, Warren makes a rough transition to his father's appearance and health: "I must now speak of my father as I remember him from my boyhood" (*PF* 9). The physical description leads to another abrupt transition: "For another preliminary but to me important general fact, there was his positive aversion to violence of any kind" (*PF* 11). To illustrate, Warren recounts an episode when his father confronted a midnight intruder in the home, and he recalls the following morning seeing blood on the snow ("Or was there snow?" Warren wonders [*PF* 14]). The next day, when one of the children (Warren speculates, "I may have been the child" [*PF* 14]) told friends about a "nigger" who broke in the house, his father rejoined with, "That word will never be used in this house" (*PF* 14). Warren comments on his father's openness toward racial differences, then comments again on how little he knows, how "sealed off" his father's past is. At this point another rough transition appears, "I must go back to my father's only remark about his mother" (*PF* 15), followed by a description of a car trip that twelve-year-old Robert took with his father.

In these ten pages, time periods shift without warning: Warren is an adult, then he has not yet been born, then he is a preteen. The father is a child, then a grown man chasing a prowler from the house and disciplining his children. There are chasms and leaps in this chronology. James Olney observes that Warren's use of autobiography is circular, with all time periods united in *Portrait of a Father*. With thoughts about one generation "sparking off" thoughts about another, it is "as if the circuit of past and future were completed in the twin acts of memory and expectation."[18] Warren begins with a general description of his subject, a conventional approach, but then zooms in on a particular event (the intruder) without any preparation or apparent justification. The narrator discusses the father's attitudes toward health, violence, and race, with no explicit rationale to explain the placement of such information at this point in the portrait. Topics change merely according to the narrator's fiat. The portrait provides no sense of logic to compel us from one page to another, or even one paragraph to another. An image leads to the recollection of another image; a section of narrative spins its way into another narrative. As in *Jefferson Davis*, in *Portrait of a Father* moments, images, and themes rush into the vacuum created by the subject, resulting in a collage rather than a conventional, linear narrative.

The narrative self-reflexively comments upon its own impressionistic, matrix structure. At one point the narrator corrects himself, noting, "I again have wandered from chronology" (*PF* 23), an idea that he develops elsewhere in the narrative: "All that I have detailed violates general chronology. I suppose, however, that it may have a chronology of its own: a chronology of vividness and sequence, not of event, but of recollection" (*PF* 30). This is the same "symbolic" chronology that Warren sets forth in the opening of *Jefferson Davis*. As in "Blackberry Winter" and *Jefferson Davis,* time in *Portrait of a Father* is not movement; it is a climate from which events emerge and into which they fade. Warren's approach to time and memory resembles Eudora Welty's recollection of her own life and parents in her autobiography, *One Writer's Beginnings* (1984): "The events in

<hr />

18. James Olney, "Parents and Children in Robert Penn Warren's Autobiography," in *Home Ground: Southern Autobiography*, ed. J. Bill Berry (Columbia: University of Missouri Press, 1991), 34.

our lives happen in a sequence in time, but in their significance to ourselves they find their own order, a timetable not necessarily—perhaps not possibly—chronological." To Warren and Welty, meaning is not a chronological "unspooling . . . like a movie film" (*JD* 1) but a "continuous thread of revelation." Perhaps a greater influence on Warren is Allen Tate's *The Fathers,* in which Lacy Buchan considers the nature of memory, at one point stating, "Memory is not what happened in the year 1860 but is rather a few symbols, a voice, a tree, a gun shining on the wall—symbols that will preserve only so much of the old life as they may, in their own mysterious history, continue to bear."[19]

The symbolic quality of time explains Warren's transitions, digressions, and speculations; it also explains why he blocks off and focuses upon particular moments. In describing the scene at his mother's deathbed, he writes, "Our father sat by the bed holding her right hand. Small and irrelevant facts may become vastly significant. I remember which hand" (*PF* 27). Memory is symbolic rather than linear. Thus, although the narrative does not prepare the reader for the intruder episode at the beginning of the portrait, the progression into that event is logical within the writer's memory. It is a significant memory of one night that shows the impression that his father's attitudes about race made on him. The shape of memory justifies the shape of the narrative.

Warren must grasp at moments as they appear to him, because his father's presence persistently eludes him. The trope of reconciliation appears as Warren struggles to fill the silences. Whereas in other biographical narratives he confronts romantic texts with a realistic text, in *Portrait of a Father* all texts are inaccessible.

The narrative is self-referential about this absence, as Warren repeatedly confronts his paucity of materials. The first sentence of the book reads, "My father, as the years since his death pass, becomes to me more and more a man of mystery" (*PF* 7). Similar

19. Eudora Welty, *One Writer's Beginnings* (New York: Warner Books, 1983), 75; Allen Tate, *The Fathers* (Baton Rouge: Louisiana State University Press, 1977), 22.

comments abound throughout *Portrait:* "My father was not secretive, but somehow he had sealed off the past, his own past. In a strange way he was depersonalized" (*PF* 15). Like the Jefferson Davis monument, his father is a blank. His father "had never been, in fact, a man to express his feelings in words" (*PF* 28), even to the extent of using withdrawal as a form of punishment by disciplining his children with cold silence. Consequently, Warren's knowledge of his father is fragmentary at best.

Warren does address some texts that he has encountered in his research about his father, but every one of them is silent. Documents such as a family Bible or a marriage certificate are lost. As a boy, he once found a book containing a poem that his father had written, but when the child asked him about the book, the father "took it, examined it, and wordlessly walked away with it. That was the last time I was ever to see it" (*PF* 41). Years later, his father sent him a poem with an attached note tersely stating, "Do not answer" (*PF* 42). The father and every document associated with him refuse to engage in dialogue with the son.

Warren encounters the same experience with oral communications. His father and maternal grandfather got along well and would engage in lengthy private conversations. Occasionally the boy would stroll near them "trying to hear that mysterious conversation," but upon his approach the topic would change or they would fall silent until he left the area (*PF* 50). Similarly, his mother and father would have long private talks, and though they were never arguments, "I had to wonder what they were talking about" (*PF* 55).

When his father dies, the silence obviously persists, but even the final document Warren finds emphasizes this fact. R. F. Warren was found slumped over his desk, in the process of composing a letter when he died. Warren discovers the unfinished letter: "Across the sheet, to the edge, was a long pen-stroke from the last word written, downward—apparently made as he fainted and fell. The pen was on the floor. I picked it up. I looked at the scarcely begun letter. It began: 'Dear Son' " (*PF* 78–79). Significantly, even the father's final statement to the son is incomplete.

As a result of the incomplete texts and absolute silences, *Portrait of a Father* is one of Warren's most self-referential narratives. Statements about how little he knows of his father persist throughout the entire narrative. Like Jack Burden in *All the King's Men* and the historian-narrator in *World Enough and Time,* Warren is forthright with the reader regarding his primary materials, particularly acknowledging himself as his own primary resource in *Portrait of a Father.* He uses speculation and memory to compensate for the absence of research materials, throughout the portrait exposing the processes and failures of both. As in *Jefferson Davis,* subjectivity is essential. When Warren introduces a new topic with a rough transition like "I must now speak of my father as I remember him from my boyhood" (*PF* 9), and when he concludes a discussion with admissions like "There must have been more, but I don't remember" (*PF* 68), he recognizes the function of subjectivity in historical construction.

Randolph Paul Runyon's *The Taciturn Text* addresses the problem of sons constructing their fathers' stories throughout Warren's work. The father of a Warren protagonist is taciturn, Runyon argues, and Warren's works are self-referential because, since the father's text does not disclose its meaning to the son, the son must himself decode and interpret it. The reader, dealing with the problems of reading and interpretation, identifies with the protagonist. In *Jefferson Davis* the monument is taciturn; in *Portrait of a Father* it is the father who is taciturn. As embodiments of the past, the monument and the father represent the silence of the past.

Runyon's thesis is important and well argued in relation to the novels. I contend, however, that the most significant point in Warren's father-son relationship is more the moment of narration. In *Portrait of a Father* the text itself enables the son to overcome the father's taciturnity. Because the portrait empowers him to create his own image of his father, Warren's writing of his father's portrait is the son's assertion of his voice into the father's silence. Warren's father was not a man given to telling stories about himself, so Warren himself tells the stories. History

redeems the son by teaching him that despite his father's power
to silence him, he does possess the power to speak.

Of course, the images and stories that the son relates are fragmentary and disjointed because he lacks information about his
father; thus, the structure of the text results from the father's
influential silence. But as the narrator, Warren confronts this paternal influence by displacing his father and casting himself as
the central character in the portrait. *Portrait of a Father* is only
incidentally a portrait of Robert Franklin Warren; it is, ultimately, a portrait of the artist.

In other Prodigal Son stories, transgression, return, reconcilia-
tion, and redemption are experienced through the act of narra-
tive: the Willie Proudfit confession in *Night Rider*, "The
Statement of Ashby Wyndham" in *At Heaven's Gate*, the Cass
Mastern diary in *All the King's Men*, the Munn Short story in
World Enough and Time, and the Hamish Bond story in *Band
of Angels*. As in "Blackberry Winter," the return of the Prodigal
Son in *Portrait of a Father* is not actual, but an act of memory.
Before discussing his father's death, Warren opens a coda section
with a powerful image: "As I backed our car out of the driveway
of the retirement home I saw his face looking out at us. He had
drawn the curtains apart at the window of his sitting room and
was watching us go. . . . We drove on past factories and other
signs of progress, down the buzzing and humming concrete slab
to the point we joined the great highway northward. That visit
to Clarksville, then the face at a window, was the last time I
was to see my father. Alive and conscious" (*PF* 77–78). Here the
father is silent again, but it is the son who, like Seth, is leaving,
forcing distance between himself and his origins. The image of
the modern highway reappears, but unlike "The World of Daniel
Boone," *All the King's Men*, *Segregation*, and other works, the
highway is now an image of separation rather than return.

Later, Warren returns to his father's deathbed, a scene that
he describes in the section of poems, "Mortmain," which was
appended to the portrait. The first poem is significantly titled,
"AFTER NIGHT FLIGHT SON REACHES BEDSIDE OF ALREADY UN-
CONSCIOUS FATHER, WHOSE RIGHT HAND LIFTS IN A SPASMODIC

GESTURE, AS THOUGH TRYING TO MAKE CONTACT: 1955." The son interprets the father's final gesture as an attempt to break the silence—perhaps wishful thinking on the son's part.

The self-conscious narrator grappling against the silence of the father and the paucity of the primary research materials appears throughout Warren's fiction, particularly *All the King's Men* and *World Enough and Time*. Burden and the *World Enough and Time* narrator return to and attempt to reconcile with their precursors in order to create a "usable past." As they attempt to construct history, they struggle to interpret the incomplete texts that precede them, and in their interpretations, they place themselves into their own texts. *Jefferson Davis Gets His Citizenship Back* and *Portrait of a Father* are the conclusion of Warren's shift toward autobiography, a shift that is observable in his novels of 1946 and 1950.

V

From "Jack Burden" to "I"
The Narrator's Transformation in *All the King's Men*

> History is the big myth we live, and in our living, constantly remake.
>
> —Robert Penn Warren, *Brother to Dragons*

In light of the central role of biographical narrative in Warren's writing, *All the King's Men* emerges as one of Warren's most significant works: the narrator's development as a biographer reflects a stage in the progression of narrators from *John Brown* to *Jefferson Davis Gets His Citizenship Back* and *Portrait of a Father*. The previous chapters have shown that from the earliest to the latest of these narratives, Warren questions the possibility of a narrator remaining neutral. In *John Brown* he exposes the biases of other biographers as a means of claiming objectivity for himself. However, with *Jefferson Davis Gets His Citizenship Back* and *Portrait of a Father,* Warren surrenders all claims to objectivity. He develops into a self-conscious narrator, exposing his subjective construction of history. As a historian and narrator, Warren becomes more involved with the dramatis personae of the past, understanding history by placing himself into historical contexts.

Burden's "historical excursions" into Stark's and Mastern's lives, and into his own life, represent an emerging knowledge of history that supersedes his sense of disconnection from history. Burden learns that although events seem divorced from human agency, individuals do act upon history by living and interpreting it. Initially, Burden evades this truth through the Great Sleep and his various theories (e.g., the Great Twitch, the Theory of Historical Costs, and the Moral Neutrality of History), but he ultimately finds himself in the existential paradox of having chosen to act merely by having chosen not to. He thus models time as a matrix of interconnected actions and consequences.

In *All the King's Men*, Warren replaces the traditional "timeline" of history (best represented by the road in the opening of the novel) with the idea of a "matrix." As we have previously discussed, this paradigm becomes a model for ethical action, a kind of secularized version of Original Sin, for it depicts all individuals in a communion with all others in what Cass Mastern calls "the common guilt of man" (*AKM* 187). Like all of Warren's protagonists, Jack Burden achieves this sense of historical connection by returning to his past (literally returning home), reconciling with the past, and being redeemed from the burden of the past through the act of confession.

As Burden discovers his connection to history, he becomes less detached as a narrator, surrendering his pose of objectivity. He becomes more involved in events, to the point that his biographical narratives of Willie Stark and Cass Mastern become autobiographical. Warren inscribes the paradigm of historical connection into the discourse of Burden's first-person narrative. While much criticism has noted Burden's philosophical development, a less-studied facet of the novel is the effect of this development on his narrative style. Joan Ray Yeatman has studied point of view in her dissertation, "Narrators and Commentators in Four Novels by Robert Penn Warren." However, both my methodology and my conclusions differ from hers. Using terminology from Henry James, Wayne Booth, and Norman Friedman, with numerous examples from the novels, Yeatman examines point of view in relation to the theme of self-knowledge and development toward perception.[1] My study shows that the "grammar" of Burden's narration (i.e., his tone, diction, levels of observation, and partic-

1. Joan Ray Yeatman, "Narrators and Commentators in Four Novels by Robert Penn Warren" (Ph.D. diss., University of Oregon, 1972).

ipation) reflects the historiographical-ethical position that he adopts. As Burden envisions himself connected to history, he places less distance between himself and the story he narrates. His development reflects Warren's development from *John Brown* to *Jefferson Davis* and *Portrait of a Father*.

Wayne Booth's distinction between "narrator-observer" and "narrator-agent" is useful here. Warren formulates his philosophy of interconnection on the narrative level by shifting his role from narrator-observer in *John Brown* to narrator-agent in *Jefferson Davis* and *Portrait of a Father*. Likewise, Burden becomes more involved with the story he tells, eventually transforming himself from an observer to a participant in the plot.

Obviously, Burden participates in the story he tells. This participation gives him both the involvement of a character and the detachment of a narrator. He is a narrator-agent rather than a narrator-observer. The problem is his failure to recognize his own agency. Burden initially attempts to evade the fact of his involvement, and his discourse reflects this failed endeavor. Charles Bohner identifies "two Jack Burdens, the one who is telling the story and the other to whom the events happened."[2] He is echoed by Yeatman, who points out that the dichotomy in the novel is not between Burden and Stark but between Burden as narrator and Burden as protagonist. Burden always participates as a protagonist, but he must progress toward acknowledging his participation and the personal responsibility that accompanies it. Marshall Walker argues that Burden is Warren's idea of a "philosophical novelist" because "Jack is involved in yet detached from the life of the book, participating in the event and then glossing its meaning." True enough, but for Burden detachment means self-isolation. He rises to the level of what Warren calls a "philosophical novelist"[3] only *after* he learns to recognize that his sense of detachment from history is both illusory and irresponsible.

2. Bohner, *Robert Penn Warren*, 91; Yeatman, "Narrators and Commentators in Four Novels by Robert Penn Warren," 91.
3. Walker, *A Vision Earned*, 98; Warren, "The Great Mirage," 160.

As in *John Brown,* "The World of Daniel Boone," *Segregation, Who Speaks for the Negro?, Jefferson Davis,* and *Portrait of a Father,* the stories of Willie Stark and Cass Mastern come to the reader through an overt narrator, what Justus calls an "intervening consciousness." Justus considers "Burden's aesthetic manipulation as an equivalent of Stark's political manipulation."[4] Indeed, there is much evidence of Burden's "aesthetic manipulation" throughout the novel. For dramatic effect, he deliberately withholds certain information (e.g., his paternity, the deaths of Judge Irwin and Adam Stanton, his marriage to Anne Stanton) until crucial moments, and he teases his reader with foreshadowings, for example, the final sentence of the first chapter: "And the Boss is dead, who said to me, 'And make it stick.' Little Jackie made it stick, all right" (*AKM* 50). Often appearing to relish the position of narrative power, Burden seems very much aware that he controls a narrative, and the reader shares that awareness. Because Burden is such an intrusive, pervasive narrator, we can chart his movement toward historical connection not only through the story he tells but also through his very audible narrating voice.

Clues to his ethical development reside in his manipulative and often hyperintellectualized rhetoric. Early in his experience he attempts to detach from history, an effort that his narrator-observer stance reflects. The effort fails. As Robert Heilman points out, Burden's tone suggests that he is "sardonic in a detachment closer to alienation than objectivity." Burden's rhetoric calls attention to his lack of neutrality, a point with which Thomas Daniel Young concurs: "Although Jack's wisecracking manner makes him seem detached from what he is observing, the reader is aware that he is deeply and profoundly affected." Burden's resistance to historical connection produces self-isolating rhetoric that he must change when he realizes that it renders him unable to understand the stories of Willie Stark, Cass Mas-

---

4. Justus, *Achievement of Robert Penn Warren,* 195; James Justus, "The Power of Filiation in *All the King's Men,*" in *Modern American Fiction: Form and Function,* ed. Thomas Daniel Young (Baton Rouge: Louisiana State University Press, 1989), 164.

tern, and himself. Some critics cite Burden's tone as the novel's major flaw. For example, Roger Sale argues that "this story of growth commits [Warren] to changes in the narrator's way of talking about the world. If Jack is just as much of a smart aleck in 1939 as he was in 1922, the whole dramatic point of the novel is evaded and finally blurred." However, as Norton Girault points out, "The manner in which he reconstructs the story gives the reader an insight into Jack's experience." Yeatman also argues, as I do, that the change in Burden's style indicates a change in his perception, though the stylistic changes we identify differ with our methodology. However, Yeatman is correct in arguing that because Burden does not narrate in chronological order, his past and present voices are mixed, and he treats his earlier misperceptions with irony. Indeed, when we examine Burden's discourse apart from the story he tells, we discover that he initially resembles the *John Brown* narrator by assuming that he can be a neutral observer. Later in the novel, like the narrators of *Jefferson Davis* and *Portrait of a Father,* he realizes that he cannot understand history until he places himself into it.[5]

To emphasize Burden's progression from neutrality to participation, Warren assigns him the career of journalist, seemingly a profession requiring objectivity. But note what happens: while reporting on Stark's first gubernatorial campaign, Burden becomes involved. He helps Stark improve his boring speeches, and when Stark gets drunk after learning that he was enlisted merely to split the Harrison vote, Burden gets him to a public appearance on time. Eventually, Burden resigns from the newspaper and accepts Stark's job offer. Leonard Casper observes, "As a

5. Robert B. Heilman, "Melpomene as Wallflower: or, the Reading of Tragedy," in *Robert Penn Warren: A Collection of Critical Essays,* ed. Lewis Longley (New York: New York University Press, 1965), 83; Thomas Daniel Young, *The Past in the Present: A Thematic Study of Modern Southern Fiction* (Baton Rouge: Louisiana State University Press, 1981), 68; Roger Sale, "Having It Both Ways in *All the King's Men," Hudson Review* 14 (1961): 75; Norton R. Girault, "The Narrator's Mind as Symbol: An Analysis of *All the King's Men,"* in *Robert Penn Warren: Critical Perspectives,* ed. Neil Nakadate (Lexington: University Press of Kentucky, 1981), 61; Yeatman, "Narrators and Commentators in Four Novels by Robert Penn Warren."

student of history, a reporter, and a political researcher, he [Burden] tries to perfect neutrality. Yet in each capacity he becomes more and more deeply, personally involved."[6] Indeed, Burden's investigations as a reporter and a researcher disabuse him of the "fiction" of neutral narration.

Consequently, his narration reveals two levels of personal involvement. There is the early Jack Burden, who believes in his own objectivity, and the mature Jack Burden, who knows what the earlier version of himself did not. For example, upon his return to Burden's Landing, described in the first chapter, he recalls his adolescence. Burden narrates in 1939, but he focalizes through the Jack Burdens from two different time periods—his teenage years in the 1910s and his graduate school experience in 1920. As I have noted, Genette's term, "focalization," clarifies and refines the earlier term "point of view," distinguishing the character who perceives from the voice that narrates. This distinction is particularly important for Burden because his narrative is both first person and subsequent to the events of the story; thus he is simultaneously the novel's voice in 1939 and the novel's primary focalizing character at various times from the 1910s through the 1930s.

As he returns to Burden's Landing with the Boss to confront Judge Irwin, Burden surveys his childhood and comments:

> [1] If the human race didn't remember anything it would be perfectly happy. [2] I was a student of history once in a university and if I learned anything from studying history that was what I learned. [3] Or to be more exact, that was what I thought I had learned. (*AKM*, 40; numbers added)

In sentence [1] Burden makes one of his many editorial statements that elevate the particulars of the story to the universal level. Because the sentence is cast in the general present tense (the tense of proverbs, aphorisms, and generalizations), we receive the impression that the statement represents the point of

6. Casper, *The Dark and Bloody Ground*, 122.

view of Jack Burden narrating in 1939. However, sentence [2] shifts to the past tense, indicating that sentence [1] was what he thought when he was a graduate student in 1920. The contrary-to-fact statement in sentence [3] clarifies that Burden-as-narrator of 1939 no longer believes what Burden-as-student thought in 1920. Thus, while Burden narrates all three statements in 1939, he focalizes the first through who he was in the early 1920s, and he focalizes the second and third through the Burden who matures in 1938 and leaves Burden's Landing in 1939. Burden's immature point of view dominates [1], and his mature point of view dominates [2] and [3]. As Girault observes, though Willie Stark's and Jack Burden's stories are told simultaneously, phrases like "'back then' remind the reader of the fact that Jack has lived through the actions he is describing and that he is trying to reorient himself in relation to them."[7]

Immediately following sentence [3], Burden continues to reminisce in the next paragraph by describing Sugar-Boy, the Boss, and himself advancing toward Judge Irwin's house:

[4] We would go down the Row—the line of houses facing the bay—and that was the place where all my pals had been. [5] Anne, who was an old maid, or damned near it. [6] Adam, who was a famous surgeon and who was nice to me but didn't go fishing with me any more. [7] And Judge Irwin, who lived in the last house, and who had been a friend of my family and who used to take me hunting with him. (*AKM* 40; numbers added)

With the pronoun "we," sentence [4] shifts point of view from 1939 to 1936. Whereas in sentence [3] Burden narrates in 1939 from his point of view in 1939, in [4], [5], [6], and [7], he narrates in 1939 but focalizes through the Jack Burden of 1936. But each of these four sentences also looks back even further. Sentence [4] introduces the pluperfect tense with "where all my pals had been," indicating that as Willie Stark's aide in 1936 in the car with Sugar-Boy and Stark, Burden recalled events of 1910–

7. Girault, "The Narrator's Mind as Symbol," 61.

15. Sentences [5] and [6] note changes that have occurred over the period 1910–15 to 1936. With sentence [7] Burden in 1939 confirms that in 1936 he recalled events of 1910–15.

As if there were not enough temporal distinctions already in this passage, there is one more. We might wonder whether every sentence here is focalized through Burden-as-narrator in 1939 rather than Burden-as-aide in 1936. Did Burden really have those recollections in 1936 in the car on the way to Burden's Landing, or is he in 1939 looking back at the car trip and revising that moment?

Probably the latter. Seymour Chatman's categories of "perceptual" point of view (literally, what a character sees and experiences) and "conceptual" point of view (a character's interpretation of perception) are useful here. When a character reflects upon a prior experience, he/she reconstructs the perceptual point of view into a conceptual point of view. When Burden-as-narrator (1939) "recalls" the thoughts of Burden-as-aide (1936), he formulates his current conception of a prior moment of perception. By explaining his earlier thoughts of even earlier events, Burden puts into words impressions that were not originally verbal. He did not construct the syntax and diction of sentences [4], [5], [6], and [7] in the car; such narration would not be written for three years. The moment of narration is, to borrow again from Genette, a "transcription" of nonverbal experience into a verbal representation.[8] Merely by transcribing his impressions from years before, Jack simultaneously reconstructs the events of two periods, 1936 and 1910–15.

As the passage continues, Burden directs Sugar-Boy toward Irwin's house, and he speculates (or, as the revisionary 1939 narrator, he inserts speculations into that night of 1936):

[8] At night you pass through a little town where you once lived, and you expect to see yourself wearing knee pants, standing all alone on the street corner under the hanging bulbs . . . .

8. Chatman, *Story and Discourse*, 151–52, 155; Genette, *Narrative Discourse*, 165.

[9] But, then, who the hell is this in the back seat of the big black Cadillac that comes ghosting through the town? [10] Why, this is Jack Burden. [11] Don't you remember little Jack Burden? [12] He used to go out in his boat in the afternoon on the bay to fish. (*AKM* 40; numbers added)

The pronoun shifts from first-person singular in [1], [2], and [3], to first-person plural in [4], to second person in [8], and, finally, to third person in [10], [11], and [12].

In [8] Burden-as-narrator (1939) addresses an unnamed "you," similar to the anonymous narratee he addresses at the beginning of the chapter to initiate his return: "To get there you follow Highway 58" (*AKM* 1). But sentence [8] also uses the reflexive pronoun ("you expect to see yourself"), indicating two different versions of the same "you," a past and a present version. In [9] he reminds "you" of Burden-aide (1936), and in [10] and [11] he reminds "you" of Burden-youth (1910). "You," then, appears to be Burden himself, a prior version of himself that he addresses, as though he functions both as his own narrator and narratee. When he speaks of his prior self in the third person, he makes himself his own main character. These various ways of speaking about himself—"you" (present), "yourself" (past), and "Jack Burden" (past)—indicates a divided modern consciousness, what Burden calls "the terrible division of our age." Burden dissociates from his experience by displacing himself in the narrative. This self-division and self-objectification make Burden, according to Richard Law, "representatively modern; his claim to be an objective seeker of 'facts' is the best clue to his alienation"; Jack's "pose of objectivity" is a "mask." Young agrees: "Like many other moderns, Jack Burden feels that he can do his job and not become personally involved in the drama of life unfolding before his eyes."[9]

Burden's historical excursions correct his false assumption that he can remain neutral. In particular, the interpolated Cass

9. Richard G. Law, " 'The Case of the Upright Judge': The Nature of Truth in *All the King's Men*," *Studies in American Fiction* 6 (1978): 6–7; Young, *The Past in the Present*, 66.

Mastern story, as a microcosm of the entire novel, acts as a corrective for Burden. Mastern's life, like Burden's, is a story of an individual's progress toward personal involvement. Furthermore, the discourse Mastern uses to record his life into his journal serves as a model for Burden to make sense of his own experience. This intercalated narrative's thematic significance makes it central to an investigation of Jack Burden's shift from observer to agent.

The Cass Mastern story, which makes up the whole fourth chapter of *All the King's Men,* was omitted from the 1974 Secker and Warburg edition of the novel (as it was omitted from the first British edition, in 1948, by publisher Eyre and Spottiswoode). We might speculate that the publisher did not see Mastern's relevance to the novel and that Warren unenthusiastically agreed to this compromise rather than risk having the British edition canceled. Whatever the reason, in "The World of Huey Long," written for the *London Times* and published (in a modified version) as the introduction to the 1974 British edition, Warren states that the Cass Mastern story is "central to the novel." When Ruth Fisher asked Warren about the function of the Cass Mastern chapter, he said that both he and Jack Burden "got stuck": "I could have stopped the action and made my narrator, Jack Burden, have a moral debate with himself. . . . He could, in other words, have gone at the question abstractly. But this is not his character. He is, in fact, trying to live a life avoiding all moral issues." Warren explains that the use of a Civil War relative gives both Burden and the reader "the image of meaning emerging from experience."[10] The Mastern story stands in for a philosophical debate about personal connection and responsibility.

The Cass Mastern chapter tells the story of a mid-nineteenth century Kentucky man (a distant relative of Jack Burden) who writes a journal notable for its confessions and expressions of repentance. Though raised by his pragmatic brother, Gilbert,

10. Robert Penn Warren, "The World of Huey Long," *London Times,* 5 January 1974, 5; Robert Penn Warren, "A Conversation with Robert Penn Warren" (Interview with Ruth Fisher, 1970), in *Talking with Robert Penn Warren,* ed. Watkins, Hiers, and Weaks, 179–80.

Cass is an idealist but one who eventually learns to act on his ideals. When his best friend, Duncan Trice, commits suicide after learning of Cass's affair with his wife Annabelle, Cass begins to see that his actions have had effects upon others. In his journal he writes, "The process had only begun of a general disintegration of which I was the center" (*AKM* 177). Cass repents by trying to save a slave, Phebe, whom Annabelle sold down the river for knowing about the affair, and he frees all of his own slaves. He joins the Confederate Army, hoping to be killed in the Civil War, a kind of noble suicide. Dying of a war wound, he writes in his journal, "I have lived to do no man good, and have seen others suffer for my sin. I do not question the Justice of God, that others have suffered for my sin, for it may be that only by the suffering of the innocent does God affirm that men are brothers. . . . Men shall come together yet and die in the common guilt of man" (*AKM* 187). As this journal entry indicates, Cass eventually accepts responsibility for the unintended consequences of his actions. He acknowledges his own and all other individuals' mutual participation in history.

But the Cass Mastern chapter also tells the story of Jack Burden, how he receives the Mastern journals and letters, how he researches Mastern's life, and ultimately what he learns from the story. Burden complicates the narrative by writing the story of a history graduate student named "Jack Burden," who wrote the story of Cass Mastern, who had written his own story in a journal. A further complication is that the narrative is not entirely fictional; the character of Cass Mastern is loosely based on Jefferson Davis. There is much evidence for this claim. In an interview for the *New England Review,* Warren says that Davis provided the "germ" for the Cass Mastern story. More specifically, Lewis Simpson observes that both Davis and Mastern attend Transylvania University, are established as planters by their brothers, and are bookish, intellectual, and poetic. In his biography of Davis, William C. Davis describes Jefferson's older brother, Joseph, as a "major influence" who "acted the part of a father, making opportunity for his brother but also maintaining a measure of control over him." The similarities to Cass Mastern's brother, Gilbert, are clear. Phebe is based on an actual slave. According to J. Winston Coleman's history of slavery in Kentucky, Eliza, a refined, poised woman with very light skin, was humiliated on the auction block in Cheapside, in Lexington, Kentucky, by an auctioneer who displayed her in a sexually explicit manner.[11] Two actual historical figures appear in the narrative of Cass Mastern: Jefferson Davis and Caroline Turner, a Lexington woman who was notorious for cruel treatment of her slaves and was subsequently killed by a slave she abused. Consequently, there are several layers of narration in the Cass Mastern story. Warren writes a third-person narrative based on Huey Long (Willie Stark) and Jefferson Davis (Cass Mastern), using a narrator (Jack Burden) who writes a first-person narrative about himself, a graduate student writing a third-person narrative about Cass Mastern, a historical figure writing a first-person account about himself.

In one of the most thorough narrative analyses of *All the King's Men,* Simone Vauthier charts the various narratees. She notes, for example, that the narratee is the first person to appear in the novel and that Burden's use of rhetorical questions, direct addresses, and conversational comments suggests different types of narratees. But as we have seen already, *All the King's Men* also presents a matrix of narrators that is particularly evident in the Cass Mastern chapter.[12]

As he narrates the story of Cass Mastern, Burden is a very audible narrator in three ways: his ironic tone, his speculations into the story, and his commentary on Mastern's story and discourse.

As in the Willie Stark narrative, Jack's tone intrudes into the

11. Robert Penn Warren, "Interview with Eleanor Clark and Robert Penn Warren" (Interview with *New England Review,* 1978), in *Talking with Robert Penn Warren,* ed. Watkins, Hiers, and Weaks, 334; Simpson, *The Fable of the Southern Writer,* 149; William C. Davis, *Jefferson Davis: The Man and His Hour* (New York: Harper Perennial, 1992), 73. See J. Winston Coleman, *Slavery Times in Kentucky* (1940; rpt. New York: Johnson Reprint, 1970), 131–35.
12. Simone Vauthier, "The Case of the Vanishing Narratee: An Inquiry into *All the King's Men,*" in *Robert Penn Warren: Critical Perspectives,* ed. Neil Nakadate (Lexington: University Press of Kentucky, 1981), 93–114.

Mastern narrative. To illustrate, upon describing Duncan Trice's death, Burden states, "It was quite obviously an accident" (*AKM* 171), rather than "it was an accident"; his addition of the unnecessary intensifiers ("quite obviously") implies the opposite. Like a classical dramatist, Burden shows his awareness of the story's outcome by foreshadowing a truth that the characters will face in a tragic moment of recognition.

Burden's tone is most clearly audible in his representation of Gilbert Mastern. When Burden describes how he came to possess the primary documents about Mastern, he explains that a relative who heard of libraries sometimes paying for archival materials sent him the journal for his opinion regarding whether it had any "financial interest"; when Burden replied that Mastern's lack of historical significance would probably not make the materials worth any money, the relative tells Burden that he can keep everything for "sentimental reasons" (*AKM* 160). Burden places the terms "financial interest" and "sentimental reasons" in quotation marks to indicate that these were his relative's actual words, but his use of direct quotation also emphasizes the contrast between his relative's pragmatic interest in exchange value and his appreciation for symbolic value. This contrast echoes the conflict between Gilbert Mastern's pragmatism and Cass Mastern's idealism, thus foreshadowing the Mastern story. This disapproving tone persists throughout Burden's descriptions of Gilbert. He writes, "How did Gilbert make his first dollar? Did he cut the throat of a traveler in the canebrake? Did he black boots at an inn? It is not recorded. But he made his fortune, and sat on the white veranda and voted Whig" (*AKM* 162). If "it is not recorded," where does Jack come up with these possible explanations? He openly speculates with possibilities that reveal his negative attitude toward Gilbert. It is not enough for him to say that Gilbert got rich; he must add "the white veranda and voted Whig."

Such speculation is the second sign of Burden's overt narratorial presence. He speculates that when Gilbert read Cass's last letter, "he must have mused over it with a tolerant irony" (*AKM* 162), for the letter was poetic, contrary to Gilbert's nature.

When the dying Cass tells Gilbert, "If one of us is lucky, it is I. I shall have rest. . . . But you, my dear brother, are condemned to eat bread in bitterness," Burden imagines "Gilbert must have smiled, looking back, for he had eaten little bread in bitterness" (*AKM* 162). These kinds of speculations continue throughout Burden's narrative. Burden assumes that Annabelle's half-sister must have known about and even assisted the two lovers in their affair, but she must have done so, "it seems, only after some pressure by Annabelle, for Cass mentions 'a stormy scene' " (*AKM* 170). Burden offers no other evidence for this inference. One of the more interesting speculations arises from the fact that Mastern never uses Annabelle's name (*AKM* 164). Burden infers Annabelle's and Duncan's identities by surveying the files of Lexington newspapers for the story of a death, reported as accidental, that would match the details related by Cass.

Finally, the most obvious sign of Burden's presence is his explicit commentary on Mastern's story. He describes the photograph of Cass through his subjective impressions: "But everything in the picture . . . seemed accidental. That jacket, however, was not accidental. It was worn as the result of calculation and anguish, in pride and self-humiliation, in the conviction that it would be worn in death" (*AKM* 161). These comments originate from Burden's interpretation of Mastern's motives. Similarly, he assesses Mastern's description of Annabelle as "conscientious . . . a kind of tortured inventory, as though . . . he had to take one last backward look even at the risk of being turned into the pillar of salt" (*AKM* 165). When we read this sentence we have not yet reached the end of the Mastern narrative, so Burden again shows his foreknowledge of the conclusion.

Because Burden is such an overt narrator throughout the Mastern narrative, the main question confronting the reader is, as Girault asks, "How aware is Jack Burden, at the time of his telling of the story?" At various times in the narration, is he speaking as the narrator of 1939 or the graduate student of 1920? These questions are important because they pertain as well to Burden's narration throughout the entire novel. Throughout his narration of Willie Stark, Burden shifts between what Casper calls "the tough-realistic and the poetic" styles and what Girault calls "reporting" and "lyrical" styles.[13] For example, Jack's report in the first chapter turns lyrical as he enters Willie's childhood bedroom and imagines what Willie must have been like as a boy: "He would lie there and shiver in the dark. . . . He wouldn't have any name for what was big inside him. Maybe there isn't any name" (*AKM* 28). Again the question obtains: Does Jack Burden stray from straight reporting into his lyrical-poetic mode in 1936 (when he visited Stark's boyhood home) or in 1939? Throughout his telling of the Cass Mastern story, whose voice speaks, and whose point of view perceives?

For answers, we may explicate the Cass Mastern chapter in relation to Cass Mastern's narration in his journal and Jack's progress from observer to agent.

Rather than begin from the beginning, that is, from Burden's explanation of how he first discovered Mastern, we must start with Mastern's account because it stands as the model for Burden's own narrative technique, particularly his voice and his shift to narrator-agent. Mastern's journal teaches Burden not only about history and ethics, it also teaches him how to narrate.

Cass Mastern is a self-conscious narrator. The "self-conscious" narrator, as the term is used by Seymour Chatman, examines and comments upon his own discourse.[14] Mastern begins his account: "I write this down . . . with what truthfulness a sinner may attain unto, that if ever pride is in me, of flesh or spirit, I can peruse these pages and know with shame what evil has been in me" (*AKM* 161). For Cass, writing the narrative is an act of self-examination; he will review his errors by writing his own story and then by reading what he has written. From the beginning of the journal, then, he recounts the story as an overt first person narrator, as in a conventional autobiography, but he also announces that the text itself is part of the redemptive process. Because he intends to be his own first reader, he announces the text's purpose primarily to himself.

13. Girault, "The Narrator's Mind as Symbol," 74; Casper, *The Dark and Bloody Ground*, 130; Girault, "The Narrator's Mind as Symbol," 73.
14. Chatman, *Story and Discourse*, 228.

Within the story Cass shows an awareness of his own behavior. He matures not only while writing the journal, but while living the experiences that he recounts. He repents not only as a narrator but as the prior self that he focalizes through. For example, after he commits adultery with Annabelle: "It was not to be believed that I was Cass Mastern, who stood thus in the house of a friend and benefactor. There was no remorse or horror at the turpitude of the act, but only the incredulity which I have referred to" (*AKM* 169). These two sentences reveal a dialectic between observation and agency. Mastern states that he could barely accept his own identity. He speaks of himself in the third person. Furthermore, he writes both sentences with impersonal constructions, saying "it was not to be believed" rather than "I could not believe," and saying "there was no remorse" rather than "I had no remorse." All of these statements reflect self-division. In the nineteenth century Mastern exhibits the same "terrible division" that Burden identifies as a twentieth-century trait.

Nonetheless, as he recalls his progression toward accepting responsibility, his syntax shifts as well. When Phebe is sold, he writes that all of the consequences, from Duncan's death to the selling of Phebe to Annabelle's rage "had come from my single act of sin and perfidy. . . . The vibration set up in the whole fabric of the world by my act had spread infinitely" (*AKM* 178). Mastern now clearly articulates accountability. He owns up to the consequences of his actions with possessive pronouns: "my single act" and "my act." This is an act of confession.

Burden earlier noted, "The impulse to write the journal sprang from the 'darkness and trouble' " that Mastern himself refers to in the journal (*AKM* 162). Nakadate notes that "confession is a means of bringing order to a problematical existence through aesthetic control."[15] The act of writing the journal becomes for Cass a full acceptance of his guilt. The confession is the culmination of his many endeavors to accept guilt (e.g.,

15. Neil Nakadate, "Robert Penn Warren and the Confessional Novel," *Genre* 2 (1969): 327.

searching for Phebe, going to war). As a penitent, Mastern returns to the past by recounting the wrongful act. He reconciles the present to the past by accepting responsibility for the act. And his repentance redeems him from the burden of the past.[16] From Mastern's narrative Burden learns how to write the narrative of Willie Stark. We might question whether the narrative of Stark would even exist had Burden not read Mastern's journal, because from that text Burden learns to place himself into history. *All the King's Men* is Burden's return to his past (Burden's Landing, Anne, Adam, his mother, Judge Irwin), his painful reconciliation (his research or "excursions") with the past, and his redemption (his realization of his connection to history and his acceptance of responsibility). Part of his redemption takes place in the act of narration itself. The novel is Burden's confession. He publishes his errors and articulates his responsibility.

Burden shows that he understands the concept of historical connection not only when he records and summarizes Mastern's statements about "the common guilt of man" and the "vibration" created by "my single act of sin." The story of Willie Stark becomes his story, an indication that he acknowledges his own role in history. *All the King's Men* is fictive autobiography. That Burden chose to write his own story truly marks his entrance into "the awful responsibility of time."

An examination of Burden's discourse reveals his transformation from observer to agent. When Burden states that "the story of Willie Stark and the story of Jack Burden are, in one sense, one story" (*AKM* 157), he acknowledges his own complicity, yet in that well-known sentence he refers to himself in the third person, as he does persistently through the Mastern narrative. He begins, "Long ago Jack Burden was a graduate student, working for his Ph.D in American history" (*AKM* 157). Rather than

16. Warren's other interpolated narratives are confessions that the protagonists must apply to their own situations. See Willie Proudfit's prodigal son story in *Night Rider*, "The Confession of Ashby Wyndham," in *At Heaven's Gate*, Munn Short's tale in *World Enough and Time*, and Hamish Bond's slave-trading story in *Band of Angels*.

begin, "When I was a graduate student," he represents himself as a separate character in the narrative, distancing himself from the experience. His sardonic tone (i.e., the clichéd "once upon a time" beginning) emphasizes this detachment. He repeats his name in the third person throughout the narrative, even in tags in the dialogue, for example, a conversation with his mother about one of his roommates: " 'Yeah,' Jack Burden said, 'on his seventy-five dollars a month.' She looked at him now, down at his clothes. 'Yours are pretty awful too,' she said. 'Are they?' Jack Burden demanded" (*AKM* 159). Further he writes: "But nothing happened to Jack Burden, for nothing ever happened to Jack Burden, who was invulnerable. Perhaps that was the curse of Jack Burden: he was invulnerable" (*AKM* 159). The striking feature of these examples is Burden's unnecessary repetition of his name. As he speaks with his mother, we know who "him" and "his" refer to; he could have just written "he demanded" rather than "Jack Burden demanded." His persistent self-objectification reflects his disconnection from his actions. Jack Burden makes himself invulnerable by speaking only in the third person.

However, we must ask why Burden would speak in a way to detach himself, since his 1939 narration takes place *after* he has learned the concept of historical connection. For the answer, we must refer back to the distinction between voice and focalization. Though writing these sentences in 1939, he focalizes through his 1920 frame of mind. His persistent self-detachment replicates the state of mind that he progressed from, giving his narratee a clear sense of how alienated he was before his association with Willie Stark changed him. His pronoun shifts show his development from narrator-observer to narrator-agent. Burden records his acceptance of responsibility into his discourse.

As Jack Burden tells the story of how "Jack Burden" started the dissertation, he does make one curious omission. He states, "When the time came for him to select a subject for his dissertation for his Ph.D., his professor suggested that he edit the journal and letters of Cass Mastern, and write a biographical essay" (*AKM* 163). However, he does not explain how the professor came to know about the Mastern materials, though it seems clear that Burden must have told him. Burden elides some interesting information here, such as his conversations with the professor. It would be interesting to know how Burden, as the graduate student in 1920, "narrated" the Mastern journal to his professor.

We have already seen from the first chapter of *All the King's Men* that Burden often focalizes through the person he was at a previous time to illustrate his development for his narratee. As he narrates in 1939 he creates conceptual points of view of his earlier perceptual points of view. Thus, rather than using the first-person pronoun, which would indicate an acceptance of responsibility in the events he narrates, he maintains an objective stance with the third-person pronoun.

As usual, this attempt at distance only emphasizes his presence. Casper observes that as Burden tells the Mastern story, "The very effort required of him to speak with unnatural objectivity of Cass Mastern is secret acknowledgement of the significance of the *exemplum*. It is an index of his resistance."[17] However, the "secret acknowledgement" of his "unnatural objectivity" can also be read as open acknowledgement of personal agency.

A significant shift to the first-person pronoun occurs at the end of the Mastern chapter. No longer trying to present himself as observer, Burden enters the narrative in the passage already quoted above:

> [1] I have said that Jack Burden could not put down the facts about Cass Mastern's world because he did not know Cass Mastern. [2] Jack Burden did not say definitely to himself why he did not know Cass Mastern. [3] But I (who am what Jack Burden became) look back now, years later, and try to say why. (*AKM* 188; numbers added)

Burden distinguishes between the "I" of the discourse and the "Jack Burden" of the story, presenting his maturity as a shedding

17. Casper, *The Dark and Bloody Ground*, 130.

of his former self. Again, to use Chatman's terminology, Burden's "perceptual" point of view in [1] and [2] is that of Burden as student, but the "conceptual" point of view in those same sentences is that of Burden as narrator. The mature voice of the 1939 narrator verbalizes what the immature consciousness of the student could not. What Genette says of "the narrative of events" also applies here to the narrative of prior perceptions: it is a verbal "transcription" of nonverbal experience.[18] Sentence [2] indicates that Burden-student did not even verbalize what he thought. By making a clear distinction between the present "I" that can "look back now, years later" and the past "Jack Burden," sentence [3] shifts from self-objectification to self-identity. The present self takes responsibility for articulating what the prior self did not know; consequently, Burden repairs the division of self. The narrative may focalize through his past "perceptual" consciousness, but the voice of his present "conceptual" consciousness supersedes it.

His return to the first person indicates that he has surrendered his pose as a neutral narrator. The "I" indicates one who participates as well as observes. It is a step toward autobiography.

Immediately after the passage quoted above, Burden interprets the Mastern story in the well-known "web" passage: "Cass Mastern lived for a few years and in that time he learned that the world is all of one piece. He learned that the world is like an enormous spider web and if you touch it, however lightly, at any point, the vibration ripples to the remotest perimeter. . . . It does not matter whether or not you meant to brush the web of things" (*AKM* 188–89). In the "web" passage, the section of Burden's most explicit editorializing, he responds to Mastern's acceptance of responsibility, situating Mastern's statements about the "common guilt of man" and "my single act of sin" within his own "web" analogy. Burden particularly seems influenced by Mastern's "fabric" metaphor for the relation between actions and consequences: "the vibration set up in the whole fabric of the world by my act had spread infinitely" (*AKM* 178). The "web"

18. Genette, *Narrative Discourse*, 165.

passage presents the novel's central statement of Warren's concept of historical connection.

John Burt suggests that this passage is very dark because the image of the spider implies an overdeterministic world (e.g., "the drowsy spider feels the tingle and is drowsy no more but springs out to fling the gossamer coils about you who have touched the web and then inject the black, numbing poison under your hide" [*AKM* 188]). That Burden can even create such an analogy indicates that he has learned Mastern's lesson. As we have seen, the point of view in this famous "web" passage is not that of Burden as student but Burden as narrator. He articulates a meaning that he could not possibly have reached at the time of researching Mastern's life. In fact, he uses the third-person pronoun to indicate that he is speaking of his former self (his 1920 self) when he states, "Jack Burden could read those words, but how could he be expected to understand them? They could only be words to him, for to him the world then was simply an accumulation of items, odds and ends. . . . One thing had nothing to do, in the end, with anything else" (*AKM* 189). The consequences of Mastern's and his own actions lead Burden to understand that in the end, everything does indeed have something to do with everything else. In 1920 though, he was unable to comprehend the meaning of Mastern's account, so he rejected the journal, though he continued to take it with him wherever he moved. After the experience with Willie Stark, Burden, unlike "all the king's men" in the nursery rhyme, is able to put together the pieces of Mastern's life.

The "web" passage thus represents his ability to formulate some general interpretation of what he had before seen as the "odds and ends" of Mastern's life. Richard Gray notes: "Burden suddenly found that the dispersed facts in the case of Cass Mastern were assuming shape and significance. The growing coherence of his 'items,' and the discovery which that coherence was precipitating, were both inviting him to recognize his involvement in history."[19] Gray's point is important, because it implies

19. Richard Gray, "The American Novelist and American History: A Revaluation of *All the King's Men*," *Journal of American Studies* 6 (1972): 305.

that the facts of history are meaningless until they are ordered into a narrative by a shaping consciousness. As a reporter and a history graduate student, Burden believed that the meaning of history was in the facts, absolute and isolated from subjective consciousness. He thought that he could observe history objectively. However, once Judge Irwin's death confronts him with his own role in events, he realizes that he must take an active role in making the facts of Mastern's life have meaning. When he discovers that he has participated in the web of events, he also discovers that he must interact as an active participant (i.e., as the narrator) in the Mastern narrative. The meaning of Mastern's experiences depends on Burden's consciousness to shape the facts into meanings.

Warren has commented that "at first he [Burden] couldn't face the fact that in his own blood there was a man who had faced up to a moral problem in a deep way. . . . Then, he couldn't face the truth otherwise, without this piece of research."[20] This statement suggests that the Mastern story gives Burden the perspective he needs to understand his relation to Stark, but the full significance of Mastern's journal is not merely that it illuminates the meaning of Burden's experience with Willie Stark. On the contrary, his association with Willie Stark enlightens his reading of Cass Mastern.

Burden read but could not understand the Mastern journal in 1920; or, as Marshall Walker states the case, Burden understands the facts about Mastern "but he evades the truth they contain." He writes the "web" passage interpreting the Mastern journal in 1939, *after* his association with Willie Stark. Burden's experiences as Stark's aide allow him to return to the Mastern journal with an improved ability to face its truth. Barnett Guttenberg points out, "When the pieces of Jack's subsequent experience finally form a new picture of the world, Jack can reformulate Cass's discovery."[21] In order to understand the Mas-

20. Warren, "The Uses of History in Fiction," (Panel discussion with Ellison, Styron, and Woodward, 1968), 108.

21. Walker, *A Vision Earned*, 103–4; Guttenberg, *Web of Being*, 52.

tern story, Burden *first* must discover his place in the "web" of history.

The publication history of the Cass Mastern chapter of *All the King's Men* also shows how Warren, like Burden, understood the chapter's significance only *after* writing the story of Willie Stark. The chapter originally appeared as "Cass Mastern's Wedding Ring," a short story in *Partisan Review* two years before the novel's publication. A footnote on the first page indicated, "This is a self-contained chapter from a novel in progress," but the story appeared without what are now the first six paragraphs and the last seven paragraphs of Chapter 4.[22] In other words, the story originally appeared without the "web" analogy. Warren must have created this central passage only after conceiving of Mastern's story in relation to the entire novel. (The final seven paragraphs of the story are also where Burden starts using the first-person pronoun.) Thus, both Warren's and Burden's constructions of the Mastern story depend upon their understanding of the Willie Stark story.

The Mastern chapter illustrates that the construction of history depends upon the subjective faculty, and that ethical action depends upon an acceptance of personal responsibility. The Mastern narrative treats these morals as two sides of the same lesson: to be ethical, one must acknowledge one's complicity in making and understanding history. As Burden accepts responsibility for his actions, he must return to the project of writing the history of Cass Mastern: "But I still had the money [from Judge Irwin's estate], and so I am spending it to live on while I write the book I began years ago, the life of Cass Mastern, whom once I could not understand but whom, perhaps, I now may come to understand" (*AKM* 438). Burden finds redemption from his illusion of disconnection by returning to Mastern's journal to reconcile it with what he has learned from working with Stark. His discourse now employs the first-person pronoun, which indicates an acceptance of responsibility in the events of history and,

22. Robert Penn Warren, "Cass Mastern's Wedding Ring," *Partisan Review* 11 (1944): 375.

emerging from that responsibility, the freedom to shape his own identity. We must reiterate Guttenberg here: "The burden of responsibility is liberating. . . . Responsibility for one's being means that one is the creator of his being, and that he is therefore free to choose what his world will be."[23]

Burden shows his growth in his explicit commentary in the "web" passage and his statements of responsibility at the end of the novel. Furthermore, as we have seen, his discourse shows that he can translate his interpretations into action. Jack's very ability to read and make meaning of Mastern's journal, and his development as a narrator-agent writing himself into the events that he narrates, are the greatest signs of his acceptance of responsibility.

Burden's development in the Mastern narrative and in the novel as a whole demonstrates the role of individual consciousness in ordering and shaping history, an important role because "in creating the image of the past, we create ourselves." Warren shows faith in the role of literature not just as a vehicle for information but as implicitly meaningful. In "Knowledge and the Image of Man," he makes the New Critical claim that literature teaches not only "knowledge by form" but also "knowledge *of* form." For Warren, according to Richard Law, "The work of art *can* directly convey knowledge, knowledge at least of the process by which man perceives."[24] If the word "history" substitutes for the words "literature" and "art" in these quotations, Warren's objective becomes clear. Jack's overt, self-conscious narration in *All the King's Men,* particularly in the Cass Mastern section, dramatizes the process with which humanity perceives its past. Burden's struggle between observing and participating illustrates his assertion, "Any act of pure perception is a feat, and if you don't believe it, try it sometime" (*AKM* 35), or as the honest attorney general Hugh Miller says, "History is blind, but man is not" (*AKM* 436). When Burden notes that the "Case of

23. Guttenberg, *Web of Being,* 55.
24. Warren, "The Use of the Past," 51; Warren, "Knowledge and the Image of Man," 191; Law, " 'The Case of the Upright Judge,' " 5.

the Upright Judge" was a historical excursion that "meant something" (*AKM* 191), he reveals his sense of connection to history. The failure to attend sufficiently to Burden's discourse has led to the popular misconception, especially prevalent in initial reviews of the novel and motion picture, that *All the King's Men* is only about Huey Long. There are probably two main reasons for this mistake. Because the novel appeared only approximately fifteen years after Long's death, Long was still much present in the public's historical consciousness. The Columbia Pictures movie (which won three Academy Awards in 1949, including Best Picture) further encouraged the error by concentrating entirely on Stark's rise and fall, completely ignoring the stories of Burden's paternity and Cass Mastern. Obviously, the discursive nature of film cannot replicate the role of the narrator as easily as literary modes can. And in *"All the King's Men*: The Matrix of Experience,"* Warren admits that if he had not lived in Louisiana and if Huey Long had not been governor, "the novel would not have been written" because the actual political scene did give him "a line of thinking and feeling that did eventuate in the novel."[25]

However, he also asserts that he became "concerned more with the myth than with the fact, more with the symbolic than with the actual." In the introduction to the Modern Library edition, Warren argues that creating Jack Burden as his narrator gave him a commentator and chorus, "a character of a higher degree of self-consciousness than my politician. . . . And the story, in a sense, became the story of Jack Burden, the teller of the tale."[26] Jack's role as narrator demonstrates what Warren meant when he insisted that Willie Stark should not be identified with Huey Long. This was a claim that Warren often made in prefaces to new editions of *All the King's Men*. For example, see

25. Robert Penn Warren, *"All the King's Men*: The Matrix of Experience,"* *Yale Review* 53 (1963): 161.

26. Ibid., 166; Robert Penn Warren, "Introduction to the Modern Library Edition of *All the King's Men*," in *Twentieth-Century Interpretations of All the King's Men,* ed. Robert H. Chambers (Englewood Cliffs, N.J.: Prentice-Hall, 1977), 95–96.

his introduction to the Modern Library edition (1953) and his essay in the *Yale Review* entitled *"All the King's Men*: The Matrix of Experience" (1963). Even the preface to the British edition, originally published as "The World of Huey Long" in the *London Times*, gives the British readers background on Louisiana politics in 1920–30 but then explains that the novel is not about Long. Clearly, for Warren, the process of constructing history became of primary importance. In his biographical narratives, Warren puts the emphasis on "narrative."

The same is true for Burden. He becomes engaged not only with the events of the story he tells (he is, after all, a participant in those events), but also with the process of representing those events in his narrative. As a self-conscious narrator, he persistently refers to the narrative he writes. For example, he refers to his experiences as chapters within larger stories (*AKM* 355), and he comments that events are meaningless until a pattern emerges into which they can be plotted (*AKM* 383–84). History for Burden is not just the past; it is the interaction between past and present, the meaning that results from the subjective consciousness of the present processing the objective data of the past. Thus the narrator becomes the most important subject in the narrative.

Again, the novel's genesis sheds light on this point. Unlike the other major character, who is based on an actual political figure, Burden is a completely fictional creation. In what is probably the most thoroughly researched comparison of *All the King's Men* to actual historical circumstances, Ladell Payne documents numerous parallels between the characters and their counterparts. In addition to the Willie Stark–Huey Long connection, many other characters appear similar to individuals close to the governor of Louisiana. Even Sugar-Boy seems a close composite of two of Long's bodyguards. However, Payne finds no prototype for Burden and concludes that he is completely fictional. In an interview with Flannery O'Connor and Joe Sills, Warren explains that when the novel originated in the late 1930s as the play *Proud Flesh,* a reporter appeared on the scene as the assassin, his childhood friend, was waiting to kill Talos (Stark), and they conversed briefly. This was necessary to create a delay for dramatic effect, Warren explains, to give the assassin a personality, and that reporter eventually developed into Jack Burden. In another interview, with Ralph Ellison and Eugene Walter, Warren explains, "It turned out, in a way, that what he [Burden] thought about the story was more important than the story itself. . . . He is an observer, but he is involved." Placing Burden into literary context, Justus notes, "Call him Ishmael or Carraway, Burden is another in a long line of American narrators who by dint of their special positions in the stories they tell end by telling their own stories as well." Justus goes so far as to call the political plot of *All the King's Men* a "subplot" to the Jack Burden story: "He [Burden] frankly presents himself as the most complex figure in his account, and he tells us finally more about himself and his difficult moral education than he does about Willie Stark."[27]

Burden's focus on his discourse in addition to his story parallels Warren's concern not for the actual facts of Huey Long's political career but for the greater questions that the Huey Long phenomenon raises, questions about good and evil, the definition of self, and the uses of the past. Richard Gray's "The American Novelist and American History" effectively makes this point: "In recasting the story of the legendary 'Boss' of Louisiana, Warren is merely doing on a large scale what his narrator does on a slightly smaller one," and more specifically, "What Robert Penn Warren has done in the case of Willie Stark, then, as far as his relationship to his historical prototype [Huey Long] is concerned, is to take authenticated facts and reproduce them so as to emphasize their tragic pattern." Recall Hayden White's assertion that a plot exists prior to events and validates an event as historical as long as the event contributes to the development of the

27. Robert Penn Warren, "Interview with Flannery O'Connor and Robert Penn Warren" (Interview with Joe Sills, 1959), in *Talking with Robert Penn Warren*, ed. Watkins, Hiers, and Weaks, 55–56; Warren, "On the Art of Fiction" (Interview with Ralph Ellison and Eugene Walter, 1956), ibid., 42; Justus, *Achievement of Robert Penn Warren*, 194; Justus, "The Power of Filiation," 166, 157.

plot.[28] Real-life events do not naturally order themselves into patterns; the historian or novelist must create the patterns. For Warren, the roles of the novelist and historian converge in that their interpretive strategies construct plots and meanings. Burden's "historical excursions," then, are microcosms of Warren's use of Huey Long. Both Burden and Warren privilege the imagination in the investigation for historical truth. Burden becomes Warren's idea of a "philosophical novelist." Thus, with the structure and style of his narration reflecting his ethical development, Burden's discourse ultimately reflects Warren's development as a writer of historical narratives.

28. Gray, "The American Novelist and American History," 307, 303; Hayden White, *The Content of the Form*, 51.

VI

"I Can Show You What Is Left"
The Historian-Narrator of *World Enough and Time*

> I chanced to lay my hand on a small package, carefully
> done up in a piece of ancient yellow parchment. This
> envelope had the air of an official record of some period
> long past.
>
> —Nathaniel Hawthorne, "The Custom House"

> Here are the diaries, the documents, and the letters, yellow
> too, bound in neat bundles. . . .
>
> —*World Enough and Time*

A s Robert Penn Warren recounts in his interview with Frank Gado, *World Enough and Time* originated during his tenure as Consultant in Poetry at the Library of Congress in the 1940s, when Katherine Anne Porter gave him a booklet containing the 1826 *Confession of Jereboam O. Beauchamp.* In what has become well known as the "Kentucky Tragedy," Beauchamp murdered Colonel Solomon Sharp for the alleged seduction of Beauchamp's wife, Ann Cook. Beauchamp believed that Sharp, a rising star in Kentucky politics, had protected his political reputation in the ensuing public scandal by publishing a broadside accusing Cook of becoming pregnant by a slave. Enraged by these charges of sexual promiscuity and miscegenation, Beauchamp sought retaliation in accordance with the southern code of honor. Arrested, tried, and convicted for stabbing Sharp, Beauchamp awaited execution. Ann lived with him in his prison cell, Beauchamp writing his *Confession* and both of them writing much romantic poetry. They attempted suicide with laudanum, but when that attempt failed they made another attempt with a smuggled knife. Cook died of her wound, but Beauchamp was hanged after his wounds were tended. On their request, their bodies were interred together in an embrace within the same tomb in a Nelson County, Kentucky, cemetery.[1]

In addition to the trial transcript, the leading players recorded their own versions of the drama. In refutation of Beauchamp's *Confession,* Leander J. Sharp wrote a vindication of his brother. Cook's letters were published. The reliability of all of these sources, particularly the authenticity of Cook's letters, has come under suspicion.[2] Nonetheless, this story contains all of the elements of a sensational and romantic tragedy: power, seduction, slander, revenge, trial, and execution. Beauchamp and Cook still plead their case from the grave. The epitaph etched on their tombstone, a poem written by Cook, asks passersby to empathize with their honorable intent to strike down the villain Sharp. Sharp's epitaph on his grave in Frankfort Cemetery argues that the victim of the assassination was noble and virtuous. It is no wonder that writers such as Edgar Allan Poe, William Gilmore Simms, Thomas Holley Chivers, and Robert Penn Warren in *World Enough and Time* have recast the Kentucky Tragedy into drama and fiction.[3]

1. See J. Winston Coleman, *The Beauchamp-Sharp Tragedy: An Episode of Kentucky History During the Middle 1820s* (Frankfort, Ky.: Roberts Printing, 1950). All of the primary sources are published in Loren J. Kallsen, ed., *The Kentucky Tragedy: A Problem in Romantic Attitudes* (New York: Bobbs-Merrill, 1963), and see the entry for Beauchamp in my Bibliography.

2. For a critical appraisal of the four primary documents, see Jack E. Surrency's, "The Kentucky Tragedy and Its Primary Sources," in *No Fairer Land: Studies in Southern Literature Before 1900,* ed. Dameron J. Lasley and James W. Mathews (Troy, N.Y.: Whitston, 1986), 110–23.

3. See William Goldhurst's article, which surveys the various fictional, dramatic, and poetic treatments of the Beauchamp-Sharp case: "The New Revenge Tragedy: Comparative Treatments of the Beauchamp Case," *Southern Literary Journal* 22 (1989): 117–27.

Warren created a fictional narrator to guide the reader through the historical documents in *World Enough and Time*, just as he created Jack Burden to narrate the Cass Mastern and Willie Stark stories in *All the King's Men*. The narrator, a historian, introduces his primary materials, foremost of which is a journal written by Jeremiah Beaumont, the fictional counterpart of Beauchamp. The plot follows the general outline of the actual Kentucky Tragedy: Beaumont's acquaintance, Wilkie Barron, tells him about Rachel Jordan's (Ann Cook) seduction and betrayal by his mentor, Colonel Cassius Fort (Sharp). Drawn to Rachel's injured innocence, Beaumont courts her and proposes marriage, but only after he presses her to show him the grave of her stillborn child and extracts from her a demand that he exact vengeance upon Fort. Beaumont challenges Fort to a duel and humiliates him in public to shame him when he declines. During the political campaign, the Relief Party raises the issue of Fort's relation with Ann to impugn Fort's character; Beaumont sees that a handbill, signed by Fort, defends Fort's honor by accusing Ann of having had an affair with a slave. Beaumont assassinates Fort, and is arrested and tried on the basis of fabricated evidence and testimony. When he attempts to counteract the lies at his trial by bribing a witness, Marlowe, he is discovered and convicted. With Rachel living in his cell, he begins to write his confession. They both attempt suicide with laudanum, but the poison fails.

Here Warren departs fully from the historical record: Barron helps them escape to the primordial region of an aged pirate named La Grand Bosse, where Rachel goes insane and Beaumont becomes atavistic. However, Beaumont decides to return to accept his guilt and execution, but he is captured and murdered by an agent of Barron, who thinks Beaumont is returning to implicate him. Barron goes on to a successful political career, though one day, seemingly inexplicably, he commits suicide. He has preserved Beaumont's journal, which has been in his possession all the years.

The political context is the nineteenth-century relief issue, in which the Kentucky state legislature passed a law to permit a twelve-month relief period for debtors. Because they favored establishing a Supreme Court that would uphold their agenda, the Relief Party was sometimes referred to as the "New Court." The opposition, the Old Court, saw debt relief as unconstitutional since it negated contracts and enforced a law ex post facto. Fort, Barron, and Beaumont are members of the Relief Party, though Fort disavows his association with the party. The opportunistic Barron is motivated by the desire to use Beaumont for political purposes; he is the one who writes and signs Fort's name to the second handbill. The idealistic Beaumont, however, is motivated by the desire to uphold a code of honor for southern womanhood. Warren's main themes are the same as in other major novels like *Night Rider* and *All the King's Men*: the capacity for good to arise out of bad circumstances and vice versa, the contrast between the inner reality of the individual and the world at large, the conflict between idealism and realism, and between the role of history and the construction of identity. Warren departs from the actual history in order to emphasize these themes. For example, Sharp actually was on the New Court side, but Warren makes Fort a defector from New Court to Old, to set up a contrast between the pragmatic concept of law as a manipulable instrument for particular needs and circumstances (New Court), and the idealistic concept of law as a means to realizing a fixed and unchanging truth and justice. In addition, Warren re-creates Beaumont's childhood to show experiences of self-isolation that contribute to making him an idealist. As a child, Beaumont rejects his maternal grandfather's proposition to change his last name in order to make him his heir. The young Beaumont baptizes himself; as an adult, he will see Fort's murder as a baptism in blood. Beaumont sees a picture of a woman in the *Book of Martyrs*, one of his first books, and wishes he could persecute her so that he could save her, an attitude that he will play out with Ann.

Throughout the novel, the modern historian functions as the principal narrating device, persistently making references to his production of the text and Beaumont's production of his own life story. During an interview with Richard Sale, Warren identified a direct connection between the narrators of *World Enough and Time* and *All the King's Men:* "Jack Burden and Cass Mastern have the same relationship as the 'I' narrator and the Jereboam Beauchamp-Beaumont fellow." Indeed, in *World Enough and Time,* the kind of excursion into the past begun in the Cass Mastern episode "is expanded to an entire novel."[4]

But there is one important difference between the two novels. Unlike Jack Burden, the Historian who narrates *World Enough and Time* does not have an immediate, personal connection to the story he tells.[5] He is not distantly related to Beaumont as Burden is related to Mastern, nor does his reading of Beaumont's confession reflect upon a larger autobiographical narrative, as is the case with Burden's reading of Mastern's journal. Throughout the Warren canon, characters shape their experiences into autobiographical narratives: Seth in "Blackberry Winter," Cass Mastern and Jack Burden in *All the King's Men,* Jeremiah Beaumont in *World Enough and Time,* Warren himself in *Segregation, Who Speaks for the Negro?, Jefferson Davis Gets His Citizenship Back,* and *Portrait of a Father.* From *John Brown* to *Portrait of a Father,* Warren develops from objective biographical narrative toward autobiographical narrative. However, *World Enough and Time,* appearing in the middle of this development, explores ways to represent another individual's experience. This is a necessary move in Warren's development. With this novel, Warren addresses the question: If he were not taking historical excursions into the lives of himself, his ancestors, and his mentors, how should a historian like Jack Burden investigate and construct a narrative about a more distant individual?

In *World Enough and Time* Warren solves this question with a modernist solution: the Historian-Narrator inserts himself into the context of history by means of self-referential discourse. To represent Jeremiah Beaumont's experience, he represents his

4. Warren, "An Interview in New Haven with Robert Penn Warren" (Interview with Sale, 1969), 128; Bohner, *Robert Penn Warren,* 106.
5. At this point I will begin to refer to the narrator of *World Enough and Time* as the "Historian" or "Historian-Narrator" in order to acknowledge him as a character and distinguish him among Warren's other narrators.

own interaction with Beaumont's experience. He revises Beaumont's story as a kind of autobiography. To borrow Wayne Booth's terminology, although the Historian-Narrator is more of a narrator-observer than a narrator-agent (because, strictly speaking, he does not participate directly in the story that he narrates), he does call attention to his own participation as one who subjectively represents past events.

Revising conventions of history in modernist fashion, Warren comes to understand autobiography as the twentieth-century alternative to traditional history. In the *story* of *World Enough and Time,* Jeremiah Beaumont's confessional narrative mirrors Warren's development toward autobiographical connection. Moreover, the modern Historian-Narrator's *discourse* iterates this growth. The modern reader, identifying with the modern Historian-Narrator, becomes involved with the Historian's reconstruction of the past into a myth that is usable for the present. The reader joins the Historian in the shift from passively receiving history as observers toward actively constructing history as agents. *World Enough and Time* is not just about the Kentucky Tragedy; it concerns a modernist's attempt to make sense of the fragments of the past.

As William Bedford Clark suggests, Warren's 1929 examination of John Brown's speeches and letters resembles the Historian's use of Beaumont's journal in *World Enough and Time.*[6] Similar to Warren's John Brown, Jeremiah Beaumont is a "self-made man" in the sense that he constructs his own public identity. Like John Brown's biographer, the Historian of *World Enough and Time* investigates the methods with which Beaumont dramatizes himself in his journal. The Historian does not permit Beaumont's illusions of heroism to be presented without challenge. Like John Brown's biographer, Beaumont's biographer discloses the fallibility of the historical record that has been created and revised by the historical person under investigation.

Both *John Brown* and *World Enough and Time* ostensibly begin as biographies of Brown and Beaumont, but this objective

---

6. Clark, *American Vision of Robert Penn Warren,* 38.

shifts. Each text examines the "making" of the historical figure, the transformation of the private person into a public persona. Because such a metahistorical agendum fosters the narrator's self-consciousness, the narrator becomes a protagonist overshadowing the historical figure being represented. The subject shifts from the life of John Brown or Jeremiah Beaumont to the methods of representing those lives. In each text, the biographer audits the primary records and documents to create a version of the figure that will be accessible to modern audiences. As Justus accurately argues, Warren's narrator in *World Enough and Time* demonstrates the necessity of searching the past "to make sense of those events that may yield a usable meaning for the present." It should be mentioned that Justus provides the most thorough survey and examination of the Historian-Narrator of *World Enough and Time,* essential to every study of the narrator's thematic, structural, and stylistic functions.[7] Like Brown, Beaumont is a text to be explicated, an embedded myth whose layers must be peeled back to reveal the individual who has become obscured by subsequent historical representations.

The major difference between *John Brown* and *World Enough and Time* is the historical figure under investigation. While Warren's Brown plays the roles of savior and martyr all the way to the scaffold, Beaumont becomes a disillusioned idealist whose journal develops into a confession. Like Jack Burden, Beaumont achieves the sense of historical connection that Cass Mastern calls "the common guilt of man" (*AKM* 187). Beaumont distances himself from the world by isolating himself within his own ideals, assuming that ideas justify actions. Once he decides to murder, he corrects this philosophy by going too far in the opposite direction: he decides that actions justify ideas, a notion that isolates him just as much. In the conclusion to *World Enough and Time,* though, Beaumont decides to seek reconciliation and communion with the human family, a sinner among sinners. Beaumont admits that his crime is "unpardonable" for "It is the crime of self. . . . The crime is I" (*WEAT* 458).

7. Justus, *Achievement of Robert Penn Warren,* 215.

He writes in his journal: "I go home through the wilderness now and know that I may not have redemption. I no longer seek to justify. I seek only to suffer. I will shake the hangman's hand, and will call him my brother, at last" (*WEAT* 460). Note that these sentences all begin with the first-person pronoun; by referring to himself as the subject of each sentence, Beaumont shows an acceptance of responsibility. His writing style here resembles Cass Mastern's confession in *All the King's Men*. His statements also resemble the "confession" of Munn Short, the jailor who briefly relates to Beaumont his own guilt at having committed adultery (a story whose relevance to his own life Beaumont fails to comprehend). Beaumont returns to his past (literally returning home), to reconcile with the community he has wronged and seek redemption through the public act of confessing in writing. Warren's John Brown does not achieve a sense of connection or reconciliation; the written documents he leaves contain attempted self-justification rather than confession, and we come to suspect the sincerity even of his most conciliatory statements. Though the Historian must work through Beaumont's unreliable self-representations, his journal, unlike John Brown's writings, contains admission and repentance, two key elements of confession.

Another major distinction between *John Brown* and *World Enough and Time* is the function of the narrators. As we have seen in Chapter III, while Warren writing as John Brown's biographer exposes Brown's agenda and the biases of Brown's subsequent biographers, he claims objectivity for himself. Yet as Warren challenges those other representations of Brown, he fails to call into question his own claim to neutrality. The overt narrator of *John Brown* persistently intrudes with explicit editorial comments delivered with a very audible tone of disapprobation. As we have seen, many critics have pointed out Warren's sarcastic tone and bias against Brown as evidence of the biography's failure, yet the *John Brown* narrator assumes that his own voice is the only objective one in the assessment of Brown's life. In contrast, the *World Enough and Time* Historian surrenders this pose of neutrality. Like the narrator of the later biographical narratives, *Jefferson Davis Gets His Citizenship Back* and *Portrait of a Father,* the Historian in *World Enough and Time* personally engages with history as a means of structuring his historical narrative. The Historian becomes self-referential, exposing his subjective construction of history. He becomes more involved with the historical subject, understanding history by placing himself into a direct and open relationship with the methods and materials of historical research. Beaumont acknowledges his own agency and complicity in events; similarly, the Historian connects with Beaumont's experience as an audible presence within his own discourse.

Warren makes his narrator a historian, working within a profession that seemingly requires objectivity. This characterization echoes Jack Burden's initial careers as history graduate student and journalist. But observe that the Historian's voice (like Burden's) is an overt presence in the narrative. The Historian's narration reveals personal involvement, evident in his pervasive and explicit interpretations, speculations, rhetorical questions, and vacillations between irony and empathy. The Historian's investigation exposes the fiction of neutrality in both his own and Beaumont's narratives.

The Historian begins as a self-conscious narrator. As Justus points out, the reader is never permitted to forget the presence of a narrator who decides which facts to present, which facts to withhold, which facts to present without comment and which facts to explicate: "We are always conscious that the Beaumont story comes to us only through him."[8]

Like Hawthorne's "Custom House" narrator, Warren's Historian begins by reporting on the materials he possesses. Unlike Jack Burden and "The Custom House" narrator, though, he does not explain how he came to possess the documents or how he decided to begin the project. But from the opening paragraph he nonetheless establishes an audible, self-conscious, and personal voice. The novel opens: "I can show you what is left. After the pride, passion, agony, and bemused aspiration, what is left is

8. Ibid., 230.

in our hands. Here are the scraps of newspaper, more than a century old, splotched and yellowed and huddled together in a library, like November leaves abandoned by the wind" (*WEAT* 3). The Historian catalogues the materials that are available to him—diaries, documents, letters, records—and he describes Beaumont's journal: "The letters of his script lean forward in their haste. Haste toward what? The bold stroke of the quill catches on the rough paper, fails, resumes, moves on in its race against time" (*WEAT* 3). Then, in the next paragraph, he defines his task as a historian: "Puzzling over what is left, we are like the scientist fumbling with a tooth and thigh bone to reconstruct for a museum some great, stupid beast extinct with the ice age" (*WEAT* 3–4).

Let us examine what has been going on in these two introductory paragraphs. With the statement, "I can show you what is left," the first-person and second-person pronouns, typical of Warren's opening passages (cf. the openings of *All the King's Men*, "The Circus in the Attic," and "The World of Daniel Boone"), invite the reader to accompany the Historian in a journey into the past. Similar to Beaumont's (and Cass Mastern's) use of the first-person pronoun, these statements focus attention not on Beaumont but on the modern Historian-Narrator's interaction with the Beaumont story. The Historian calls attention to his own participation with the text.

The opening sentences are cast in straightforward prose, but each statement departs from a conventional history text. The Historian lists qualitative factors—"pride, passion, agony, and bemused aspiration"—rather than more traditional, quantitative components of history such as geography, demographics, and so forth. The narrator lists the primary materials that are available for him to research, but he describes the newspaper with a simile more lyrical than factual ("like November leaves"). He also invites the reader's participation with rhetorical questions ("Haste toward what?"). The Historian clearly interprets his materials as he introduces them, and he departs from neutrality further by imagining the forward-leaning style of Beaumont's handwriting to be a "race against time."

In the second paragraph the Historian compares his occupation with that of a scientist, but the Historian's discourse undermines any claim to scientific objectivity: his imagined scientist attempts to reconstruct some "stupid beast extinct with the ice age," a clear example of the Historian's attitude emanating from his opinionated diction. These opening lines set the stage for a highly intrusive narrator who is, to borrow Seymour Chatman's terms, very "audible" or "overt."

This sifting through the records exposes "the difficulties of reconstructing the whole truth," but Casper also makes this distinction between the two narrators of the novel: "An anonymous and neutral historian tabulates the facts in an objective discourse; Jeremiah discloses his own story in frantic subjectivity." Referring to Jack Burden's failed neutrality in *All the King's Men,* Casper argues that "the singular detachment of the narrator in *World Enough and Time* illustrates such neutrality. . . . Warren satirizes the historian's professional blindness to the truth that surrounds him."[9] Granted, the Historian's discourse is much calmer than Beaumont's "frantic subjectivity," but as the opening passages illustrate, the Historian is certainly subjective.

Observing the probable influence of *The Scarlet Letter* and *Absalom, Absalom!* upon Warren, Justus points out that *World Enough and Time* "is a critique of conventional scientific historiography. . . . Since the truth of history is difficult to know, imaginative reconstruction may come as close to truth as we are likely to get."[10] Warren's Historian does demonstrate an awareness of his own "imaginative reconstruction." Many examples illustrate that the Historian is not entirely detached, not neutral, and not blind to the greater universal and moral truths of the Beaumont story. The Historian comments on Beaumont's conflicts between idea and fact, between private identity and the public self, showing that he is clearly aware of the philosophical implications of the story he narrates. For example, in the first chapter's back-

9. Casper, *The Dark and Bloody Ground,* 137, 148.
10. Justus, *Achievement of Robert Penn Warren,* 233–35.

ground of Jeremiah Beaumont's life, we see Beaumont's first affirmation of his identity. Grandfather Marcher, his maternal grandfather, who never approved of Jeremiah's father, offers to make the boy his heir if Jeremiah will deny his father and adopt the Marcher name. Jeremiah refuses and leaves Marcher's land, never to see his grandfather again. The Historian, however, can see Marcher's future. He writes that the old man "married a sluttish wench" who bore him a son, though "perhaps the son was not his" (*WEAT* 23). One Marcher descendant becomes governor, another dies in the Civil War, and a third becomes a professor of French who loses his university position amid charges of pederasty. The Historian informs us that the Marcher mansion is now "only a few heaps of stone and disintegrating brick" (*WEAT* 23). The Historian's selection of details undercuts grandfather Marcher's pride in his name. The Historian, relating the family's uncertain genealogy and the decaying mansion, seems to relish presenting this Faulknerian decline of the family. This is not a neutral narrator, but one whose critique of Marcher implicitly aligns his sympathies with Beaumont.

The Historian's introduction of Rachel shows the same subjective narration. While he wonders, "Was she beautiful? There is no picture for us to see," he also speculates, "even if the pictured face was beautiful it could not be beautiful enough to account for the story," and then comments, "or perhaps we have lost our faith in beauty" (*WEAT* 45). The Historian wonders why Rachel's diary concludes, and he speculates, "Did she know why she closed it? Did she feel that . . . when you truly begin to live you must construct your own world and therefore have no need for words written on paper, words that can only give the shadow of a world already lived?" (*WEAT* 54). The Historian here not only speculates upon Rachel's motives but also entertains the question of the efficacy of language to represent experience. These are not the disinterested comments of a neutral biographer.

Similarly, in presenting Jeremiah's reaction upon hearing the story of Fort's seduction of Rachel, the Historian uses free indirect discourse, more indicative of the Historian's voice than Jeremiah's: "Ah, where was the greatness of life? Was it only a dream? Could a man not come to some moment when . . . he could live in the pure idea?" (*WEAT* 57). As a conscientious archivist, the Historian is careful with the facts of the seduction, introducing several statements with qualifying clauses such as "we cannot be entirely sure" (*WEAT* 58), "we know this much" (*WEAT* 58), and "we can be certain" (*WEAT* 59). He does not always permit himself to bridge gaps in chronology; nonetheless, he does permit himself full license to speculate upon the thoughts and motives of the characters.

The Historian speculates as to why Jeremiah, after committing the crime, joins other people in condemning the murder "as though he would cloak himself in the language of common report" (*WEAT* 245). The Historian wonders: "Or did his motive lie deeper? Did that language cleanse his hands for the moment, and restore him to the society of men?" (*WEAT* 245). Knowing of Jeremiah's intention to return and admit guilt, the Historian wonders whether his denials of guilt were also motivated by the desire to connect with his community. Near the conclusion of the novel, the Historian notes that for information about Jeremiah's return journey, "we must make inferences from scanty evidence" (*WEAT* 460). Again, the Historian attends to the accuracy of his facts but freely speculates in his search for truth.

All of these examples illustrate that the Historian is meticulous about factuality but receptive to any interpretation that is potentially meaningful. His movement from facts to interpretations demonstrates that he is what Warren refers to as a "philosophical novelist," a writer "for whom the documentation of the world is constantly striving to rise to the level of generalizations about values." As a philosophical historian, the *World Enough and Time* narrator "is willing to go naked into the pit, again and again, to make the same old struggle for his truth."[11]

Critics have debated the Historian's intrusiveness. Some, like James Justus, assert that Warren's narrator is too quick to judge Jeremiah, arguing that the narrator's representations of Beau-

11. Warren, "The Great Mirage," 160.

mont's "humanistic virtues . . . are often enough cancelled out by bursts of condescension and impatience." Others, such as Joseph Frank, argue that the narrator does not employ enough of the same irony that made *All the King's Men* a success, balancing the irony with too much sympathy.[12] It is not too equivocal to say that both of these positions are correct, for the Historian certainly vacillates from empathy and agreement to condescension and irony.

The significance of these tonal shifts, however, is not so much in whether the narrator employs too much of one and too little of the other, but in the fact that the narrator employs such shifts at all. If the Historian were completely sympathetic or completely condescending toward Beaumont, he would be an unengaged and unengaging narrator. The Historian's variant tones show that he is a modern individual attempting to negotiate with the experiences of the nineteenth-century Jeremiah Beaumont. The narrator struggles between contradictory attitudes toward the Beaumont story because, like Jack Burden grappling with the Cass Mastern journal, as a modern narrator he *must* engage in the struggle. While every historian must assess the accuracy of data and the validity of interpretations, the *World Enough and Time* Historian writes a self-referential discourse that discloses a highly subjective struggle with his connection to his subject. The novel is about the journey of a modern narrator entering "the awful responsibility of Time."

Warren's choice of a modern, distanced narrator is very significant. In the Richard Sale interview, Warren identifies with his modern Historian-Narrator as he recalls Katherine Anne Porter introducing him to the Kentucky Tragedy: "There was a document written by a man. The prototype of my character and the me who read that document were the germ of the novel. So me, a modern man, reading that historical document, was the germ of the novel itself." Warren further emphasizes that *World*

12. James Justus, "Warren's *World Enough and Time* and Beauchamp's *Confession*," *American Literature* 33 (1962): 510; Justus, *Achievement of Robert Penn Warren,* 226; Joseph Frank, "Romanticism and Reality in Robert Penn Warren," *Hudson Review* 4 (1951): 255.

Enough and Time is based on the "counterpoint" and "interplay" between "the modern man writing the book, the 'I' of the book" and "the Jeremiah narrative."[13] The problem that Warren deals with is modernist because it is epistemological: the construction of the text becomes a problem of knowing and interpreting.

The modern narrator provides a double perspective, enabling the reader to focalize through the narrator of the story (Beaumont) while identifying with the narrator of the discourse (the Historian). Justus offers some essential observations on this point. Though Beaumont's story is set in the nineteenth century, "the enveloping vision is aggressively twentieth century." The novel juxtaposes "a deluded young idealist in the early nineteenth century" against the "inquiring intelligence of a twentieth-century man of reason" whose voice is "closer to the sensibilities of the reader"; the narrator is "one of us."[14]

Like Jack Burden's narratorial relationship to the stories of Willie Stark and Cass Mastern, the Historian's discourse in *World Enough and Time* serves as a critical gloss on the story of Jeremiah Beaumont. Beaumont casts himself in the role of Avenging Hero, Rachel in the role of Wronged Innocent, and Fort in the role of Villain. Beaumont attempts to reason that his motives are pure, his pursuit of an ideal (avenging the dishonor of womanhood) imbuing the murder with an innocence of its own. For all of his high style, Beaumont presents his experience in simplistic terms, compartmentalizing all of the people and situations within his romantic narrative. But the Historian discloses the complexity of the events, revealing Beaumont's true impulses and refusing to permit Beaumont to wallow in his self-justification.

Thus the Historian "corrects" Beaumont's narrative. With persistent, interlinear commentary, he exposes the dramatic characteristics of Beaumont's journal. Examples are numerous.

13. Warren, "An Interview in New Haven with Robert Penn Warren" (Interview with Sale, 1969), 127.
14. Justus, *Achievement of Robert Penn Warren*, 223–25.

He describes the journal as a script: "The drama which Jeremiah Beaumont prepared was to be grand, with noble gestures and swelling periods, serious as blood. It was to be a tragedy, like those in the books he read as a boy" (*WEAT* 5). According to the Historian, all others in Beaumont's life "stumbled into the drama he was devising" (*WEAT* 33). The Historian relates that when introduced to Beaumont, Colonel Fort had "spoken his first lines" and "retired into the wings to wait for the cue" (*WEAT* 38). As Beaumont and Rachel await his execution, they spend their days making love and writing poetry, and the Historian comments, "They assumed their perfect shapes, took their perfect roles for a drama enacted on a high and secret stage with no vulgar eye to leer. We can fancy them as high allegorical figures acting out their ritual" (*WEAT* 300). Beaumont's days in prison form the "sequel" to the "secret drama" of his crime (*WEAT* 302). Beaumont pays Captain Marlowe to give false testimony that he scripts, a document that the Historian identifies as "a speech for the drama he had contrived . . . with stage directions complete" (*WEAT* 308). As execution nears, Rachel finally tells Jeremiah that she loves him, and the Historian wonders why. Does she do this because it is the truth, "Or because the unwritten text of the drama that she and Jeremiah Beaumont acted out on their high and secret stage demanded this in the end? Without it there would be no climax" (*WEAT* 374). Every one of these instances illustrates an ironic, twentieth-century perspective, a perspective on life as "text," which undermines and even taunts Beaumont's ideals.

The Historian's most piercing irony appears in his comment upon Jeremiah's and Rachel's failed suicide attempt: "So after the fine speeches and the tragic stance, the grand exit was muffed. The actors trip on their ceremonial robes, even at the threshold of greatness, and come tumbling down in a smashing pratt-fall, amid hoots and howls from the house, and the house gets its money's worth" (*WEAT* 401–2). The Historian notes that the audience ("the house" in theatre parlance) "never really believes in the fine speeches and the tragic stance. . . . It knows that the speech and the stance are only an illusion" (*WEAT* 402).

This passage echoes a passage from the first chapter: "But the actors were not well trained. At times even he, the hero, forgot his lines. At times it all was only a farce" (*WEAT* 5). The Historian notes that "we may find the pathos only in those moments when the big speeches are fluffed or the gestures forgotten. . . . We find the pathos then, for that is the kind of suffering with which we are most fully acquainted" (*WEAT* 5). As is evident from the use of first-person plural pronoun, the Historian identifies with his audience; the audience that the Historian criticizes thus includes the modern reader. Because the modern reader is part of a critical audience of realists whose refusal to suspend disbelief enables them to see through the illusions, this passage seems to place modern readers into a position superior to Beaumont. Yet the Historian brings the reader down to the level of Beaumont's experience. By noting that the audience shares the pathos, the Historian reminds the reader that moderns cannot merely observe Beaumont from a distance, for they join him in a communion of suffering. The Historian echoes Cass Mastern's realization that "only by the suffering of the innocent does God affirm that men are brothers" (*AKM* 187).

Justus notes that "the historian tempts us into that unarticulated position of generational superiority from which most moderns instinctively regard the past, only to reprimand us for doing so." Beaumont's story explains how he discovers his position within what Cass Mastern calls "the common guilt of man" (*AKM* 187). Similarly, the Historian-Narrator's discourse reminds readers of their connection to the past. As John Burt argues, "There is no superior standpoint from which Beaumont may be judged, no way that we can look down upon him without betraying our own emptiness."[15] Beaumont's pathos becomes the Historian's and our own.

In such passages the Historian resembles Jack Burden, who often exposes the dramatics of a scene. Burt also makes this connection between the novels: "The narrator, like Jack Burden, en-

15. Ibid., 227; Burt, *Robert Penn Warren and American Idealism* (New Haven: Yale University Press, 1988), 178.

joys undermining 'drama' and speaks of Beaumont's story as a piece of stagecraft."[16] For example, Burden explains how Willie Stark constructs a public identity through speeches and staged photographs. At the conclusion of *All the King's Men,* Burden turns this critical eye inward, observing his own self-dramatization in his confrontation with Tiny Duffy: "I had sure-God brought off that scene. I had hit him where he lived. I was full of beans. I had fire in my belly. I was a hero. I was St. George and the dragon, I was Edwin Booth bowing beyond the gaslights, I was Jesus Christ with the horsewhip in the temple. I was the stuff" (*AKM* 415). Burden's overstatement illustrates his ineffectiveness, which he later admits when he realizes that he and Duffy are "bound together under the unwinking eye of Eternity" (*AKM* 417). Just as Burden first confronts Duffy but later admits his error in perspective, the Historian "corrects" not only Beaumont but his own modern perspective as well.

The Historian even employs empathy to temper his critique of Beaumont. Although he argues that Beaumont prepares a drama, he also admits, "But it may have been the drama Jeremiah Beaumont had to prepare in order to live at all, or in order, living, to be human. And it may be that a man cannot live unless he prepares a drama, at least cannot live as a human being against the ruck of the world" (*WEAT* 5). When Rachel is arrested for being an accessory to the crime, the Historian sympathizes with her being treated "as though she were a common criminal who might take to the woods and hide out like an animal" (*WEAT* 348). The Historian criticizes but also grants the empathy that the *John Brown* narrator would deny. As Beaumont acknowledges his role in the community of fallible humanity, the Historian does the same, as is evident in his tempering his criticism of Beaumont with empathy. The narrator and the audience are part of the same human community as Beaumont. The narrator is as critical of the modern world as he is of Beaumont's world, for in the matrix of time, they are the same world.

At times, the *World Enough and Time* narrator is overtly crit-

---

16. Burt, *Robert Penn Warren and American Idealism,* 177.

ical of modernity. Whereas John Brown's omniscient biographer blatantly condemns as if he could transcend the events of the world and the motives of common humanity, the Historian does not pretend to be neutral. Perhaps the most apparent instance is his editorial on the *code duello*. As Beaumont challenges Fort, the Historian briefly summarizes the history of duelling. Quoting from an 1820s Frankfort, Kentucky, newspaper article critical of "dunces" who duel, he comments, "We are complacent as we look back on those dunces, and we congratulate the newspaper editor in old Frankfort for being so much like ourselves" (*WEAT* 118). "But," the Historian continues, "on second thought, we may be like the dunces," for even though we no longer duel, we conduct war on a level never dreamed of in Beaumont's time (*WEAT* 118). Again, with the first-person plural pronoun, the Historian identifies himself with his reader. Woodward notes that "we are tempted by his [the narrator's] implicit invitation to join him on the peaks of twentieth-century rationality to survey the sad wreckage of nineteenth-century delusions and pretensions,"[17] but the Historian turns this invitation against us.

The italicized epilogue, surveying the wreckage of the twentieth century, presents the novel's most blatant critique of modernity. In this passage the Historian recounts the changes in Kentucky since the time of the Beaumont-Jordan-Fort tragedy.[18] Like the narrators of "The World of Daniel Boone" and *Jefferson Davis Gets His Citizenship Back,* the Historian notes the passage of time and modern society's failure to negotiate with the past:

> *Things went on their way, and the Commonwealth of Kentucky has, by the latest estimate, 2,819,000 inhabitants, and the only Shawnee in the country is in a WPA mural on a post-office wall, and Old Big Hump and his brass cannon are lost in the mud of the swamps, and tourists occasionally visit the grave of Daniel*

17. C. Vann Woodward, *The Future of the Past* (New York: Oxford University Press, 1989), 230.
18. See Casper, *The Dark and Bloody Ground,* 148; Justus, *Achievement of Robert Penn Warren,* 233.

> *Boone and the log cabin in Larue County where Abraham Lin-*
> *coln was born and the log cabin in Todd County where Jefferson*
> *Davis was born and the Old Kentucky Home at Bardstown in*
> *Nelson County, and some 400,000,000 pounds of tobacco are*
> *grown annually, and in a good year over 60,000,000 tax gallons*
> *of whisky are distilled, and the State University now has 8000*
> *students and a championship basketball team.* (WEAT 463–64)

Because he records facts about great men and statistics about production, the Historian relates history in conventional terms, the only place in the novel where he does so. He notes how many inhabitants live in the state, how many pounds of tobacco are grown, how many gallons of whiskey are distilled, and the amount of money spent on horse racing. He then claims, *"Things are improving as all statistics show and civilization is making strides"* (WEAT 464), a highly ironic statement. By juxtaposing such statistics with more romantic observations (*"the only Shawnee in the country is in a WPA mural"*), he achieves an irony that questions the capacity of facts and figures to communicate a complete, accurate history. He has shown that Beaumont's story is a cyclical drama that every age plays out for itself, so we are left to question whether demographics and highway construction indeed demonstrate improvement.

Some critics suggest that Warren himself narrates this epilogue, the novel's one instance of authorial intervention. However, no evidence has yet been presented to prove a distinction between Warren's and the Historian-Narrator's voices. Given that Warren directly identifies himself with his Historian-Narrator (see the Richard Sale interview), it is plausible to view Warren and the Historian as the same character. Because the epilogue presents a modern perspective, the speaker could be either Warren or the Historian or both.

The epilogue concludes with the Historian quoting from the last page of Beaumont's journal: Beaumont wonders whether his longing for nobility and justice, even though it "was born in vanity and nursed in pride," might have had some redeeming worth, or "Was all for naught?" (WEAT 465). The Historian repeats this final question, and as Guttenberg notes, that he ends "not with a conclusion, but with a question" indicates the narrator is split by what Jack Burden calls "the terrible division of our age."[19] The novel ends by questioning how the modern desire for an idealized past should be balanced against realism. This question, because it reveals the Historian-Narrator's own need for an answer, again shows the focus to be not Beaumont's story but the modern Historian's interaction with that story. The final question shows the anxiety within the modernist.

The Historian tempers his criticism of Beaumont's nineteenth-century romanticism with a criticism of twentieth-century realism. As an objective archivist, the Historian attends to the accuracy of Beaumont's account, but as a subjective narrator he approves of the mythical dimension that gives history relevance. Warren again appears to be a romantic realist, straddling the line between verisimilitude and myth just as Beaumont finds himself caught between law and justice. Justus points out that the Historian-Narrator's "tensions between personal involvement and professional discipline parallel the tensions in Beaumont— between the private dream and public drama, the idea and the fact, the word and the flesh."[20] Other Warren narrators such as Jack Burden and the narrator of "The World of Daniel Boone" face this same struggle.

As Casper points out, Warren's Historian-Narrator resembles the narrator of "How Texas Won Her Freedom." In that article Warren shows Houston aware of the larger drama of which he was a part: "He [Sam Houston] was an actor in the deepest sense—the sense that makes a man see himself in history" (72). During his trial Houston sees the courtroom as a political theatre (73). During a discussion of Sam Houston in his interview with Bill Moyers, Warren explores how the story's romantic or Homeric qualities make Houston significant to American history. Warren acknowledges the necessity and usefulness of myth, but he also objects to myths obscuring rather than illuminating the

19. Guttenberg, *Web of Being*, 69–70.
20. Justus, *Achievement of Robert Penn Warren*, 228.

facts of history. Warren resists an oversimplification of history. Commenting on Sam Houston, Warren states, "It's the complexity that is engaging."[21] Complexity necessitates the ordering function of narrative.

Neil Nakadate observes, "Confession is a means of bringing order to a problematical existence through aesthetic control. . . . Jeremiah Beaumont learns to know himself through his confession." We might observe that the Historian's narrative is also an aesthetic means of controlling and bringing order to Beaumont's experience. If Beaumont comes to know himself through his journal, we come to know Beaumont through the historian's archival, editorial, narrative, and ultimately modern manipulation of the journal. Guttenberg argues that "man's rage for order and the incoherence of the world" is the main existential problem in *World Enough and Time*,[22] but we may add that order versus incoherence is also the principal textual problem. Beaumont "prepares a drama . . . against the ruck of the world" (*WEAT* 5); likewise, the historian constructs a narrative to counter the interstices of Beaumont's narrative.

As a modern individual confronting the chaos of the past, Jack Burden finds a model of order in Cass Mastern's journal. For all of the Historian's critical assessment of Beaumont's journal, Beaumont's confession does teach the Historian something about how to order events into a narrative. The Historian's use of narrative to confront the complexity of the story reflects Warren's revisionary ordering of the Beauchamp-Sharp story.

Although the Historian-Narrator does not examine other literary treatments of the Kentucky Tragedy, they are in the background of Warren's project. Some of the major texts (those most likely to have been familiar to Warren) illustrate other types of narrators. Thomas Holley Chivers wrote *Conrad and Eudora* (1834), a play in which the seducer, Alonzo (Sharp), gives an

21. Casper, *The Dark and Bloody Ground*, 143–44; Warren, "A Conversation with Robert Penn Warren" (Interview with Moyers, 1976), 217–18.

22. Nakadate, "Robert Penn Warren and the Confessional Novel," 327, 333; Guttenberg, *Web of Being*, 68.

opening monologue that shows his awareness of his part in the drama:

> This lower world, says Shakespeare, is a stage,
> Where every mortal acts a comic part;
> Who, now and then, in Tragedies engage,
> Which break up every fountain of the heart!
> For marriages have been so long the rage,
> Each actor seems to play it with an art.

Later, upon seeing a sylvan valley near Frankfort, the perfect spot for his seduction plot, he says, "There is the place where I'm to play the devil."[23] In Chivers's version, Alonzo is like any number of Shakespearean protagonists, self-conscious of his own plots and deceits. Because Warren bases his version on Beauchamp's journal, he shifts the role of self-conscious plotter to Beauchamp.

The most critically significant and popular treatment of the Kentucky Tragedy before Warren is *Beauchampe,* by William Gilmore Simms (1842). Like Warren's Historian-Narrator, in his preface Simms claims license for the novelist to interpret and speculate upon the historical materials, arguing that "newspapers are lying things at best—they have told sundry fibs on this very subject. Pamphlets . . . are scarcely better as authorities." Later in the novel the narrator comments, "The novel only answers half its uses when we confine it to the simple delineation of events." Occasionally, Simms is self-conscious of his own literary production. For example, like a classical tragedian, he has the murder occur off stage, explaining that "we shall not fatigue the reader" with all of the details: "We make short a story which, long enough already, we apprehend, might, by an ingenious romancer, be made a great deal longer." Simms also employs the drama metaphor, for example, calling his characters "our figures in our drama," and announcing near the beginning, "we raise the curtain upon other scenes and characters," and at

---

23. Thomas Holley Chivers, *Conrad and Eudora; or, The Death of Alonzo* (Philadelphia: 1834), 5, 17.

the end, "Let us drop the curtain." Warren's narrator echoes Simms's occasional sympathy toward Beauchampe: while not approving of the murder, Simms argues that there are mitigating circumstances. Law cannot redress every wrong; therefore, "Give us, say I, Kentucky practice, like that of Beauchampe, as a social law."[24]

At this point, the difference of Warren's Historian-Narrator becomes clear. Unlike Simms's narrator, Warren's Historian is modern and distanced. The Historian's comments on the *code duello* condemn the violent practices of both the nineteenth and twentieth centuries. Moreover, the Historian uses self-reflexive comments and the drama metaphor as interpretive rather than conventional devices. Simms's narrator refers to the drama he writes as a means of carrying on a conversation with his popular audience, but Warren's Historian uses these devices to evaluate the very construction of history. Simms is content to permit his characters their drama. Beauchampe is allowed to write himself into history unexamined: Awaiting execution, he speaks to his wife, "I tell you, Anna, the wives and daughters of Kentucky will bless the name of Beauchampe!" Simms's characters also dramatize themselves melodramatically; Anna delivers a soliloquy over her seduction and ruin: "Love is impossible to me now. The dream is gone! the hope—every hope! Even ambition is impossible! Alas, what a dream it was! how wild, how impossible from the first! Yet, I believed it all. Fool! Fool!"[25] Such highly stylized passages characterize every page of Simms's novel.

It is such romanticizing that Warren writes against in *World Enough and Time*. When characters do dramatize themselves, Warren's Historian presents their dramas ironically. As a modern realist who acknowledges the complexity of experience, Warren will not permit the players to simplify their experiences into clearly defined categories. In one of the best examinations of the conflict between realism and romanticism in *World*

24. William Gilmore Simms, *Beauchampe; or, The Kentucky Tragedy* (Chicago: Belford, Clarke, 1885), 8, 46, 337, 52, 402, 342.
25. Ibid., 398, 37.

Enough and Time, Steven Ryan explains that the novel is an "anti-tragedy which insists upon a complexity beyond conventional unification." Ryan contrasts Warren's novel with Poe's drama, *Politian,* noting that the Beauchamp story appealed to Poe's belief in idealized love. Warren, however, manages "to oppose the drama envisioned by both the historical Beauchamp and by Edgar Allan Poe with a complex, illusive reality which refuses to conform to the tragic paradigm." In Warren's version, Beaumont is unable to carry out pure vengeance; the world will not permit his idealism to go unchecked by reality. Recognizing Warren's demythicizing process, Ryan notes that "Warren relies upon comic irony to deflate heroic pretensions."[26]

Unlike the previous literary treatments of the Kentucky Tragedy, Warren's novel deals primarily with the interaction between the modern Historian and past events. As Ryan observes, Warren recognizes that the Beauchamp-Sharp case became tragedy through two means: "the participants saw themselves as performers enacting great drama," and readers, desirous of frontier romances, "imagined the murder case as romantic tragedy." Warren examines both of these agents that transformed history into tragedy: "the romantic posturing of the historical participants," and "the way the Kentucky Tragedy captured the imagination of the period."[27]

It has been much noted that Warren uses mainly primary sources in *World Enough and Time,* particularly Beauchamp's *Confession.*[28] What Richard Gray says of *All the King's Men* applies to *World Enough and Time.* Discussing Warren's departure from the Huey Long story in *All the King's Men,* Gray argues that Warren's objective "is to take authenticated facts and reproduce them so as to emphasize their tragic pattern. . . . War-

26. Steven T. Ryan, "*World Enough and Time:* A Refutation of Poe's History as Tragedy," *Southern Quarterly* 31, no. 4 (1993): 88, 90.

27. Ibid., 86, 87.

28. See Casper, *The Dark and Bloody Ground,* 136, 143–45; Justus, "Warren's *World Enough and Time* and Beauchamp's *Confession,*" 500; Wilford Eugene Fridy, "Robert Penn Warren's Use of Kentucky Materials in His Fiction as a Basis for His New Mythos" (Ph.D. diss., University of Kentucky, 1968), 103–105.

ren is merely doing on a large scale what his narrator does on a slightly smaller one."[29] Likewise, the Historian's use of Beaumont's journal iterates Warren's use of Jereboam Beauchamp's *Confession*. Warren examines how Beauchamp patterns his life as romance and as tragedy in his *Confession*. Beauchamp's *Confession* begins with a preface in which he notes the fragmentary nature of his own narrative: "The short time I have to live, together with the multiplied duties I have to perform, towards consolating my family and friends, will unavoidably render the detail of facts, which I shall leave for the perusal of my countrymen, greatly disconnected and confused. I shall abandon all studied style; I shall only in laconic language record facts."[30] Warren takes these comments as an invitation to interpretation, speculation, revision, and reconciliation.

Both the Historian's and Warren's uses of the primary documents of the Kentucky Tragedy demonstrate the insufficiency of neutrality, for there are many blanks in the historical record that a historian must fill. The history of the Kentucky Tragedy is full of such gaps. Jack Surrency advises great caution in using the primary materials of the Jereboam Beauchamp case, locating numerous inconsistencies, contradictions, and agenda in the trial transcript, journals, and letters. As if anticipating the same charge of self-dramatization against Jereboam Beauchamp that the Historian cites against Jeremiah Beaumont, J. Winston Coleman argues that Beauchamp "attempted, with his usual flair for melodramatics, to make himself the great hero of his narrative," for Beauchamp wanted to transform himself "from the role of a brutal murderer into the noble champion and martyred protector of female virtue." Coleman accuses Beauchamp of dramatizing himself even at the point of attempting suicide with the knife: "The arch-criminal and killer seemed to be careful not to inflict upon himself any injury which would deprive him of the high drama which he anticipated on the gallows."[31] Coleman charges

29. Gray, "The American Novelist and American History," 303, 307.

30. Jereboam Beauchamp, "The Confession of Jereboam O. Beauchamp," in *The Kentucky Tragedy*, ed. Kallsen, 3.

31. Coleman, *The Beauchamp-Sharp Tragedy*, vii–viii, 54.

Beauchamp with creating melodrama even as Ann was dying and as he was riding toward the gallows. Noting such melodramatics, along with contradictions and inconsistencies throughout the *Confession,* Coleman strongly doubts Beauchamp's reliability as a narrator. Such is the incomplete, unreliable, and in the case of Ann Cook's letters, even fictional state of the materials the historian has to work with.

Warren responds in a manner similar to Coleman's preface: he proceeds not from the events themselves but from the difficulties that the primary materials present. Justus categorizes Warren's numerous factual changes in transforming the Kentucky Tragedy into fiction: "(a) a selectivity of details which emphasize the moral patterns in the actual events, and (b) an expansion of details which give historical and personal meaning to a larger theme." Events do not occur already ordered into neat patterns; the historian or novelist must envision the patterns. As Hayden White argues, a plot exists prior to events and validates an event as historical when the event contributes to the plot's development.[32] In *World Enough and Time,* the roles of novelist and historian converge, for both employ interpretive strategies to construct plots and meanings, questioning the narrator's neutrality.

As stated earlier, Warren directly identifies his own reading of Jeremiah Beauchamp's *Confession* as the origin of the *World Enough and Time* narrator (see the Sale interview). The Historian-Narrator's revision of the Beaumont journal is a microcosm of Warren's use of the Kentucky Tragedy. Warren and the Historian privilege the imagination in the investigation for historical truth. The Historian, like Jack Burden, becomes Warren's idea of a "philosophical novelist."

By demonstrating the role of individual consciousness in the construction of history, the Historian also reflects Warren's development from an objective pose in *John Brown* to direct participation in *Jefferson Davis Gets His Citizenship Back* and *Por-*

32. Justus, "Warren's *World Enough and Time* and Beauchamp's *Confession,*" 508; Hayden White, *The Content of the Form,* 51.

trait of a Father. Recall Richard Law's comment on Warren's idea of the "knowledge of form": "the work of art can directly convey knowledge, knowledge at least of the process by which man perceives."[33] The writing of history also serves as a vehicle for "knowledge of form." The discourse of the *World Enough and Time* Historian demonstrates the process by which humanity perceives the past, a project that reflects Warren's overall development as a writer of biographical narratives.

33. Law, " 'The Case of the Upright Judge,' " 5.

VII

Biography and the Poet
Chief Joseph of the Nez Perce

Andrea: Unhappy the land that has no heroes.
Galileo: No, unhappy the land that needs heroes.
—Bertolt Brecht, *The Life of Galileo*

As we see in his biographical narratives, Warren creates a sense of historical connection by surrendering all pretense of neutral or objective narration, and by revising the myths and misconceptions of the past. A basic and significant tactic within this revisionary project is his questioning of the process that transforms men into heroes. Warren makes past heroes more accessible to a modern audience by humanizing them, an objective that is apparent in his poetry, particularly his long poems on Thomas Jefferson, *Brother to Dragons*, and John James Audubon, *Audubon: A Vision*. Appearing at the end of a long line of prose and poetic texts about American heroes, *Chief Joseph of the Nez Perce* is a text that defends a man's heroic stature. Warren's final narrative poem is an answer to the "deheroizing" of "The World of Daniel Boone," *Brother to Dragons*, and *Audubon: A Vision*. In *Chief Joseph of the Nez Perce* Warren acknowledges a hero, revising a man into a hero rather than revising a hero into a man.

As we have seen, after his initial attempt at biography, *John Brown: The Making of a Martyr*, Warren no longer attempts to dislodge heroes merely for the sake of destroying well-ensconced cultural icons. His intentions become much more constructive.

The process of making a man into a hero necessarily causes the true identity of the individual to fragment because, as Justus observes, the personae of history are dehumanized by "the confining categories invariably designed for them, not merely by the needs of historians but by certain impulses in us all to reduce and compartmentalize."[1] Turning an individual person into a hero requires re-figuring his/her life into a heroic narrative so that he/she will conform to an ideal image. Flaws and foibles of human nature must be excised from the plot so that the hero may embody every expectation of perfection. As a late modernist, Warren seeks to reverse this process, but demythicizing does not mean debunking. It means reintegrating the fragments of historical identities that have been restructured into heroic patterns. The oversimplified patterns of mythical narratives are reformulated as realistic narratives that acknowledge the complexity of real lives. The merely heroic becomes fully human.

The demythicizing process reconciles the disjunction between idealism and realism. In Warren's formulation, one cannot truly love without full knowledge of that which one loves. One must recognize the flaws as well as the virtues that inhere within the object of one's love. Loving America, for example, would require evolving beyond a simple monological patriotism to a full acknowledgement of America's faults. Love is not genuine unless informed by knowledge,

> For nothing we had,
> Nothing we were,
> Is lost. All is redeemed,
> In knowledge. (*BD* 120)

Knowledge is not useful unless tempered by love, for "what is knowledge / Without the intrinsic mediation of the heart?" (*BD* 130). In the sixth section of *Audubon: A Vision*, entitled "Love and Knowledge," knowledge is a name for love. By shooting the birds so that he may study and paint them, and thereby place

1. Justus, "Robert Penn Warren," 452.

them in our imaginations, Audubon demonstrates a strong love for the natural world. Similarly, by removing American heroes from their privileged status to embrace their actual human experiences, Warren shows a deep love for America.

Equally significant for *Chief Joseph of the Nez Perce*, the deheroizing process enables the culture to reformulate its identity. We may recall that "The Use of the Past" asserts that a sense of identity originates in a sense of time. Although the past is never fully or easily available to us, such indeterminacy is precisely its value, for "in creating the image of the past we create ourselves."[2] Warren makes a similar argument about hero-making in his *American Heritage* essay, "A Dearth of Heroes." Considering America in the postmodern age, Warren concludes that heroes are now produced by the media rather than achieving prominence through great deeds. Warren reiterates Daniel Boorstin's observation in *The Image*: the celebrity has replaced the hero.

Warren's biographical poems reverse this modern trend, recuperating American heroes by reintegrating their images from the fragments strewn through time as America has represented them in its history. As the Historian-Poet of *Brother to Dragons* and *Audubon*, Warren introduces repressed facts into Jefferson's and Audubon's biographies, and in *Chief Joseph of the Nez Perce* he reintroduces Chief Joseph into canonical American history. The following summaries illustrate the distinction.

The central episode and sine qua non of *Brother to Dragons* is the brutal murder of a slave by two of Jefferson's nephews. Though Warren does not implicate Jefferson, he does suggest that Jefferson's dream of human perfectibility, to be embodied by the new nation, was corrupted by a family sin. Curiously, Warren notes in the Preface, Jefferson never referred to the crime in any journal, letter, or public appearance. As a historian, Warren infers that this is a silence of repression, so he speculates about the psychological and spiritual turmoil that might have tortured Jefferson upon discovering an affront to his political

---

2. Warren, "The Use of the Past," 51.

ideals within his own family and, by implication, within the nation he founded. The Historian calls upon Jefferson and the other participants to fill the silences in the historical record.

Brother to Dragons encompasses all of Warren's major themes: the search for self-identity, the mutual existence of good and evil, the conflict between idealism and pragmatism, the interconnection and shared guilt of all human beings, the burden of the past and the dream of the future. All of the major tropes—return, reconciliation, and redemption—appear. Warren visits and revisits the region and the Jefferson family house, his father traveling with him. As a reconciler of past and present, in the Foreword Warren offers himself as a historian like the Historian of *World Enough and Time*, sifting through bundles of faded court records in a basement. Warren justifies his revision of history, arguing that the poem may not violate "the spirit of his history" or "the nature of the human heart," though "what he takes those things to be is, of course, his ultimate gamble" (xiii). He continues: "Historical sense and poetic sense should not, in the end, be contradictory, for if poetry is the little myth we make, history is the big myth we live, and in our living, constantly remake" (xiii). This book offers Warren's most hopeful statement, for he concludes that despite the presence of evil in our history, we can be redeemed by facing the evil and admitting our own complicity with it. The poem concludes with R.P.W.'s hopeful apostrophe to the river, a statement of faith that regardless of what flows from the past we can control what will flow into the future:

> I take you as image and confirmation
> Of some faith past our consistent failure,
> And the filth we strew. (130)

The central theme in *Chief Joseph of the Nez Perce* is the paradox of a nation that violates its ideals in the pursuit of those very ideals. America putatively expanded westward to bring the rights of life and liberty, and the values of individualism, family, community, and economic prosperity to every corner of the continent. Yet in this process they denied the life, liberty, and individuality of the land's aboriginal peoples, whose families, communities, and economies they displaced. The march toward the Pacific was the Manifest Destiny of one nation and the destruction of many others. *Chief Joseph of the Nez Perce* resurrects the voice of a Native American who believed in the same ideals championed by those who destroyed his people. At the same time, Chief Joseph's reverence for the land and his people's history become correctives to the American sense of detachment and abstraction from place and past. Thus, the poem proposes Chief Joseph as an ideal image for modern America, a true American hero.

Both *Brother to Dragons* and *Chief Joseph of the Nez Perce* reconcile traditional heroic records with a modern critical agenda. By exposing neglected information to the present, these poems destabilize fundamental misconceptions about American history. On the one hand, *Brother to Dragons* forces some acknowledgment that a horrible crime spots the mythically spotless image of the man who defined America's ideals and aspirations. *Chief Joseph of the Nez Perce*, on the other hand, argues for accepting a hero into American history. The poems are two sides of the same revisionary coin.

This distinction is what makes *Chief Joseph of the Nez Perce* a significant work in Warren's canon. *John Brown: The Making of a Martyr*, *Brother to Dragons*, *Audubon*, and other texts inform us who the hero is not. The Chief Joseph narrative poem nominates a hero.

As Warren's final long poem, *Chief Joseph of the Nez Perce* forms part of a frame around Warren's life and career, the other part of the frame being his first major long poem, "The Ballad of Billie Potts." Recall that Warren's early biography of John Brown highlights his development toward the final biographical narratives of Jefferson Davis and Robert Franklin Warren. Similarly, Warren's agenda in the narrative poem about Chief Joseph becomes more apparent with reference to his earliest major narrative poem.

Originally published in 1943, "The Ballad of Billie Potts" is what John Bradbury has called a transition between the early "semi-narrative" poetry and the "full-length novel-poem" that Warren began writing in the 1950s.[3] The poem is based on a folktale about a boy who grows up in western Kentucky in the late eighteenth century. Little Billie's parents provide room and board to travelers, some of whom they rob and murder with the aid of accomplices. One day, their usual runner fails to show up, so Billie is sent ahead to notify the accomplices that a wealthy traveler is approaching their way. Aspiring to his father's approval, Billie decides to waylay the traveler himself, but he is thwarted and humiliated in the attempt, and flees West. Having made his fortune many years later, he returns home to his parents who, failing to recognize him, kill and rob him. After burying the body, they discover their tragic error.

The form of "The Ballad of Billie Potts" is significant to the later narrative poetry. Not a true ballad, the poem shifts between the story of Billie Potts and the discourse of the modern, philosophical narrator. The overt presence of the narrator dominates the poem as the interpretive sections, encased in parentheses, eventually overtake the sections that advance the story. This presence of a highly audible, even intrusive, narrative voice mirrors the development of Warren's narrators in *All the King's Men* and *World Enough and Time*, making Warren what Peter Stitt calls a "philosophical poet."[4] The poem not only makes a statement about human experience; it "dramatizes the way in which a contemporary consciousness formulates such a statement out of the raw stuff of life."[5] The reader watches two stories unfold: the lives of the ballad's subjects and the modern narrator's attempt to locate meaning.

Many critics have observed that the running commentary

3. John Bradbury, *The Fugitive: A Critical Account* (Chapel Hill: University of North Carolina Press, 1958), 185.

4. Peter Stitt, *The World's Hieroglyphic Beauty* (Athens: University of Georgia Press, 1985), 215.

5. William Bedford Clark, "A Meditation on Folk History: The Dramatic Structure of Robert Penn Warren's 'The Ballad of Billie Potts,'" *American Literature* 49 (1978): 641.

leads to problems. Bradbury notes that the form of the entire poem is weakened as the commentaries break into the story and overtake it with their increasing length. Floyd Watkins suggests that the "mechanical device" of the "philosophical lyric poems in parentheses" does not "fuse" with the historical narrative. In fact, Warren's attempt to merge subjective commentaries with the ballad proper undermines itself. As Justus points out, the use of parentheses around the philosophical sections serves only to reinforce their separation from the story. And in the most significant insight on this point, John Burt writes, "The very fact that the commentator must work as hard as he does in order to bring us close to the action announces how far from it we both are." The presence of the commentary demonstrates that the story itself is unable to embody the truths that the narrator wants to communicate.[6]

After the introductory descriptions of the setting and before the inciting action of Billie's father sending him on the fateful errand, the narrator comments:

(There was a beginning but you cannot see it.
There will be an end but you cannot see it.
They will not turn their faces to you though you call,
Who pace a logic merciless as light,
Whose law is their long shadow on the grass,
Sun at the back. . . .

And heedless, their hairy faces fixed
Beyond your call or question now. . . .

And [they] breathe the immaculate climate where
The lucent leaf is lifted, lank beard fingered, by no breeze,
Rapt in the fabulous complacency of fresco, vase, or frieze. . . .
(BBP 289)

---

6. Bradbury, *The Fugitives*, 186; Floyd Watkins, *Then and Now: The Personal Past in the Poetry of Robert Penn Warren* (Lexington: University Press of Kentucky, 1982), 81; Justus, *Achievement of Robert Penn Warren*, 58; Burt, *Robert Penn Warren and American Idealism*, 87.

In these passages the narrator refers to a past "they" and an ambiguous "you." Thus we have here a disjunction between past and present. "You" are disconnected from the past, unable to access the far reaches of time, as the first two lines indicate. "You" of the present may wish to see them, but "their faces" in the past are an unavailable image. Figures from the past have no obligation to come to those who summon them across time; the "sun at the back" and "their long shadow" signify a passage of time, a sunset, which now commands their attention. The ancestors answer only to the past; they are "beyond your call or question now." In an allusion to Keats's "Grecian Urn," the narrator states that they are now frozen in time, available to the present only in an "immaculate climate." To preserve the past one must freeze it, but because time requires motion, to freeze the past is to terminate it.

In a later section the narrator sketches a portrait of "you." In a passage reminiscent of T. S. Eliot, the narrator describes a modern "wanderer with slit-eyes adjusted to distance":

> And the clock ticked all night long in the furnished room
> And would not stop
> And the El-train passed on the quarters with a whish like a
>   terrible broom
> And would not stop
> And there is always the sound of breathing in the next room
> And it will not stop
> And the waitress says, "Will that be all, sir, will that be all?"
> And will not stop. . . . (BBP 294–95)

Many critics from Bohner (1964) to Blotner (1997) have pointed out the major influence of *The Wasteland* upon Warren, evident in the city imagery here (e.g., the waitress's call, which echoes the bartender's "HURRY UP PLEASE ITS TIME" in "A Game of Chess"). I would like to suggest that this passage best resembles Eliot's city description in "Preludes," for example:

> With the other Masquerades
> That time resumes,

> One thinks of all the hands
> That are raising dingy shades
> In a thousand furnished rooms.[7]

"Preludes" is even more of a "city poem" than *The Wasteland*, with its central theme of disconnection coinciding exactly with Warren's "Ballad." Both Eliot and Warren envision one isolated individual in a room that is not his own, alienated from the very crowds of people who surround him. Warren's poem replicates the isolation of a character who plods through masquerades because, without a clear sense of the past, he has no identity to connect himself with others past or present. At issue is not just time running out, as the Wasteland bartender reminds, but time persistently moving on. In "Preludes," "time resumes" but without discernible direction, for "The worlds revolve like ancient women / Gathering fuel in vacant lots."[8] Similarly, Warren's narrator reminds us of time's relentless movement with the repetition of the clause "and would not stop" and the lack of terminating punctuation at the ends of the lines.

As one would expect, the later biographical poems sharply contrast with "The Ballad of Billie Potts," even as they use the same techniques of overt narration and interpolated interpretation. The focus of later poems becomes the narrator's engagement with the subject at hand rather than his involvement in his own philosophizing: "In this new period poems began to proceed from a particular concrete thing, whereas the earlier ones at least seem to have derived from a concept." In the later biographical poems, Warren develops from the particular incident to the larger meaning, whereas in "The Ballad of Billie Potts" Warren seemed to be moving from meanings to the episode at hand.[9]

Consider *Brother to Dragons*, which Blotner calls a "turning

---

7. T. S. Eliot, *The Waste Land and Other Poems* (San Diego: Harcourt Brace Jovanovich, 1934), 13.

8. Ibid., 15.

9. Watkins, *Then and Now*, 81; Floyd Watkins, "Billie Potts at the Fall of Time," *Mississippi Quarterly* 11 (1958): 27.

point in Warren's career, accomplishing for his poetry what *All the King's Men* did for his fiction." Initially, Warren anticipated that *Brother to Dragons* would be in the same form as "The Ballad of Billie Potts."[10] In the beginning of Part II of *Brother to Dragons*, R.P.W. notes that he had intended to write a ballad about the murder and its aftermath, and he quotes the opening lines of that proposed ballad:

> *The two brothers sat by the sagging fire,*
> *Lilburne and Isham sat by the fire,*
> *For it was lonesome weather.*
> *"Isham," said Lilburne, "shove the jug nigher,*
> *For it is lonesome weather.*
> *It is lonesome weather in Kentucky. . . ."* (BD 31)

In light of the resonance and lyricism that characterize *Brother to Dragons*, these lines sound like cruel parody. As his own ellipses at the end of the passage imply, the project was literally abandoned. R.P.W. then comments,

> It began about like that, but the form
> Was not adequate: the facile imitation
> Of folk simplicity would scarcely serve. (BD 31)

Warren apparently realized that neither the ballad form nor his earlier, detached, academic voice was effective. As he discovered after *John Brown: The Making of a Martyr*, he would need to surrender the fiction of neutral narration. The results are Jack Burden's discovery of his complicity within the web of history in *All the King's Men*, the Historian-Narrator's self-conscious construction of history from raw materials in *World Enough and Time*, and Warren's autobiographical meditations on history in *Segregation, Who Speaks for the Negro?, Jefferson Davis Gets*

---

10. See Joseph Blotner, *Robert Penn Warren: A Biography* (New York: Random House, 1997), 289, 284; see also Robert Penn Warren, "A Dialogue with Robert Penn Warren on *Brother to Dragons*" (Interview with Floyd Watkins, 1980), in *Talking with Robert Penn Warren*, ed. Watkins, Hiers, and Weaks, 336–56.

His Citizenship Back and *Portrait of a Father*. Warren journeys toward discovering a kind of narrative that can replace conventional historical narrative, so as to reformulate history into myths that are more available and appropriate to a cynical modern age.

With Chief Joseph, Warren creates a myth that is necessary for the survival of the industrialized, technologized world. The creation of Chief Joseph as an American hero becomes a corrective to a dehumanized modern society. Perhaps the best statement of Warren's attitude about modernity appears in the Bill Moyers interview. Echoing the 1930 Agrarian manifesto, *I'll Take My Stand*, Warren voices concern about American society's abandonment of traditional values as it has defined itself in terms of its industrial and technological progress. Warren recounts meeting a representative from the Xerox corporation. The young man introduced himself with the statement, "I'm Xerox." Warren comments: "Now he has given up his identity already; he says, 'I'm Xerox.' He's not Mr. Jim Jones any more even in his own mind; he has no self. . . . He's the organization of which he's a part. I'm Xerox. And this is a symbol to me of the whole state of mind of the self ceasing to exist. . . . It's part of a machine." Using Coleridge's *Rime of the Ancient Mariner* as an example for modern humanity, Warren suggests that the Mariner used the crossbow simply because it existed; the inanimate instrument determined the man's action and therefore defined his identity. According to Agrarian arguments, such fragmentation of self inevitably leads to isolation, which in turn causes unethical behavior. The solution that Warren proposes is the humanities. The study of literature, history, and philosophy can help students to create selves, find meaning, and negotiate with technology. The entire Moyers interview is well worth reading as a complete statement of Warren's mature Agrarianism or Traditionalism. Particularly notable is that Warren qualifies his criticisms of technology, pointing out that technology per se is not bad, rather, how it is used: "We want our technology and we should have it, should want it. It's how we use it, that's important. It's the attitude toward it, it seems to me is important, not its presence."[11]

With his strong sense of history and attachment to the land, Chief Joseph provides an antidote to modern America. Part I opens with a pastoral landscape, as yet untouched by the encroaching Europeans:

> The Land of the Winding Waters, Wallowa
> The Land of the Nimipu,
> Land sacred to the band of old Joseph,
> Their land, the land in the far ages given
> By the Chief-in-the-Sky. (*CJNP* 3)

The initial words of the narrative are "the land," emphasizing connection to the landscape and its life-sustaining power. The modern narrator, whom we may call the "Historian-Poet," thus implicitly endorses the Nimipu (Nez Perce). Reflecting the nobility of the Nez Perce with high rhetorical style, the narrator employs appositives and repetition ("The land of the Winding Waters," "Land sacred," "Their land," "the land in the far ages," etc.). Because this land originates "in the far ages" and was "given / By the Chief-in-the-Sky," it comes to the Nez Perce from the secular realm of history and the metaphysical realm of the gods. The land is their birthright and destiny.

One facet of the Nez Perce mythos might initially appear similar to the American notion of Manifest Destiny. "The Sky-Power thus blessed the Nimipu" with "abundance" just as the Puritan settlers in the New World believed themselves to be the modern incarnations of the wandering Israelites making their exodus to the Promised Land. But any resemblance is deceiving. The earliest European settlers and their descendants see the landscape, and all native tribes within it, as resources to be exploited or obstacles to be removed as "Westward the course of empire takes its way," to use Bishop Berkeley's prophetic declaration. The Nez Perce theology calls for more responsibility. They con-

---

11. Warren, "Talking with Robert Penn Warren" (Interview with Moyers, 1976), 222–23, 210.

sider themselves stewards of the land, required to nurture the land, to give to it as they take from it. This attitude is apparent in Part II, as Chief Joseph comments on the treaty with which some of the Nez Perce chiefs sold their land at the disapproval of others including Joseph. He speaks "the Truth that no / White man can know":

> ". . . the Great Spirit
> Had made the earth but had drawn no lines
> Of separation upon it, and all
> Must remain as He made, for to each man
> Earth is the Mother and Nurse, and to that spot
> Where he was nursed, he must,
> In love cling." (*CJNP* 14)

Identifying themselves as stewards of the land has several pragmatic effects. First, it assures the Nez Perce that the land will continually produce for them. Second, it assures that the Nez Perce will identify themselves as a unified people. Joseph recalls his father telling him, "You must never sell the bones of your fathers—/ For selling that, you sell your Heart-Being" (*CJNP* 10). In a landscape where the dead ancestors are present, the living are continually held accountable. In their interactions among themselves and with others, the Nez Perce apply Warren's dictum from "The Use of the Past": "Without a sense of time, there can be no sense of identity."[12]

The young Joseph's ceremonial naming is a ritual of identification through the lens of the past. Upon his birth he is given a name, "but not my true name" (*CJNP* 5). When ten years old, he is sent alone to the mountain where he fasts and remains motionless, "heart open / To vision" (*CJNP* 5). His guardian spirit, the apparition of an old man, appears and gives him his name. We are immediately struck by the contrast with other biographical texts that identify their subjects by who they are not. *Audubon: A Vision*, for example, begins with a prefatory section that

---

12. See Warren's essay "The Use of the Past," perhaps his most significant articulation of the purpose of history.

states the "official version of his identity" but then corrects the legend, noting that John James Audubon "encouraged the other version, along with a number of flattering embellishments," such as the legend that he was the lost Dauphin of France. The poem's first section, entitled "Was Not the Lost Dauphin," refutes the popular stories of Audubon's birth:

> Was not the lost dauphin, though handsome was only
> Base-born and not even able
> To make a decent living, was only
> Himself, Jean Jacques. . . . (*Audubon* 84–85)

Similar to the first chapter of *John Brown: The Making of a Martyr*, this opening defines Audubon in terms of who he was not, a revision of the trope, conventional in nonfiction biography, of defining the subject in terms of his place of birth and parentage. *Chief Joseph of the Nez Perce* reverses this revisionary development in Warren's canon, as though presenting Joseph as an antidote to figures like Brown and Audubon. Unlike Brown, Audubon, Willie Stark, Jeremiah Beaumont, and others from Warren's canon, Joseph does not manufacture his identity through public representations. His name is an identity earned through the myth constructed by his community; however, it is an identity that is earned privately in communion with his ancestors. He has nothing to prove to his people; rather, he has much to give them. Joseph has more in common with Jefferson Davis and Robert Franklin Warren, the heroes of Warren's later biographical narratives. These men know who they are. For the young Joseph, that knowledge originates in his connection to his community, through their ancestral land. It should be noted, though, that Chief Joseph's identity was later revised and reconstructed by popular white culture. The same culture that fought against him would later praise his courage and honor; he would become a "noble savage."

Joseph's connection to the land creates his sense of responsibility to the land itself and to his people. His relationship to his tribe emerges from his relationship to the past, which in turn results from his relationship to the land. When Jack Burden in *All the King's Men* realizes that history is a web of interrelated events, in which all are acted upon and in turn act upon others, he acknowledges his own accountability to others. He learns the lesson that Chief Joseph represents: ethical action is the direct result of an acknowledgment of one's place in the matrix of history.

This connection to history is illustrated in the discourse of the poem. Like Warren's prose biographical narratives, the narrative poetics of *Chief Joseph of the Nez Perce* parallels the theme. Ethical action through historical connection is apparent in the presence of audible, overt narrators who are participants in events and agents in making meaning.

Chief Joseph of the Nez Perce represents the final stage of Warren's development toward autobiography within biography. However, in this case it is not only the author-narrator's voice that evolves toward autobiographical participation with the historical plot; rather, Joseph himself is given his own voice. This strategy echoes Jack Burden's quotations from Cass Mastern's journals in *All the King's Men*, the Historian-Narrator's quotations from Jeremiah Beaumont's journals in *World Enough and Time*, and even Amantha Starr's first-person narration in *Band of Angels*. Every character's voice is actually a palimpsest of voices, ultimately originating with the author himself. Cass Mastern is, to some extent, Jack Burden's creation, but Burden is, of course, Warren's creation.

These layers of voices are not so problematic with fictional narratives because we always know that behind every fictional character and narrator stands an author. According to Wayne Booth's distinctions between authors, implied authors, and narrators, we should not necessarily identify the author with the voices within the story. But as Gerard Genette points out, the distinguishing feature between fiction and nonfiction is the relation between the narrator's and author's voices. When we identify a narratorial voice with a real-life counterpart, we interpret the text as nonfiction history or biography (or even autobiography, if the author's voice is also that of a character).[13]

Given that Chief Joseph was an actual person, the question is: Who narrates his autobiography in *Chief Joseph of the Nez Perce?* Just as Warren cites the journals, letters, and speeches of John Brown, Daniel Boone, Jefferson Davis, and Robert Franklin Warren in his prose biographical narratives of those figures, we might expect such quotations from Chief Joseph. *Chief Joseph of the Nez Perce* offers such quotations, but it goes further. It is the only biographical text that is presented in part as autobiography. Joseph narrates much of his own life; yet, the text being a long narrative poem, we know that we are not reading Joseph's actual words. Warren appropriates and revises Chief Joseph's autobiography, thereby appropriating his voice as well.

Some critics have therefore accused Warren of distorting Chief Joseph's voice with clichéd Indian idioms or "Injun talk," a product of Warren's own racist consciousness as a descendant of Anglo stock. One reviewer writes, "Though *Chief Joseph of the Nez Perce* recognizes some of the ways in which narrative can distort history, it does not apply this recognition to its own operations." For example, Warren criticizes white culture for praising the nobility of the natives after exerting much effort to eradicate them, "but [Warren] conveys no sense that his own poem may be colluding in such a process." In short, Warren is accused of denigrating Chief Joseph in the very narrative act of trying to represent him as a noble American figure.[14]

Countering these assertions, James Finn Cotter points out that Chief Joseph's speech is typical of Warren's "tight-jawed

13. See Wayne Booth, *The Rhetoric of Fiction* (Chicago: University of Chicago Press, 1961); Genette's essay, "Fictional Narrative, Factual Narrative."

14. Nicolas Tredell, "Shaman and Showmen," review of *Chief Joseph of the Nez Perce*, by Robert Penn Warren, *Times Literary Supplement*, 27 April 1984, 454. In addition, see James Finn Cotter, "Poetry Encounters," review of *Chief Joseph of the Nez Perce*, by Robert Penn Warren, *Hudson Review* 36 (Winter 1983–84): 711–23. Particularly see page 718 of Cotter's review, which defends Warren's style. See also Monroe K. Spears, "Robert Penn Warren: A Hardy American," review of *Chief Joseph of the Nez Perce*, by Robert Penn Warren, *Sewanee Review* 91 (Fall 1983): 655–64.

style." Cotter is correct. Evidence for his defense is traceable throughout Warren's poetry. Warren's use of short poetic lines should not be taken as a lack of fluidity in Chief Joseph's speech, for such short, abrupt lines appear throughout much of Warren's lyric and narrative poetry, including *Brother to Dragons*. Let us take as an example Thomas Jefferson's opening soliloquy:

> My name is Jefferson. Thomas. I
> Lived. Died. But
> Dead, cannot lie down in the
> Dark. Cannot, though dead, set
> My mouth to the dark stream that I may unknow
> All my knowing. . . . (*BD* 5)

These brief lines, characteristic of the entire text, contain little subordination and few connectives. This style is hardly indicative of any disparaging attitude toward Jefferson. The shortness and abruptness of such lines lend the text a directness and clarity necessary to convey significant meaning. Similarly, an instance from *Chief Joseph of the Nez Perce*, where the chief says:

> ". . . My father
> Waits thus in his dark place. Waiting, sees all.
> Sees the green worm on green leaf stir. Sees
> The aspen leaf turn though no wind, sees
> The shadow of thought in my heart—the lie
> The heel must crush. Before action, sees
> The deed of my hand. My hope is his Wisdom." (*CJNP* 10)

In these brief lines, the repetition of the subject ("my father") is elliptically implied rather than explicitly stated. Yet the notion of the father who is now dead (i.e., "in his dark place") being a constant presence, inspiration, and influence upon his son represents for Warren the epitome of historical and ethical consciousness. This is the point that Jack Burden and Jeremiah Beaumont strive toward, a point which Chief Joseph has inhabited long before they arrive. The brevity and abruptness of the lines emphasize—they do not impede—the insights of the speaker.

An even more convincing argument may be made with reference to Warren's other autobiographical narrators. Warren permits characters to tell their stories in their own dialects. Examples of first-person narrators abound: Jack Burden, Cass Mastern, Jeremiah Beaumont, Amantha Starr, Hamish Bond, Jed Tewksbury. Some of these voices reflect a superior education and higher class status, but their voices do not necessarily ennoble them. In some cases, such as Jack Burden and Jeremiah Beaumont, the ability to rationalize and articulate themselves well becomes a weapon. In contrast, Willie Proudfit in *Night Rider*, Munn Short in *World Enough and Time*, and Ashby Wyndham in *At Heaven's Gate* are examples of characters whose voices reflect their more provincial and less educated roots. Yet these characters, despite their stereotypical speech, are among the most insightful in all of Warren's work.

For example, in his confession, Ashby Wyndham recalls a time when he failed to realize the interrelatedness among human beings: "I taken no thought and it was my sin. . . . You throw a rock in a pond and it don't make but one splash but they is ripples runs out from it" (*AHG* 120). Ashby's "sin" is his ignorance of the effects of his own actions, and he is redeemed as a Christian when he acknowledges his accountability in the matrix of human experience. His growth parallels Cass Mastern's, who realizes that many harmful consequences had resulted from his actions. Wyndham's statement, with its perceptive analogy of the rock thrown into the pond, demonstrates a wisdom that is out of reach for the more "educated" characters in *At Heaven's Gate*. Bogan Murdock, for instance, is educated, wealthy, and highly skilled in rhetoric and public relations, but he cannot approach Ashby Wyndham's intellectual and ethical development.

As this example demonstrates, we should not suppose that characters who speak in their native dialects are to be taken less seriously. This is not to excuse any stylistically weak passages, if indeed there are any. But we should not dismiss them outright. Recall Chief Joseph's famous proclamation of surrender: "Hear me, my chiefs, I am tired. Heart is sick and sad. From where the sun now stands, I will fight no more forever" (*CJNP* 46). While some dispute the authenticity of these lines, arguing that they were written by a white man who reconstructed Joseph's statement after the fact, the issues of textual accuracy and historical reconstructions of Joseph lie somewhat beyond the scope of this study. I would argue that the lines exhibit eloquence regardless of their authorship, and it is surely misguided to suppose Chief Joseph incapable of such moving speech. Warren's idiom for Chief Joseph does not diminish or distract from his insightfulness. The dialect that he created for Chief Joseph is no more a hindrance than the dialect that Samuel Clemens created for Huckleberry Finn.

Chief Joseph is the first narrator in the poem. Joseph is refigured into an overt narrator-participant with unobstructed connection to the past and his people. The second narrator is the autobiographical Historian-Poet, Warren himself, who journeys to the Nez Perce region in a kind of return, reconciles historical records with his present need to find significance for a modern audience, and departs with knowledge that redeems. The Historian-Poet appropriates the task of narration in the prefatory note and opening of Part I, and then from Part V to the end. By telling Chief Joseph's story in the third person, Warren places him into history. The poem makes no claim or pretense to the nonparticipatory or detached narration of "The Ballad of Billie Potts." *Chief Joseph of the Nez Perce* completes Warren's shift from the fiction of neutral narration and toward autobiography.

Floyd Watkins has documented this shift through Warren's poetry, showing, as Joseph Blotner does in his biography of Warren, how Warren's poetry has often incorporated autobiographical materials. Warren's early poetry (e.g., "The Ballad of Billie Potts") is aloof, but the later work is personal, a change that occurs in 1953 with *Brother to Dragons*. Justus argues that "the use of himself, both as a persona and as a fully developed character" in *Brother to Dragons* pushed the later poetry into a more confessional mode. Indeed, Warren himself stated that poems "grow out of your life," a statement he made in an article appropriately entitled "Poetry Is a Kind of Unconscious Autobiography."[15]

Chief Joseph establishes greater connection to the historical figure by means of the autobiographical engagement of the narrator, and in this respect it departs from "The Ballad of Billie Potts" and owes a debt to *Brother to Dragons*, in which Warren enters the discussion as himself, renamed "R.P.W." He is the moderator of the drama, and he connects with the other characters' experiences by visiting the scene of the crime with his father, Robert Franklin Warren. In *Chief Joseph of the Nez Perce*, the Historian-Poet enters the narrative, bringing to the text a larger, more abstract vision of history. Like Jack Burden or the Historian-Narrator of *World Enough and Time*, he possesses the powers of speculation and interpretation. As General Howard talks to General Miles about surrender, the Poet peers into Howard's mind: "And hearing his own words, he knew a pure / And never-before-known bliss swell his heart" (*CJNP* 42). Like R.P.W. in *Brother to Dragons*, he visits the region where the events occurred. He now appears in the construction of history as a character representing the modern individual's creation of heroes.

The final section is a kind of return. Although the Historian-Poet does not return to his own home in any literal sense, in a figurative sense he journeys to a region with which he is already familiar, an area that has lived in his thoughts and imagination. He returns to a territory of the mind. Throughout the return section he attempts to negotiate past and present, reconciling the violent reality of the Nez Perce destruction and the dehumanized reality of the modern world with his own needs for a mythical west of the past.

Immediately preceding his journey, section eight concludes with the Historian-Poet's observations of modernity:

Frontiersmen, land-grabbers, gold-panners were dead.
Veterans of the long chase skull-grinned in darkness.

15. Watkins, *Then and Now*, 1–6; Justus, *Achievement of Robert Penn Warren*, 61; Warren, "Poetry Is a Kind of Unconscious Autobiography," *New York Times Book Review*, 12 May 1985, 9.

A more soft-handed ilk now swayed the West. They founded
Dynasties, universities, libraries. . . . (*CJNP* 54)

This section echoes Warren's lament for the loss of the frontier
and great men in "The World of Daniel Boone" and in the final
passages of *World Enough and Time*. Of course, what makes
this passage ironic is that with his academic career and literary
awards, Warren himself depended upon dynasties, universities,
and libraries. Once again, we find him caught between realism
and idealism. Warren insists that we embrace the realities of
American history before we claim to embrace America; otherwise, it is a false, ill-informed embrace. Yet the realities are useless without some overriding myth to give significance to the
facts of history. One cannot live among mere facts, for facts
without meanings are lifeless. With its images of a lost romantic
West, this passage expresses nostalgia for a myth of the past.

We see in this passage Warren attempting to strike some balance between the love for America and the knowledge of American history. After showing the reality of nineteenth-century
American history through Chief Joseph's story, the Historian-
Poet longs for a myth that he himself has helped to destroy.
However, the myth is problematic. The Historian-Poet laments
the loss of a time that brought about the destruction of the Nez
Perce. The frontiersmen, land grabbers, and gold panners were
among those taking and exploiting the western landscape, evacu-
ating or exterminating the Native Americans in the process.

Shortly after the passage quoted above, a similar passage appears, this one commenting on another myth of the American
West:

> Great honor came, for it came to pass
> That to praise the red man was the way
> Best adapted to expunge all, all, in the mist
> Of bloodless myth. (*CJNP* 55)

Chief Joseph and the other aboriginal peoples of North America
become pictured as noble savages, but this American fascination

and admiration with Native Americans comes conveniently too late to save them. It is a myth that expunges guilt. The passage continues by describing how Joseph has been historically represented next to myths like Buffalo Bill, accompanied by clowns and magicians "who could transform . . . The blood of history into red ketchup, / A favorite American condiment" (*CJNP* 55). The contrast between "blood" and "ketchup" accuses Americans of being locked into their preference for myth over reality. The problem articulated by the Historian-Poet here is that the myth is so irrelevant to actual experience that it forms a veil over truth.

Warren touches upon a theme that Robert F. Berkhofer has extensively investigated in his landmark study, *The White Man's Indian*. Pointing out that Native Americans neither referred to themselves as "Indians" nor any other single term, nor saw themselves as a single entity, Berkhofer demonstrates that "the *Indian* was a white invention" that American culture categorized into stereotypes (e.g., noble savage, demon) "for the convenience of simplified understanding."[16]

This categorizing process results from a need to make real historical people and events conform to a priori expectations. As Hayden White has shown, an event becomes understandable once it is plotted according to a genre, such as tragedy or comedy, that gives significance to the event. We may apply White's argument to the construction of historical characters. Real human beings are complex; few fit neatly into the roles of hero and villain. Yet historical figures become available to popular audiences when they are plotted into history according to established roles. The problem with constructing real events and people as history is that it creates what White calls an "illusory coherence," the mistaken belief that events naturally follow patterns of tragedy or comedy and that real people in history naturally fall into particular archetypal functions.[17]

16. Robert F. Berkhofer, *The White Man's Indian* (New York: Vintage, 1978), 3.
17. See Hayden White, *The Content of the Form*. The discussion about the plotting of historical events into genres is taken from pages 14, 43–44, 51, and ix.

We have seen Warren's narrators exposing the processes by which John Brown, Daniel Boone, and Jefferson Davis were reconstructed into history. The Historian-Poet of *Chief Joseph of the Nez Perce* also exposes the making of history, the transformation of Chief Joseph into a simplistic image. The Historian-Poet examines the making of history, how Joseph acted upon history and how historians and the popular imagination transformed Joseph into an unreal figure. By being praised for his nobility and honor, Joseph has been figured into a role and plot commensurate with America's heritage of Manifest Destiny. Modern America has prepared a role for him to place him into history.

In Part IX, the journey to the Snake Creek region, Warren places himself into the making of history so as to recuperate Joseph's experience: "To Snake Creek, a century later, I came" (*CJNP* 58). Like the conclusion of *World Enough and Time*, this section becomes very autobiographical, to the point that the identities of Warren and his Historian-Poet merge. In contrast to the Edenic imagery that opens Part I, Warren traverses a wasteland:

> Vacant of cattle, horse, man, the color
> Gray-brown, the season October, not yet
> Snowfall. (*CJNP* 58)

After arriving by airplane, he travels by car, noticing "the scraggle of villages dropped by history on Route 87." He and his companions consult "a large map outspread" in the automobile. Their unfamiliarity with the region indicates their disconnection from the land, as opposed to the Nez Perce's close affiliation with the land. The scene is far different from the image of the Native who, a century earlier, rode on horseback and navigated his way by reading the signs of the landscape.

The tourists arrive at some "modest monuments" featuring a soldier and Indian in bronze relief and reproducing Joseph's famous statement, "From where the sun now stands, I will fight no more forever." An official map on the site recounts and ana-

lyzes the action of the battle. The spot resembles the tourist at-
tractions at Boonesborough and Todd County, where one may
visit monuments to Daniel Boone and Jefferson Davis (see "The
World of Daniel Boone" and *Jefferson Davis Gets His Citizenship Back*). Through these descriptions Warren leads us to question whether monuments and plaques are capable of making
history accessible.

Standing at the spot of a mass grave, Warren notes what the
guidebooks and markers do not say, that some are buried in
other places where they had tried to find shelter:

> [when] shells began lobbing in,
> The Indians tried to dig caves for children,
> The women, the old. (*CJNP* 60)

The spot where Joseph's tepee stood is now marked by a cold
image of modernity:

> There, southward, a steel pipe,
> With marker screwed on, defines the spot
> Of the tepee of Joseph. (*CJNP* 61)

This spot is just beyond Snake Creek:

> . . . Snake Creek is near-dry, only
> A string of mossy-green puddles where Joseph,
> In the same season,
> Had once found water fresh for people and horse herd. (*CJNP* 60)

The pastoral, historical landscape that once sustained the lives of
people who lived and died in earnest is now a modern wasteland.

As a late modernist, Warren seeks some resolution or redemption for the detritus of history that he sees in this landscape. Like
Jack Burden addressing an unnamed "you" as he drives down
the highway of time, he invites the reader to empathize with Joseph's experience and acknowledge modern America's neglect of
the true history:

If you climb the slope, say a mile and a half,
Or two, to the point where Miles must first
Have debouched from the Bear Paws, and look north,
You see what he saw—or what erosion has done. (*CJNP* 61)

He invites the reader to join him in imaginatively reconstructing
history, to create significance for the present: "Northward, you
see what you guess he saw"; "All / Now only a picture there in
my head"; "I, / In fanatic imagination, saw—/ No, see—the old
weapon" (*CJNP* 61–62). For Warren, memory becomes a symbolic rather than chronological experience, a matrix in which
the past is always present.

As we observe throughout Warren's historical narratives, the
roles of the novelist and historian often converge in the matrix.
In this text, the roles of historian and poet intersect in that both
employ interpretive strategies as they construct plots. Warren's
journey to Snake Creek is a "historical excursion" similar to
Jack Burden's return to his own history. Both Burden and the
Historian-Poet of *Chief Joseph of the Nez Perce* privilege the
imagination in the investigation for historical truth.

The journey to Snake Creek becomes an occasion for reconciling the events of the Nez Perce wars with the insufficient
reconstruction or loss of history in the present. In fact, the reconciliation process dominates the entire text, with the Historian-
Poet interpolating quotations from actual primary sources: journals, speeches, proclamations, laws, and letters. The use of historical documents is the most distinguishing feature of the form
of *Chief Joseph of the Nez Perce*. Blotner explains that publish-
ers originally rejected the manuscript because they were uncertain about its genre, whether it was poetry or "an unclassifiable
form of journalism" or something else. No doubt, the prepon-
derance of actual documents fueled this confusion. In form,
Chief Joseph of the Nez Perce owes a debt to its predecessor.
Brother to Dragons is a verse drama, what Nakadate calls a
"verse colloquium," wherein Warren (R.P.W.) is one of the characters, though as the modern writer he also acts as a stage man-

ager.[18] Although parts of *Chief Joseph of the Nez Perce* are narrated by Joseph himself, the overt Historian-Poet orchestrates a colloquium of quotations from historical sources. The Historian-Poet does not comment on these sources, nor does he expose his struggle with interpreting his primary sources, as the Historian-Narrator of *World Enough and Time* does. Seemingly, he presents them objectively.

Chatman's terminology from narrative theory is applicable here. *Chief Joseph of the Nez Perce* represents a genre that could be called a "nonnarrated story": it uses a free direct style; that is, the speech is quoted, not reported, with minimal use of tags or no tags at all. Chatman explains that indirect discourse "implies a shade more intervention by a narrator, since we cannot be sure that the words in the report clause are precisely those spoken by the quoted speaker." Types of nonnarrated stories would be soliloquy, dramatic monologue, and written records of which the author is a "mere collector or collator."[19] Although the narrator purports to allow the quoted historical figures to speak for themselves, *Chief Joseph of the Nez Perce* is not a pure nonnarrated story since a narrator or writer's persona does appear and participate overtly and audibly. There are no neutral narrators here.

This denial of objectivity may seem contradictory, since throughout the poem the Historian-Poet engages in what may be the most "objective" performance from a historian: he merely presents his primary source materials without comment. As Callander points out, the prose quotations lend a note of authenticity to the poem.[20] Indeed, it would seem that the only objective voices in the poem are the documents. However, they are often presented precisely for the lack of objectivity. The documents are used because of their biases or agenda.

18. Blotner, *Robert Penn Warren*, 467; Neil Nakadate, "Voices of Community: The Function of Colloquy in Robert Penn Warren's *Brother to Dragons*," in *Robert Penn Warren's Brother to Dragons: A Discussion*, ed. James A. Grimshaw (Baton Rouge: Louisiana State University Press, 1983), 114.

19. Chatman, *Story and Discourse*, 200, 169, 180.

20. Marilyn Berg Callander, "Robert Penn Warren's *Chief Joseph of the Nez Perce*: A Story of Deep Delight," *Southern Literary Journal* 15, no. 3 (1983): 29.

The primary sources are given new significance by their placement or juxtaposition in the text. The first such quotations appear paratextually before the prefatory note. These are three epigrams by, respectively, Thomas Jefferson, William Tecumseh Sherman, and Chief Sealth of the Duwamish. Jefferson indicates connection with the Natives; since whites and Indians are "made by the same Great Spirit, and living in the same land," they are part of the same family and should share the same interests. Not surprisingly, Sherman expresses a different view, one of pragmatism and total detachment: "The more we can kill this year, the less will have to be killed in the next war." According to Chief Sealth, the past will always be a present, available experience. Chief Sealth proclaims that even when all tribes have vanished, "These shores will swarm with the invisible dead of my tribe. . . . The White Man will never be alone" (*CJNP* ix). The sequence of these statements makes a prophetic argument. Jefferson expresses an ideal of ethical conduct, Sherman would violate that code, and Chief Sealth follows as if in response to Sherman.

The sequence and interrelatedness of the quotations thus serve an implicitly narrative function. Interpolated into the pastoral description of Part I is a statement by Jean Baptiste le Moyne de Bienville, observing the honesty and religious nature of the natives. Yet on the next page appears a passage from the *Journals* of Lewis and Clark. Its very presence foretells the destruction of the Nez Perce, all the more so because the passage recounts the two explorers encountering a storm in which "the heavens became suddenly darkened by a black cloud" (*CJNP* 5), surely an omen of the war to follow.

For the most part, most of the quotations do not carry such implicit ironies or unspoken arguments, so we must be careful not to push this analysis too far. However, the criticism, which appeared in at least one of the early reviews, that the quotations break up the narrative and deny the reader transitions, is simply wrong. All of the quotations make the retold events more real by making the historical voices accessible to a modern audience.

The quotations enable the reader to hear the debates of the 1870s. For example, Part I concludes with a quotation from one of Ulysses S. Grant's executive orders to the commissioner of Indian Affairs, declaring the Nez Perce territory off limits to white settlement. Part II concludes with a quotation from Chief Joseph to the commissioner: "The earth, my mother and nurse, is very sacred to me: too sacred to be valued, or sold for gold or for silver . . . and my bands have suffered wrong rather than done wrong" (*CJNP* 14). The juxtaposition conveys irony.

So, too, does the juxtaposition of some quotations within individual sections. Part IV recounts the violence of war against the Nez Perce. A few lines appear from an interview with an Indian warrior:

> *Query: You did not really hear the soldiers crying, did you?*
> *Narration: I heard them cry like babies. They were bad scared.*

This is followed by a quotation from General Howard suggesting the white Americans' inability to see the truth of the war: "Some method must be found to encourage and properly reward such gallantry and service hardly ever before excelled" (*CJNP* 26–27).

Part VII describes the hardships suffered by the Nez Perce. Supplementary quotations include a report of the Indian Commission of 1878 describing their conditions and a statement of Chief Joseph wondering why the "Great Spirit Chief who rules above" seems to be ignoring his people. Chief Joseph longs for divine concern for his people's troubles. The quotation from a Portland, Oregon, newspaper on the following page compounds the problem with human unconcern for these troubles: "A party of miners returned to Owyhee from a raid on Indians with twenty scalps and some plunder. The miners are well" (*CJNP* 49).

The ultimate ironies appear in Part VIII, in which the Historian-Poet reflects on the loss of the romantic myths of the American West. Several sources that have contributed to unrealistic historical representations of the Indian punctuate this section. A statement from General Sherman praises the courage and military skill of the Natives. Another quotation is taken from the *American Sculpture Catalogue of the Collection of the Metro-*

politan Museum of Art; it describes a bronze sculpture of Chief Joseph.

In Part VI, two significant quotations from Chief Joseph communicate the pathos of surrender, and while these two passages speak to each other, they stand on their own. The first states, "I believed General Miles or I never would have surrendered." The second recapitulates his well-known speech; "I am tired of fighting. Our chiefs are killed. Looking Glass is dead. The old men are killed. . . . Our little children are freezing to death. . . . Hear me, my chiefs, I am tired. Heart is sick and sad. From where the sun now stands, I will fight no more forever" (*CJNP* 45–46). Such use of primary sources supplements the content of the poem proper. We are persistently reminded that the verse we are reading emerges from real events.

The final presentation of a primary source appears in Part IX, after Warren announces that he made the journey to Snake Creek: "*La Guardia to O'Hare, American Airlines, October 9, 1981, Ticket 704 982 1454 4, Chicago*" (*CJNP* 58). While this seems like a trite inclusion, perhaps more suitable for a scrapbook, it precedes the most significant observations of the poem. By giving his itinerary, Warren emphasizes the shift to modernity, which has led him to struggle with his project of correcting the past in order to create a usable myth for the present. The poem concludes with Warren struggling to discover how a modern American can appreciate and learn from the past. He creates an image reminiscent of the lone city dweller in "The Ballad of Billie Potts":

> Now soon they would go back, I too,
> Into the squirming throng, faceless to facelessness,
> And under a lower sky. (*CJNP* 64)

But departing from "The Ballad of Billie Potts," he now prescribes a method for interconnection with history, envisioning, "some stranger," a visitor or tourist "standing paralyzed in his momentary eternity" and looking into his own heart to determine "From what undefinable distance, years, and direction,/ Eyes of fathers are suddenly fixed on him" (*CJNP* 64). This passage reiterates Warren's argument from "The Use of the Past" and numerous novels, essays, and interviews. The only way to negotiate our way into the future is to use the past as a guide. In these lines he suggests a method: to look not merely to monuments or museums or even the landscape where history occurred, but into the heart. One must stand outside of time in a "momentary eternity," like the young Seth in "Blackberry Winter," for whom time has no linear quality: "Time is not a movement, a flowing, a wind then, but is, rather, a kind of climate in which things are" (BW 63–64).

What is most significant about this historiographical method is not just that one must look *into* oneself to discover the past but that one must look *through* oneself. One must look into oneself to discover the presence and influence of one's ancestors within, but one must also look to oneself to make meaning out of the examples of the ancestors' lives. In a review of *Chief Joseph of the Nez Perce*, Michael Garcia-Simms creates a perceptive analogy to describe the operation of Warren's self-conscious, overt, and audible narration in his construction of history: "It is as if the poet were standing in a brightly lit room and looking out a window into darkness where the shapes and shadows of history dance out of reach, while superimposed on those images the poet's own face is reflected in the glass."[21] This is a precise image of Warren's method throughout his later biographical narratives in prose and poetry. The concluding lines of the *Chief Joseph of the Nez Perce* instruct the reader how to use this method. The "some stranger" he refers to in his final statement, like the ambiguous "you" that appears so often in his work, suggests that at the end of his life and career, Warren was looking for successors for his historical-ethical program. Often writing his novels, poems, and other narratives from the point of view of a son in search of a father, Warren was unfailingly conscious of the presence of fathers in the lives of sons. Warren concludes the Chief Joseph biographical poem from the point of view of one who hopes to leave an inheritance to others.

21. Michael Garcia-Simms, "Time and the Maker," review of *Chief Joseph of the Nez Perce*, by Robert Penn Warren, *Southwest Review* 68 (1983): 401.

Conclusion
Making American Literary History

In the 1970s Warren published biographical-critical essays concerning some of his literary predecessors—Nathaniel Hawthorne, John Greenleaf Whittier, Theodore Dreiser, and Herman Melville (though the Melville essay, concentrating on Melville's later poetry rather than on his entire life, is less biographical than the others). Like the other biographical narratives, these essays personalize history by humanizing historical or, in this case, literary figures. In Warren's assessment, their works were inevitable products of their lives. Hawthorne's fictions resulted from his family's fall from greatness and his subsequent alienation from family, region, and history. In contrast, Whittier's ambition originated in his privilege of looking back into his family's history, always to find the founding fathers of a new nation. His greatest poem, *Snowbound*, was an autobiographical "backward glance," an examination of how present perception shapes the past, and a struggle with the past on personal and national levels. Dreiser's art and life created each other. His fiction documents his life, from the poverty of his childhood and corruption of his family, to his failures in love and business. His life was the living document of his characters' financial and interpersonal disasters.

These portraits form a coda to this study, because even though they are not, strictly speaking, autobiographical, together they constitute a portrait of Warren's identity as a poet, novelist, and historian. Warren superimposes his image upon his biographical constructions of other writers, discovering the same themes and techniques in their works that he explores in his own work. As he reconstructs their identities into narratives, he constructs his identity as a writer of biographical narrative. We might recall the metaphor in Garcia-Simms's review of *Chief Joseph of the Nez Perce*: Warren examines the past as if he were having to search beyond his reflected image while gazing at a dark landscape through a window in a well-lighted room.[1] To paraphrase Jack Burden, taken as a whole, the "stories" of these four writers and the "story" of Warren "are, in one sense, one story."

Thematically the "stories" are the same, for many of Warren's observations about these writers' responses to history, family, region, sin, and responsibility correspond to his treatment of these issues in his own work. Technically, the "stories" are the same, for Warren's descriptions of their poetics echo the strategies employed in his narratives and poems. Warren's biographical essays on other writers document influences upon his development. They are portraits of his literary fathers.

Critics have already noted Hawthorne's influence upon Warren's treatment of the conflicts between individual and community, and between good and evil. For example, Justus observes traces of Hawthorne in Warren's "web" metaphor, noting that both writers perceive humanity as united in a "brotherhood of evil."[2] The correspondence between Hawthorne and Warren receives its most explicit articulation in Warren's essay "Hawthorne Revisited: Some Remarks on Hell-Firedness," which he expanded into an introduction to the "Hawthorne" section in *American Literature: The Makers and the Making*.[3] Both texts open with a description of conflicts in Hawthorne's work; the following passage is remarkable for its convergence with Warren's work and is therefore worth quoting at length:

1. Garcia-Simms, "Time and the Maker," 401.
2. Justus, *Achievement of Robert Penn Warren*, 37.
3. R. W. B. Lewis recounts the production of this textbook in collaboration with Warren and Cleanth Brooks, in "Warren's Long Visit to American Literature," *Yale Review* 70 (1981), 568–91. Warren was predominantly responsible for writing the introductions to the nineteenth-century American Romantic writers.

He lived in the right ratio—right for the fueling of his genius—between an attachment to his region and a detached assessment of it; between attraction to the past and its repudiation; between attraction to the world and contempt for its gifts; between a powerful attraction to women and a sexual flinch; between a faith in life and a corrosive skepticism; between a capacity for affection and an innate coldness; between aesthetic passion and moral concern; between a fascinated attentiveness to the realistic texture, forms and characteristics of nature and human nature, and a compulsive flight from the welter of life toward abstract ideas; and between, most crucially of all, a deep knowledge of himself and an ignorance of himself instinctively cultivated in a fear of the darker potentialities of self.

Warren's literary and personal relation to the South resonates in this passage and in another passage, which describes Hawthorne's knowledge of his ancestors' culpability in the Salem witch trials: "[Hawthorne's] tales were the first manifestations of the nostalgic appeal of a lost glory and a lost certainty of mission, the sense of a curse intertwined with the glory of the past."[4] For both Hawthorne and Warren, for Robin Molineux and Jack Burden, the past is both burden and source of identity.

Most significant for the purpose of this study, Warren defines Hawthorne's employment of autobiography and his use of the past in passages that clearly characterize his own development toward participatory, self-referential narration. Hawthorne is an engaged and engaging narrator, for "the characters, situations, and issues are created with a passionate urgency of imagination which bespeaks the involvement, intellectual and emotional, of the creator and which, therefore, involves us." Indeed, Hawthorne's personal confrontation with the past is evident in "The Custom House," as the narrator notes the autobiographical nature of his work: as an editor he assumes what he calls "a personal relation with the public." The "Custom House" narrator also explains that while he has taken liberties with the narrative

4. Warren, "Hawthorne Revisited: Some Remarks on Hell-Firedness," in *New and Selected Essays* (New York: Random House, 1989), 69–70.

"as if the facts had been entirely of my own invention," he also ensures the "authenticity of the outline." The autobiographical impulse, accounting for Hawthorne's concern for accuracy but repudiation of mere factuality, results in romance rather than history or the popular "historical novel." In a significant passage, as Warren contrasts the novelist and the writer of romance, he defines his own aesthetic objectives: "The writer of romance would use the actualities of the past as a means of validating and generalizing—at a distance for clarity of outline—the moral and psychological drama. *The historical novelist aims, then, at converting the past into a kind of virtual present; the writer of romance aims at converting the past into a myth for the present.*"[5] These statements clarify Warren's resistance to critics who labeled his novels "historical fiction," in the popular sense of the term. If we did not know the origin of this passage, we might assume that Warren wrote it to define his own work rather than another writer's.

Echoes of Warren's autobiographical development similarly appear in his description of Whittier's boyhood in "John Greenleaf Whittier: Poetry as Experience": "He was already steeped in the legends and folklore of his region, which he had absorbed as naturally as the air he breathed." In Warren's childhood, history was the climate in which he lived: "I didn't get my impression of the Civil War from home. I got it from the air around me" (*JD* 9). Seth in "Blackberry Winter" reconstructs childhood as a time of pastoral innocence, before the flood that awakens him to death and corruption. Whittier, according to Warren, also envisioned childhood with nostalgia: "Almost everyone has an Eden time to look back on, even if it never existed and he has to create it for his own delusion."[6]

5. Cleanth Brooks, R. W. B. Lewis, and Robert Penn Warren, *American Literature: The Makers and the Making* (New York: St. Martin's Press, 1973), 433; Nathaniel Hawthorne, *The Scarlet Letter* (New York: W. W. Norton, 1978), 7, 29; Brooks, Lewis, and Warren, *American Literature*, 459 (italics are Warren's).

6. Warren, "John Greenleaf Whittier: Poetry as Experience," in *John Greenleaf Whittier's Poetry: An Appraisal and a Selection*, ed. Robert Penn Warren (Minneapolis: University of Minnesota Press, 1971), 6, 34.

While these one-to-one correspondences are worth noticing, they do not dominate here as they do in the Hawthorne essay. What makes the Whittier essay most significant is Warren's personal engagement with the subject. Like Jack Burden writing himself into the Cass Mastern narrative, Warren becomes an audible narrator in telling the story of Whittier's life. A similar personal appearance occurs briefly in the introductory note to Melville's selected poems: "I have called this book *A Reader's Edition*, and the reader I refer to is myself. The book may be regarded as a log of my long reading of Melville's poetry."[7] The narrator explicitly presents himself as an agent in the construction of the narration.

Warren's personal engagement with Whittier is even more pronounced, accounting for an extended discussion about abolitionism. Coming across as a southern loyalist, Warren shows that he is not a mere recorder of Whittier's life and surrenders any claim to neutral narration. He states that Whittier was initially more interested in politics than poetry, noting, in counterpoint, that Whittier also suffered from depression, withdrawals, chronic headaches, and insomnia, all symptomatic of some "deep inner conflict." The juxtaposition of these two statements implies that Whittier may have been at conflict with himself over abolition. Enlisted in the cause by William Lloyd Garrison, Whittier was a committed abolitionist throughout his life; however, Warren also notes that Whittier agreed more with Lincoln rather than Emerson, Thoreau, Garrison, or the "Secret Six" who funded John Brown. A Quaker who believed in pacifism and reform, Whittier was a mediator; thus, he could condemn Brown's actions and condemn the South for creating an atmosphere in which men like Brown could take action. He believed that if the nation could place the South on "moral quarantine," slavery would die out on its own; after the Civil War he was disappointed that emancipation was brought about only by violence.[8]

7. Warren, Introduction to *Selected Poems of Herman Melville: A Reader's Edition*, ed. Robert Penn Warren (New York: Random House, 1970), vii.

8. Warren, "John Greenleaf Whittier," 9–24. Subsequent quotations are cited parenthetically by page number in the text.

Six pages of overt editorial commentary on abolitionism appear. Warren announces his authorial entrance in the narrative: "Since for more than thirty years abolitionism was the central fact of Whittier's life, it is worth trying to say what it was, and what some of the assumptions behind it were" (14). Although he justifies an analysis of abolitionism by citing Whittier's involvement in it, his approach to the topic may lead us to infer that he is motivated by his own interest as well. Rather than offer a direct definition of the term, Warren suggests that we might best understand the "essential nature" of abolitionism "by focusing on the radical variety that is associated with the name of Garrison," and that "the simplest way to start is to say what it was not" (14–15). With these two sentences, Warren narrows his subject to a scope and methodology that place him in position not merely to define abolitionism but also to make an argument and offer rebuttals. Warren chooses to define abolitionism by concentrating on an extreme variety, a strategy that provides him with an opportunity to maximize his opposition. (It is more difficult to argue against a moderate or general political perspective.) By explaining what abolitionism was not, he may present abolitionism as a set of myths to refute. We have seen him use this strategy before, in *John Brown: The Making of a Martyr*, which begins with a section demythologizing Brown's ancestry and identity.

An agenda is at work here, which becomes apparent as he presents arguments to divest the nineteenth-century North of any claim to moral superiority. Not all northerners were abolitionists, he explains; moreover, abolitionists might also be racists, for "racism was as prevalent in the North as in the South" (15). Notwithstanding any possible validity in these claims, they are a rhetorical strategy to lessen the guilt of the South. He does concede that racism was probably less prevalent among abolitionists than among the general population: "even an abolitionist *might* be, in one way or another, a racist; but it is true that there was less of this attitude among abolitionists than among the population at large, certainly of the more obvious kind" (15–16; italics are Warren's). In this passage, he immediately undermines his concession by adding "certainly of the more obvious kind," a phrase that modifies "[racist] attitude" and thereby implies that abolitionists were perhaps guilty of more subtle racism. An asterisk then leads to a footnote: "Ironically enough . . . there was a great deal less racism in the South than in the North," apparent in the South's greater acceptance of miscegenation (and here he cites, for evidence, "many works of southern literature, for instance the novels of William Faulkner") (16).

According to Warren, abolitionism is based upon abstraction, the same extreme reliance upon idealism that becomes the tragic flaw of John Brown and Jefferson Davis, Willie Stark and Jeremiah Beaumont. Warren contrasts abolitionism with its more moderate form, emancipationism. The latter treated slavery "in a general context, social, political, moral, or theological. . . . But for an abolitionist the problem of slavery was paramount, central, burning, and immediate. The context did not matter" (16). Abolitionists discovered a theological justification for calling slavery the "greatest sin"; Warren comments upon this position with a footnote: "See, for instance, Hawthorne's 'Ethan Brand' for a different primary sin" (17). Warren clearly establishes a taxonomy of sin. Slavery is the sin of exploiting other human beings as means to an end rather than ends in themselves. Abstraction is the sin of perceiving philosophical, theological, or political ideals as ends in themselves, without regard for any possible negative consequences. In Warren's formulation, the slaveholder is concerned only with pragmatics, to the exclusion of ideals; the abolitionist is concerned only with ideals, to the exclusion of practical effects.

The "higher law" absolutism of the abolitionist could lead to the kind of violence that John Brown committed, for it set up "a naked and absolute individualism," an attitude that "struck not only at an evil in society, but at the roots of the democratic process." Yet Warren concedes that while this attitude strikes against the process, it is part of the process, "the claim of the individual intuition to be heard in protest against an order established by a majority" (19). Whether one should follow the majority or his own conscience is ultimately a gamble. Another footnote comments that if history determines a man's gamble to be correct, "then the man gets a statue to his memory. But if history says that the gamble was 'wrong,' then the best the man can expect, in lieu of the statue, is a grudging recognition of his 'courage' or 'sincerity'" (20). Such "grudging recognition" typifies remembrances of Confederate soldiers. Warren's tone here is that of a narrator in ambivalent relation to his home region. He will take up this matter—the man, the gamble, and the monument—a few years later in *Jefferson Davis Gets His Citizenship Back*. In that book, the monument becomes a symbol of Warren's struggle with history. For now, his concluding description of Whittier's struggle with abolitionism summarizes his own inner conflict; it is a passage that echoes Warren's thesis in "The Use of the Past": "[He] spent a large part of his active life trying to master, resolve, or mediate these tensions. . . . And he came to see that man's fate is that he must learn to accept and use his past completely, knowingly, rather than to permit himself to be used, ignorantly, by it" (20).

Like the Whittier essay, *Homage to Theodore Dreiser* illustrates the narrator's engagement with the subject, evident in several paratextual elements. Similar to the titles of other biographical works (e.g., *Portrait of a Father, Audubon: A Vision*), the title of the Dreiser book indicates that the subject is not the facts of the writer's life but the narrator's perception of those facts. The book is prefaced by a poem sequence entitled "Portrait," which includes the subsections "Psychological Profile," "Vital Statistics," and "Moral Assessment." Footnotes throughout the text do more than document sources; they discuss problems with determining the validity of certain factual claims. One footnote, typical of the kind of interpretation that characterizes many of the notes, attempts to locate the psychological causes for Dreiser's behavior in a desire to protect his mother. Warren's objective is not to present the man and artist, but to assess his life and work. By setting the biography into the mode of homage, Warren grants himself, as historian, the liberty of an artist.

Like the "Custom House" narrator and the Historian-Narrator of *World Enough and Time*, Warren commences the narrative with self-referential comments: "The career of Theodore Dreiser raises in a peculiarly poignant form the question of the relation of life and art. . . . It is tempting to think of him as a kind of uninspired recorder blundering along in a dreary effort to transcribe actuality. And the next temptation is to think that what is good is good by the accident of the actuality that he happened to live into—not by any power that he, as artist, might have achieved." This paragraph and the one that follows it begin the narrative with a discussion of the problems of factuality, which the biographer confronts, or realism, which the novelist confronts. At issue is not only whether Dreiser was an "uninspired recorder," but whether the novelist or historian will be an "uninspired recorder . . . transcrib[ing] reality." Although Warren understates these issues as "temptations" that divert him as he progresses with his project, they are essential epistemological questions that must be answered, at least temporarily, before the biographer can construct a narrative of the life. In the case of Dreiser, the question is, where is the line that divides the life from the work? With every writer (and here, Warren must be including himself), "Art is the artist's way of understanding—of creating even—the actuality that he lives." The problem with Dreiser, though, is that there are numerous direct correspondences between himself and his work. Even Dreiser's directly "autobiographical writings are scarcely distinguishable from his fiction." The objective for Warren's narrative, then, is to illustrate the direct relation between the life and the work, an enterprise fit for a realist. In the process, just as Warren discovered much of himself in Hawthorne and Whittier, he makes discoveries in his portrait of Dreiser.[9]

There are many themes in the Dreiser narrative that correspond to Warren's work. For example, the conflict between ideals and experience (or between idealism and pragmatism), which appears throughout Warren's canon, appears in Dreiser as well:

9. Warren, *Homage to Theodore Dreiser: August 27, 1871–December 28, 1945, On the Centennial of His Birth* (New York: Random House, 1971), 9. All quotations in this paragraph are from page 9. Subsequent quotations are cited parenthetically by page number in the text.

"The fundamental fact is that for Dreiser ideas had to be absorbed into life, had to interpenetrate with experience" (92). In discussing *An American Tragedy*, Warren notes that there is a "rhythm of detachment and involvement" in the novel. For example, the reader is involved with Clyde Griffiths's story, but the chapter following the murder begins with a wide perspective, creating detachment. And the reader is distracted from Clyde's story by the introduction of other perspectives, for "the narrative is conceived as a drama involving both the individual and the universe" (117). We have seen the vacillation between detachment and involvement in Jack Burden's relation to his subject. We also see Warren's familiar theme of the relationship between responsibility and identity, as Warren argues that Clyde Griffiths denied himself full knowledge of his own identity when he denied accountability for his actions. In the process of escaping responsibility, he runs from himself; changing his name is a repudiation of self. Thus the American tragedy is "the story of the individual without identity, whose responsible self has been absorbed by the great machine of modern industrial secularized society, and reduced to a cog, a cipher, an abstraction" (129). (And here we might recall Warren's interview with Bill Moyers, in which he discussed this theme of the lost self in contemporary American society.) Warren disagrees with Dreiser's acceptance of social determinism: "If in the world of complicities and ambiguities, it is hard to understand responsibility, then how, ultimately, can one understand the self? . . . If one is passive, how can there be a self?" (128). Jack Burden and Jeremiah Beaumont confront the same problem as Dreiser's characters. One comes to a sense of identity only through connection.

Warren charts much of Dreiser's youth, and he observes how several people and events in Dreiser's life ended up, perhaps not surprisingly, as characters and plot elements in his fictions. Like Melville, Dreiser grew up with the burden of a father who failed in business. When his father was injured physically and financially after his mill burned down (he had neglected to keep an insurance policy), young Theodore learned what it was to feel like "a pawn in the hands of a blind or malevolent fate." Like

Melville, then, his philosophy was based in "the early disaster of the father" (11). At this point, we may recall Jack Burden's relation to his biological father, Jeremiah Beaumont's rise above his father's social level, and Warren's own sympathetic reaction to his father's business difficulties in *Portrait of a Father*.

Dreiser's reliance upon his personal experience for material in his fictions occasionally leads to problems of realism. Warren calls *The "Genius"* a "crashing bore" because, as he explains in a significant passage,

> The kind of realism here practiced by Dreiser is based on the assumption that whatever is literally true . . . is justified by that truth—that all that is required of the author is to report that truth. This assumption, in that it takes the literal truth as the basic criterion, justifies the telling of all, for no one thing, by this basis, is "truer" than anything else. Furthermore, the assumption makes superfluous the art of fiction, the shadings of emphasis, the imaginative renderings of depths and subtleties, the sense of the inwardness of action; the assumption reduces all to a monotone of mere chronicle with an occasional passage of commentary.

Any critic who accuses Warren of taking too much liberty with facts should consult this passage, because, like the passages in "Hawthorne Revisited" that define Hawthorne's sense of autobiography, this passage defines Warren's sense of the function of realism in fictional narrative. The passage also has application to historical narrative, for, Warren continues, "Most destructive of all, the assumption makes into a virtue the self-indulgence and self-vindication of merely pouring out recollections, or pseudo-recollections" (51). Recollections, real or imagined, become solipsistic when not submitted to the scrutiny of analysis and interpretation. In contrast, Warren discusses Dreiser at his best: "And this returns us to the difference between the historical novel and the kind of fiction represented here. Here Dreiser is trying to invent a genre, a novel in which all the outer facts are certified and the inner facts are imaginatively extrapolated from that evidence, and the whole, outer and inner, is offered as a document"

(76). In "Hawthorne Revisited," Warren makes a distinction between the popular notion of the historical novelist and the writer of romances; the romance reconstructs the past into a myth for the present. Although Dreiser is hardly a romantic, Warren finds in his novels a productive use of the past, wherein the writer takes authenticated facts and imaginatively searches for the truth that makes those facts meaningful. Warren distinguishes between factuality, the conventional historian's concern, and truth, the ultimate concern of novelist and historian alike. These passages comprise an aesthetic philosophy that we find put to practice in the best of Warren's autobiographical poems and narratives.

Throughout the Warren canon, we see a willingness to embrace the truth of American history and, as the essays on Hawthorne, Whittier, and Dreiser illustrate, the truth of American literary history. Shortly after Warren's death, the *Southern Review* published a collection of essays in memoriam. In his tribute, Cleanth Brooks reflected upon "Warren's love of truth": "One cannot truly love something unless he truly knows it, including its defects; and to know something thoroughly, completely, becomes a form of love."[10] We may recall the conclusion of *Brother to Dragons*, which articulates this relationship between love and knowledge. When R.P.W. leaves the Smithland estate, he exits the gate but enters a world that is "sweeter than hope in that confirmation of late light" (*BD* 132). After spending a lifetime sifting through both the glory and the detritus of history, Warren emerged with a usable past and a faith that did not flinch from the future. In his biographical narratives he converted American history into a usable myth for artists, historians, and all citizens. In this life-long process, Warren became a literary father to others.

10. Cleanth Brooks, "A Tribute to Robert Penn Warren," *Southern Review* 26 (1990), 4.

Bibliography

All the King's Men. Produced, directed, and with screenplay by Robert Rossen. Columbia Pictures, 1949.

Barthes, Roland. "The Discourse of History." Translated by Stephen Bann. In *Comparative Criticism,* edited by E. S. Schaffer, 3–20. Cambridge: Cambridge University Press, 1981.

Beauchamp, Jereboam. "The Confession of Jereboam O. Beauchamp." In *The Kentucky Tragedy: A Problem in Romantic Attitudes,* edited by Loren J. Kallsen, 2–109. New York: Bobbs-Merrill, 1963.

Berkhofer, Robert F. *The White Man's Indian.* New York: Vintage, 1978.

Blotner, Joseph. *Robert Penn Warren: A Biography.* New York: Random House, 1997.

Bohner, Charles H. *Robert Penn Warren.* New York: Twayne, 1964.

Boorstin, Daniel. *The Image; or, What Happened to the American Dream.* New York: Atheneum, 1962.

Booth, Wayne. *The Rhetoric of Fiction.* Chicago: University of Chicago Press, 1961.

Bradbury, John M. *The Fugitives: A Critical Account.* Chapel Hill: University of North Carolina Press, 1958.

Brooks, Cleanth. "Homage to R. P. Warren." In *"To Love So Well the World": A Festscrift in Honor of Robert Penn Warren,* edited by Dennis L. Weeks, 13–18. New York: Peter Lang, 1992.

———. "A Tribute to Robert Penn Warren." *Southern Review* 26 (1990): 2–4.

Brooks, Cleanth, and Robert Penn Warren. *Understanding Fiction.* 2nd ed. New York: Appleton-Century-Croft, 1959.

Brooks, Cleanth, R. W. B. Lewis, and Robert Penn Warren. *American Literature: The Makers and the Making.* New York: St. Martin's Press, 1973.

Brooks, Van Wyck. "On Creating a Usable Past." In *The Early Years,* edited by Claire Sprague, 219–26. New York: Harper and Row, 1968.

Brown, Norman D. Review of *Jefferson Davis Gets His Citizenship Back*, by Robert Penn Warren. *Southwestern Historical Quarterly* 85 (1981): 93–94.

Bryan, Daniel. *The Mountain Muse: Comprising the Adventures of Daniel Boone; and the Power of Virtuous and Refined Beauty.* Harrisonburg, Ky.: Davidson and Bourne, 1813.

Burt, John. *Robert Penn Warren and American Idealism.* New Haven: Yale University Press, 1988.

Callander, Marilyn Berg. "Robert Penn Warren's *Chief Joseph of the Nez Perce*: A Story of Deep Delight." *Southern Literary Journal* 15, no. 3 (1983): 24–33.

Casper, Leonard. *Robert Penn Warren: The Dark and Bloody Ground.* Seattle: University of Washington Press, 1960.

Chambers, Robert H., ed. *Twentieth-Century Interpretations of All the King's Men.* Englewood Cliffs, N.J.: Prentice-Hall, 1977.

Chatman, Seymour. *Story and Discourse.* Ithaca: Cornell University Press, 1978.

Chivers, Thomas Holley. *Conrad and Eudora; or, The Death of Alonzo.* Philadelphia, 1834.

Clark, William Bedford. *The American Vision of Robert Penn Warren.* Lexington: University Press of Kentucky, 1991.

———. "A Meditation on Folk History: The Dramatic Structure of Robert Penn Warren's 'The Ballad of Billie Potts.'" *American Literature* 49 (1978): 635–45.

Coleman, J. Winston. *The Beauchamp-Sharp Tragedy: An Episode of Kentucky History During the Middle 1820s.* Frankfort, Ky.: Roberts Printing, 1950.

———. *John Filson, Esq.: Kentucky's First Historian and Cartographer.* Lexington, Ky.: Winburn, 1954.

———. *Slavery Times in Kentucky.* Chapel Hill: University of North Carolina Press, 1940. Reprint, New York: Johnson Reprint, 1970.

Connelly, Thomas. "Robert Penn Warren as Historian." In *A Southern Renascence Man: Views of Robert Penn Warren*, edited by Walter B. Edgar, 1–17. Baton Rouge: Louisiana State University Press, 1984.

Cooke, J. W. Review of *Jefferson Davis Gets His Citizenship Back*, by Robert Penn Warren. *Modern Age* 25 (1981): 310–12.

Cotter, James Finn. "Poetry Encounters." Review of *Chief Joseph of the Nez Perce*, by Robert Penn Warren. *Hudson Review* 36 (Winter 1983–84): 711–23.

Craven, Avery. Review of *John Brown: The Making of a Martyr*, by Robert Penn Warren. *New York Herald Tribune Book Review*, 12 January 1930, 17.

Daniel Boone, Trailblazer. Produced and directed by Albert C. Gannaway. Republic Pictures, 1956.

Davis, William C. *Jefferson Davis: The Man and His Hour*. New York: Harper Perennial, 1992.

Eliot, T. S. *The Waste Land and Other Poems*. San Diego: Harcourt Brace Jovanovich, 1934.

Faulkner, William. *Absalom, Absalom!*. New York: Vintage, 1987.

Filson, John. *The Adventures of Colonel Daniel Boon, Formerly a Hunter: Containing a Narrative of the Wars of Kentucky*. London: John Stockdale, 1793.

Frank, Joseph. "Romanticism and Reality in Robert Penn Warren." *Hudson Review* 4 (1951): 248–58.

Fridy, Wilford Eugene. "Robert Penn Warren's Use of Kentucky Materials in His Fiction as a Basis for His New Mythos." Ph.D. diss., University of Kentucky, 1968.

Gabriel, R. H. "Seven American Leaders." Review of *John Brown: The Making of a Martyr*, by Robert Penn Warren. *Yale Review* 19 (1930): 590–96.

Garcia-Simms, Michael. "Time and the Maker." Review of *Chief Joseph of the Nez Perce*, by Robert Penn Warren. *Southwest Review* 68 (1983): 400–406.

Genette, Gerard. "Fictional Narrative, Factual Narrative." *Poetics Today* 11 (1990): 755–74.

———. *Narrative Discourse*. Translated by Jane E. Lewin. Ithaca: Cornell University Press, 1980.

Girault, Norton R. "The Narrator's Mind as Symbol: An Analysis of *All the King's Men*." In *Robert Penn Warren: Critical Perspectives*, edited by Neil Nakadate, 60–76. Lexington: University Press of Kentucky, 1981.

Goldhurst, William. "The New Revenge Tragedy: Comparative Treatments of the Beauchamp Case." *Southern Literary Journal* 22 (1989): 117–27.

Gray, Richard. "The American Novelist and American History: A Revaluation of *All the King's Men*." *Journal of American Studies* 6 (1972): 297–307.

———. *The Literature of Memory: Modern Writers of the American South*. Baltimore: Johns Hopkins University Press, 1977.

Grimshaw, James A. *Robert Penn Warren: A Descriptive Bibliography,
    1922–1979.* Charlottesville: University Press of Virginia, 1981.

––––––, ed. *Robert Penn Warren's Brother to Dragons: A Discussion.*
    Baton Rouge: Louisiana State University Press, 1983.

Guttenberg, Barnett. *Web of Being: The Novels of Robert Penn Warren.*
    Nashville: Vanderbilt University Press, 1975.

Harper, Margaret Mills. "Versions of History and *Brother to Drag-
    ons.*" In *Robert Penn Warren's Brother to Dragons: A Discussion,*
    edited by James A. Grimshaw, 226–43. Baton Rouge: Louisiana
    State University Press, 1983.

Havard, William C. "The Burden of the Literary Mind: Some Medita-
    tions on Robert Penn Warren as Historian." In *Robert Penn Warren:
    A Collection of Critical Essays,* edited by Lewis Longley, 178–94.
    New York: New York University Press, 1965.

Hawthorne, Nathaniel. *The Scarlet Letter.* New York: W. W. Norton,
    1978.

Heilman, Robert B. "Melpomene as Wallflower; or, the Reading of
    Tragedy." In *Robert Penn Warren: A Collection of Critical Essays,*
    edited by Lewis Longley, 82–95. New York: New York University
    Press, 1965.

Inge, M. Thomas. Review of *Jefferson Davis Gets His Citizenship Back,*
    by Robert Penn Warren. *South Atlantic Review* 47, no. 3 (1982):
    74–75.

Justus, James H. *The Achievement of Robert Penn Warren.* Baton
    Rouge: Louisiana State University Press, 1981.

––––––. "The Power of Filiation in *All the King's Men.*" In *Modern
    American Fiction: Form and Function,* edited by Thomas Daniel
    Young, 156–69. Baton Rouge: Louisiana State University Press,
    1989.

––––––. "Robert Penn Warren." In *The History of Southern Literature,*
    edited by Louis D. Rubin, Jr., et al., 450–59. Baton Rouge: Louisiana
    State University Press, 1985.

––––––. "Warren and the Narrator as Historical Self." In *Time's Glory:
    Original Essays on Robert Penn Warren,* edited by James A. Grim-
    shaw, 109–18. Arkansas: University of Central Arkansas Press,
    1986.

––––––. "Warren's *World Enough and Time* and Beauchamp's *Confes-
    sion.*" *American Literature* 33 (1962): 500–511.

Kelly, Florence Finch. "John Brown Sits for a Critical Portrait." Review
    of *John Brown: The Making of a Martyr,* by Robert Penn Warren.
    New York Times Book Review, 12 January 1930, 7.

Kentucky. Department of Parks. *Fort Boonesborough Historic Walking Trail Guide*, 1994.

———. *Jefferson Davis Monument State Historic Site*, 1994.

Koppelman, Robert S. *Robert Penn Warren's Modernist Spirituality*. Columbia: University of Missouri Press, 1995.

LaCapra, Dominick. *History and Criticism*. Ithaca: Cornell University Press, 1985.

Law, Richard G. " 'The Case of the Upright Judge': The Nature of Truth in *All the King's Men*." *Studies in American Fiction* 6 (1978): 1–19.

Lewis, R. W. B. "Warren's Long Visit to American Literature." *Yale Review* 70 (1981): 568–91.

Longley, Lewis, ed. *Robert Penn Warren: A Collection of Critical Essays*. New York: New York University Press, 1965.

MacDonald, William. Review of *John Brown: The Making of a Martyr*, by Robert Penn Warren. *Nation*, 2 July 1930, 22–23.

Moore, Arthur K. *The Frontier Mind: A Cultural Analysis of the Kentucky Frontiersman*. Lexington: University of Kentucky Press, 1957.

Moore, L. Hugh. *Robert Penn Warren and History: "The Big Myth We Live."* Paris: Mouton, 1970.

Nakadate, Neil. "The Narrative Stances of Robert Penn Warren." Ph.D. diss., Indiana University, 1972.

———. "Robert Penn Warren and the Confessional Novel." *Genre* 2 (1969): 326–40.

———, ed. *Robert Penn Warren: Critical Perspectives*. Lexington: University Press of Kentucky, 1981.

———. "Voices of Community: The Function of Colloquy in Robert Penn Warren's *Brother to Dragons*." In *Robert Penn Warren's Brother to Dragons: A Discussion*, edited by James A. Grimshaw, 112–24. Baton Rouge: Louisiana State University Press, 1983.

Napier, Cameron Freedman. Review of *Jefferson Davis Gets His Citizenship Back*, by Robert Penn Warren. *Alabama Historical Quarterly* 43 (1981): 153–54.

Nevins, Allan. "Martyr and Fanatic." Review of *John Brown: The Making of a Martyr*, by Robert Penn Warren. *New Republic*, 19 March 1930, 134–35.

Olney, James. "Parents and Children in Robert Penn Warren's Autobiography." In *Home Ground: Southern Autobiography*, edited by J. Bill Berry, 31–47. Columbia: University of Missouri Press, 1991.

Payne, Ladell. "Willie Stark and Huey Long: Atmosphere, Myth, or Suggestion?" In *Robert Penn Warren: Critical Perspectives*, edited by Neil Nakadate, 77–92. Lexington: University Press of Kentucky, 1981.

Perkins, Dexter. "Figures in Perspective." Review of *John Brown: The Making of a Martyr*, by Robert Penn Warren. *Virginia Quarterly Review* 6 (1930): 614–20.

Poe, Edgar Allan. *Politian*. Edited by Thomas Ollive Mabbott. Menasha, Wis.: George Banta, 1923.

Quinlan, Kieran. Review of *Portrait of a Father*, by Robert Penn Warren. *Mississippi Quarterly* 42 (1989): 197–200.

Quinn, Sister M. Bernetta, O.S.F. "Robert Penn Warren's Promised Land." *Southern Review* 8 (1972): 329–58.

Review of *John Brown: The Making of a Martyr*, by Robert Penn Warren. *Historical Outlook* 21 (1930): 186.

Robbins, F. L. Review of *John Brown: The Making of a Martyr*, by Robert Penn Warren. *Outlook*, 13 November 1929, 153.

Rubin, Jr., Louis D. *The Wary Fugitives: Four Poets and the South*. Baton Rouge: Louisiana State University Press, 1978.

Runyon, Randolph Paul. *The Taciturn Text: The Fiction of Robert Penn Warren*. Columbus: Ohio State University Press, 1990.

Ruppersburg, Hugh. *Robert Penn Warren and the American Imagination*. Athens: University of Georgia Press, 1990.

Ryan, Steven T. "*World Enough and Time*: A Refutation of Poe's History as Tragedy." *Southern Quarterly* 31, no. 4 (1993): 86–94.

Sale, Roger. "Having It Both Ways in *All the King's Men*." *Hudson Review* 14 (1961): 68–76.

Simms, William Gilmore. *Beauchampe; or, The Kentucky Tragedy*. Chicago: Belford, Clarke, 1885.

Simpson, Lewis P. *The Fable of the Southern Writer*. Baton Rouge: Louisiana State University Press, 1994.

Smith, Henry Nash. *Virgin Land: The American West as Symbol and Myth*. Cambridge: Harvard University Press, 1950.

Souvenir of Fairview, Kentucky. Dedication Day, June 7th, 1924. Sturgis, Ky.: Ezell Publishing, 1924.

Spears, Monroe K. "Robert Penn Warren: A Hardy American." Review of *Chief Joseph of the Nez Perce*, by Robert Penn Warren. *Sewanee Review* 91 (Fall 1983): 655–64.

Stewart, John L. *The Burden of Time*. Princeton: Princeton University Press, 1965.

———. "Robert Penn Warren and the Knot of History." *English Literary History* 26 (1959): 102–36.

Stitt, Peter. *The World's Hieroglyphic Beauty*. Athens: University of Georgia Press, 1985.

Surrency, Jack E. "The Kentucky Tragedy and Its Primary Sources." In *No Fairer Land: Studies in Southern Literature before 1900*, edited by Dameron J. Lasley and James W. Mathews, 110–23. Troy, N.Y.: Whitston, 1986.

Tate, Allen. *The Fathers*. Baton Rouge: Louisiana State University Press, 1977.

———. "The New Provincialism." In *Essays of Four Decades*, 535–46. Chicago: Swallow Press, 1968.

Tredell, Nicolas. "Shaman and Showmen." Review of *Chief Joseph of the Nez Perce*, by Robert Penn Warren. *Times Literary Supplement*, 27 April 1984, 454.

Vauthier, Simone. "The Case of the Vanishing Narratee: An Inquiry into *All the King's Men*." In *Robert Penn Warren: Critical Perspectives*, edited by Neil Nakadate, 93–114. Lexington: University Press of Kentucky, 1981.

Walker, Marshall. *Robert Penn Warren: A Vision Earned*. New York: Barnes and Noble, 1979.

Walton, John. *John Filson of Kentucke*. Lexington: University of Kentucky Press, 1956.

Warren, Robert Penn. *All the King's Men*. San Diego: Harcourt Brace Jovanovich, 1984.

———. "All the King's Men: The Matrix of Experience." *Yale Review* 53 (1963): 161–67.

———. *At Heaven's Gate*. New York: New Directions, 1985.

———. *Audubon: A Vision*. In *Selected Poems, 1923–1975*, 83–100. New York: Random House, 1976.

———. "The Ballad of Billie Potts." In *New and Selected Poems, 1923–1985*, 287–300. New York: Random House, 1985.

———. *Band of Angels*. New York: Random House, 1955.

———. "Blackberry Winter." In *Circus in the Attic and Other Stories*, 63–87. San Diego: Harcourt Brace, 1963.

———. *Brother to Dragons: A Tale in Verse and Voices*. Baton Rouge: Louisiana State University Press, 1996.

———. "Cass Mastern's Wedding Ring." *Partisan Review* 11 (1944): 375–407.

———. *Chief Joseph of the Nez Perce*. New York: Random House, 1982.

———. "Circus in the Attic." In *Circus in the Attic and Other Stories*, 3–62. San Diego: Harcourt Brace, 1963.

———. "Conversation: Eleanor Clark and Robert Penn Warren." Interview with Roy Newquist, 1967. In *Talking with Robert Penn Warren*, edited by Floyd Watkins, John T. Hiers, and Mary Louise Weaks, 86–99. Athens: University of Georgia Press, 1990.

———. "A Conversation with Robert Penn Warren." Interview with Ruth Fisher, 1970. In *Talking with Robert Penn Warren*, edited by Floyd Watkins, John T. Hiers, and Mary Louise Weaks, 170–89. Athens: University of Georgia Press, 1990.

———. "A Conversation with Robert Penn Warren." Interview with Frank Gado, 1966. In *Talking with Robert Penn Warren*, edited by Floyd Watkins, John T. Hiers, and Mary Louise Weaks, 68–85. Athens: University of Georgia Press, 1990.

———. "A Conversation with Robert Penn Warren." Interview with Bill Moyers, 1976. In *Talking with Robert Penn Warren*, edited by Floyd Watkins, John T. Hiers, and Mary Louise Weaks, 205–26. Athens: University of Georgia Press, 1990.

———. "A Dearth of Heroes." *American Heritage*, October 1972, 4 + .

———. "A Dialogue with Robert Penn Warren on *Brother to Dragons*." Interview with Floyd Watkins, 1980. In *Talking with Robert Penn Warren*, edited by Floyd Watkins, John T. Hiers, and Mary Louise Weaks, 336–56. Athens: University of Georgia Press, 1990.

———. *Flood: A Romance of Our Time*. New York: Signet, 1965.

———. "Fugitives' Reunion: Conversations at Vanderbilt." Panel Discussion, 1956. In *Talking with Robert Penn Warren*, edited by Floyd Watkins, John T. Hiers, and Mary Louise Weaks, 7–24. Athens: University of Georgia Press, 1990.

———. "The Gamecock." Review of *High Stakes and Hair Trigger: The Life of Jefferson Davis*, by Robert W. Winston, and *Jefferson Davis: Political Soldier*, by Elisabeth Cutting. *New Republic*, 25 March 1931, 158–59.

———. "The Great Mirage." In *New and Selected Essays*, 137–61. New York: Random House, 1989.

———. "Hawthorne Revisited: Some Remarks on Hell-Firedness." In *New and Selected Essays*, 69–101. New York: Random House, 1989.

———. *Homage to Theodore Dreiser: August 27, 1871–December 28, 1945, On the Centennial of His Birth*. New York: Random House, 1971.

———. "How Texas Won Her Freedom." *Holiday*, March 1958, 72 + .

———. "An Interview in New Haven with Robert Penn Warren." Interview with Richard B. Sale, 1969. In *Talking with Robert Penn Warren*, edited by Floyd Watkins, John T. Hiers, and Mary Louise Weaks, 110–46. Athens: University of Georgia Press, 1990.

———. "Interview with Eleanor Clark and Robert Penn Warren." Interview with the *New England Review*, 1978. In *Talking with Robert Penn Warren*, edited by Floyd Watkins, John T. Hiers, and Mary Louise Weaks, 318–35. Athens: University of Georgia Press, 1990.

———. "Interview with Flannery O'Connor and Robert Penn Warren." Interview with Joe Sills, 1959. In *Talking with Robert Penn Warren*, edited by Floyd Watkins, John T. Hiers, and Mary Louise Weaks, 52–67. Athens: University of Georgia Press, 1990.

———. "Interview with Robert Penn Warren." Interview by Peter Stitt, 1977. In *Talking with Robert Penn Warren*, edited by Floyd Watkins, John T. Hiers, and Mary Louise Weaks, 233–46. Athens: University of Georgia Press, 1990.

———. "Introduction to the Modern Library Edition of *All the King's Men*." In *Twentieth-Century Interpretations of "All the King's Men*," edited by Robert H. Chambers, 93–97. Englewood Cliffs, N.J.: Prentice-Hall, 1977.

———. Introduction to *Selected Poems of Herman Melville: A Reader's Edition*, edited by Robert Penn Warren, 3–88. New York: Random House, 1970.

———. *Jefferson Davis Gets His Citizenship Back*. Lexington: University Press of Kentucky, 1980.

———. *John Brown: The Making of a Martyr*. Southern Classics Series. Nashville: J. S. Sanders, 1993.

———. "John Greenleaf Whittier: Poetry as Experience." In *John Greenleaf Whittier's Poetry: An Appraisal and a Selection*, edited by Robert Penn Warren, 3–62. Minneapolis: University of Minnesota Press, 1971.

———. "Knowledge and the Image of Man." *Sewanee Review* 63 (1955): 182–92.

———. *The Legacy of the Civil War: Meditations on the Centennial*. New York: Random House, 1961.

———. *New and Selected Essays*. New York: Random House, 1989.

———. *Night Rider*. Southern Classics Series. Nashville: J. S. Sanders, 1992.

———. "On the Art of Fiction." Interview with Ralph Ellison and Eugene Walter, 1956. In *Talking with Robert Penn Warren*, edited by Floyd Watkins, John T. Hiers, and Mary Louise Weaks, 25–51. Athens: University of Georgia Press, 1990.

———. *A Place to Come To*. New York: Dell, 1977.

———. "Poetry Is a Kind of Unconscious Autobiography." *New York Times Book Review*, 12 May 1985, 9–10.

———. *Portrait of a Father*. Lexington: University Press of Kentucky, 1988.

———. "Remember the Alamo!." *Holiday*, February 1958, 52 +.

———. "Robert Penn Warren: An Interview." Interview with Marshall Walker, 1969. In *Talking with Robert Penn Warren*, edited by Floyd Watkins, John T. Hiers, and Mary Louise Weaks, 147–69. Athens: University of Georgia Press, 1990.

———. *Segregation: The Inner Conflict in the South*. In *A Robert Penn Warren Reader*, edited by Albert Erskine, 229–69. New York: Vintage, 1987.

———. *Selected Poems, 1923–1975*. New York: Random House, 1976.

———. "A Self-Interview." In *Talking with Robert Penn Warren*, edited by Floyd Watkins, John T. Hiers, and Mary Louise Weaks, 1–3. Athens: University of Georgia Press, 1990.

———. "Speaking Freely." Interview with Edwin Newman, 1971. In *Talking with Robert Penn Warren*, edited by Floyd Watkins, John T. Hiers, and Mary Louise Weaks, 190–204. Athens: University of Georgia Press, 1990.

———. "The Use of the Past." In *New and Selected Essays*, 29–53. New York: Random House, 1989.

———. "The Uses of History in Fiction." Panel discussion with Ralph Ellison, William Styron, and C. Vann Woodward, 1968. In *Talking with Robert Penn Warren*, edited by Floyd Watkins, John T. Hiers, and Mary Louise Weaks, 100–109. Athens: University of Georgia Press, 1990.

———. "The Way It Was Written." *New York Times Book Review*, 23 August 1953, 6 +.

———. *Who Speaks for the Negro?* New York: Random House, 1965.

———. *Wilderness*. New York: Random House, 1961.

———. "William Faulkner." In *New and Selected Essays*, 197–215. New York: Random House, 1989.

———. *World Enough and Time: A Romantic Novel*. New York: Random House, 1950.

———. "The World of Daniel Boone." *Holiday*, December 1963, 162 +.

———. "The World of Huey Long." *London Times*, 5 January 1974, 5.

Watkins, Floyd. "Billie Potts at the Fall of Time." *Mississippi Quarterly* 11 (1958): 19–28.

————. *Then and Now: The Personal Past in the Poetry of Robert Penn Warren*. Lexington: University Press of Kentucky, 1982.

Watkins, Floyd, John T. Hiers, and Mary Louise Weaks, eds. *Talking with Robert Penn Warren*. Athens: University of Georgia Press, 1990.

Wecter, Dixon. *The Hero in America: A Chronicle of Hero-Worship*. New York: Scribner's, 1941.

Welty, Eudora. *One Writer's Beginnings*. New York: Warner Books, 1983.

White, Hayden. *The Content of the Form: Narrative Discourse and Historical Representation*. Baltimore: Johns Hopkins University Press, 1987.

White, Robert. "Robert Penn Warren and the Myth of the Garden." *Faulkner Studies* 3 (1954): 59–67.

Woodward, C. Vann. *The Future of the Past*. New York: Oxford University Press, 1989.

————. Introduction to *John Brown: The Making of a Martyr*, by Robert Penn Warren. Southern Classics Series. Nashville: J. S. Sanders, 1993.

Yeatman, Joan Ray. "Narrators and Commentators in Four Novels by Robert Penn Warren." Ph.D. diss., University of Oregon, 1972.

Young, Thomas Daniel. *The Past in the Present: A Thematic Study of Modern Southern Fiction*. Baton Rouge: Louisiana State University Press, 1981.

Index